D1047879

YOU WILL DREAM NEW DREAMS

INSPIRING PERSONAL STORIES
BY PARENTS OF CHILDREN
WITH DISABILITIES

*Stanley D. Klein, Ph.D.
and Kim Schive, Editors*

KENSINGTON BOOKS
http://www.kensingtonbooks.com

KENSINGTON BOOKS are published by

Kensington Publishing Corp.
850 Third Avenue
New York, NY 10022

All Kensington titles, imprints and distributed lines are available at
special quantity discounts for bulk purchases for sales promotion, pre-
miums, fund raising, educational or institutional use.

Special book excerpts or customized printings can also be created to fit
specific needs. For details, write or phone the office of the Kensington
Special Sales Manager: Kensington Publishing Corp., 850 Third
Avenue, New York, NY 10022. Attn. Special Sales Department.
Phone: 1-800-221-2647.

ISBN-13: 978-0-7582-2282-4
ISBN:-10: 0-7582-2282-3

First Printing: April, 2001
10 9 8

Printed in the United States of America

ACKNOWLEDGMENTS

We are grateful to all the parents who took the time to write and submit essays for this book. We are also grateful to the organizations that published our request for essays in their publications.

We appreciate the suggestions and patience of Sheree Bykofsky, our literary agent, and Tracy Bernstein, our editor at Kensington Publishing Corporation. We also appreciate the wisdom of Ginny Thornburgh, vice president and director, Religion and Disability Program at the National Organization on Disability, for suggesting her husband, Dick, as a fine person to write the Foreword. We also thank Sarah B. Klein for her assistance.

We gratefully acknowledge permission to adapt essays published previously in the following publications:

FamilyFun magazine. Valle Dwight's essay "Aidan's Gift."

Liguorian magazine, January 2000. Karen Ciaccio's essay "Getting to Know My Son."

Annals of Internal Medicine, January 15, 1996, vol. 124, no. 2, pp. 271–272. Eric C. Last's essay "For Corrie." With the permission of the American College of Physicians–American Society of Internal Medicine.

Emily Perl Kingsley's essay "Welcome to Holland" was first published in 1987.

NICHCY (National Information Center for Children and Youth with Disabilities) *News Digest,* vol. 3, no. 1, 1993. Patricia McGill Smith's essay "You Are Not Alone."

Carolyn Schimanski's essay "The Woman in the Picture" and portions of Robert Naseef's essay "The Rudest Awakening" were previously published in *Exceptional Parent* magazine.

CONTENTS

FOREWORD

You are not alone. My wife and I have been there, and we have learned to dream new dreams. On July 1, 1960, our son, Peter, then an infant only four months old, was involved in a terrible automobile accident which took the life of his mother, my first wife. For a considerable period of time, his very survival was in doubt. He had multiple skull fractures and serious brain injuries which resulted in mental retardation.

Peter received intensive hospital care under the loving supervision of the Sisters of Mercy in our hometown of Pittsburgh, Pennsylvania. While in the hospital with tubes running in and out of his tiny body, he was baptized. He returned home just before Christmas, and our family life began anew.

After I had spent three years as a single parent to Peter and his two older brothers, God sent me Ginny Judson, a schoolteacher whom I met and married in 1963. In 1966, Ginny and I added a fourth son to our family.

Although there are now more community supports for parents and more programs for children with disabilities than there were when Peter was growing up, it has always been very special for us to meet and talk with other parents who have shared similar experiences. We have been comforted and nourished by other parents; we have wept together and we have laughed together. We never perceived one another as superstars or martyrs; we were mothers and fathers discovering our gifts while trying to be the best parents we could be.

I have also been uniquely blessed with opportunities to apply the lessons I have learned as a parent in public life. In 1978, I ran successfully for governor of Pennsylvania; I served two four-year terms. Peter was a fine campaigner, a popular subject for campaign photos, and a frequent participant in official activities after I was elected. Our feeling was one of pride in Peter's accomplishments, not reluctance to share his shortcomings. Everyone in Pennsylvania knew that the governor had a son with a serious disability.

While I served as governor, we put a heavy emphasis on providing community-based services for persons with disabilities as an alternative to large and isolated institutional settings. We emphasized "mainstreaming" for all persons with disabilities. We promoted independent living and supported work and other employment opportunities to help provide the dignity and financial independence that can only come from being in the workforce. All these things were accomplished because parents and parent organizations helped us, supported us, and often prodded us.

Later when I served in Washington, D.C., as attorney general of the United States, one of my principal tasks for President Bush was to spearhead the effort to obtain congressional passage of the Americans with Disabilities Act (ADA), the civil rights law designed to end discrimination against persons with disabilities and remove barriers to their participation in all aspects of community life. Once again, it was parents, parent organizations, and organizations of people with disabilities who helped develop bipartisan support for this legislation.

When I served at the United Nations, I had an opportunity to observe how the needs of some 500 million persons with disabilities around the world are beginning to be met—through the UN's own program of action and in many nations that are using our ADA as a model. Today determined advocates throughout the world, including many parents, are stimulating new thinking about how persons with disabilities can best serve and be served in their societies.

When I look back on all that has been accomplished through the passage of the ADA as well as those laws dating back to

Section 504 of the Rehabilitation Act of 1973 and the Education for All Handicapped Children Act in 1975—now called the Individuals with Disabilities Education Act, or IDEA—I realize that none of these laws were on the books when our family first had to face up to the implications of Peter's disability. It is only during his lifetime that we have taken these giant steps forward.

In this book, more than sixty parents who have "been there" reach out to new parents by sharing their stories and their wisdom. They describe their deepest emotions and reflect on how they have become seasoned, veteran parents. Because of their sons and daughters, their lives and their values have changed. They have become informed experts about their children and have found new ways to grow and serve. As veteran parents ourselves, Ginny and I know firsthand that parents' strongest allies will always be other parents, and we count ourselves fortunate to have been able to share our experiences with others.

To new parents, grandparents, and other family members reading these fine essays, we say with special feelings of respect: "Welcome to a wonderful worldwide community! Keep this book nearby and share it with your family and friends. You are not alone.

—*Dick Thornburgh*
Washington, D.C.

INTRODUCTION

This book is all about human connections—"veteran" parents reaching out to parents who have recently learned that their child has a disability or special health care need. The compassion and caring of these very special connections can be healing at a critical time in the life of a family.

Every expectant parent plans on having a healthy child. From the time a pregnancy is identified, most parents begin building hopes, dreams, and expectations for their new baby. These dreams can be suddenly shattered when a child is diagnosed with a disability or special health care need. This can happen as early as a prenatal checkup, because some conditions are diagnosed even before a baby is born. Other types of disabilities are evident at birth or shortly thereafter. Still others may be diagnosed later in infancy and early childhood, or not until a child enters school.

Few parents ever forget the moment their child was first diagnosed with a disability. Although compassionate physicians, nurses, social workers, and therapists may try to provide emotional support and useful information, most parents describe feeling terribly alone with emotions they may find hard to put into words. Many parents and professionals have suggested that the diagnosis of a child's disability initiates a mourning process in parents, much like the grief felt when a child dies. Yet the child is alive and parenting must proceed.

This is a time when parents' need for support may never be greater. But many parents have a difficult time reaching out to family members and friends. Nor are physicians and other professionals typically perceived as particularly helpful. Where can mothers and fathers turn at a time like this?

For many parents, a turning point occurs when they first begin hearing the stories of other parents who have been through similar experiences. Such connections have proven to be so helpful that formal outreach programs have been established to match veteran parents with parents who have only recently learned about their child's diagnosis.

The disappointment and anguish felt by parents of a newly diagnosed child have often been compared to an open wound that will heal only gradually. Hearing the stories and hard-earned wisdom of more experienced parents can be an important part of the healing process. In hearing these stories, parents often report feeling a sense of validation—validation that feelings of grief and despair are normal and, perhaps more importantly, validation that others have survived, even thrived, after similar heartbreaks. Often this sense of validation is followed by the first stirrings of hope. No longer alone, these "new" parents begin to realize that shattered dreams and expectations can be replaced with new ones. To create this book, we asked veteran parents of children with disabilities to tell the stories they wish they could have heard at that emotionally difficult time, to share words of validation, affirmation, support, and encouragement. Hundreds of veteran parents submitted essays.

Our book includes more than sixty short essays from mothers and fathers of children with different kinds of disabilities who learned about their child's disabilities at different times in the child's life and in the life of their families. The essays are presented in a manner that invites new parents to pick up the book just long enough to read an essay or two, in any order and at any time. We believe this format will be particularly appropriate for parents of newly diagnosed children, who may feel deluged with and overwhelmed by too much information provided all at once. The book begins with essays by parents of younger children and concludes with essays by parents of children who are now adults. When children's names are mentioned in authors' biographies, each child's name is followed by the child's year of birth in parentheses.

At the end of the book, specific resources are provided that can enable parents to make connections in their own communities. Although the authors of these essays have had very different experiences—differences that are reflected in the stories they tell—similar messages of hope and encouragement come through in each essay. The basic messages of the essays include:

- You are not alone.
- The wide range of difficult feelings you are experiencing are a normal part of the human experience. We, too, have been there when everything seemed hopeless; yet we have survived, and our lives have continued. You can go on and grow.
- Although there are no easy answers, you will find ways to cope. You are likely to discover inner resources you did not know existed.
- There is sadness; some dreams are lost. You will mourn, but you can heal. You will be happy again; you will dream new dreams.

1

WHAT CAN I SAY?

by Geralyn Anderson Arango

What can I tell you about my journey that will offer you hope as you embark on yours? What do you need to know now—to get you through, to get you going, to keep you going?

I wish I could be there to listen. I think it would be the best thing I could do for you. Still, I hope these few words will help.

Nicolas, our second child, has Down syndrome. We found out eighteen weeks into the pregnancy, because, though we did not want amniocentesis, we consented to a targeted ultrasound. Just for reassurance, they told us.

Given a fifty-fifty chance that what the doctor had seen would turn out to be nothing at all, we continued to hope that this was all just the result of smudges on the ultrasound monitor. And then we could get back to the business of morning sickness and weight gain.

It was nine days before we found out for sure. The business of morning sickness and weight gain was still there, but now the news was, too. We held tight to each other and to the support of family, friends, and our amazing midwife. We lashed out at the genetic counselor whose first question to us was: "Will you be terminating?"

The diagnosis of Down syndrome was almost good news, we told ourselves. Given the other possibilities—chromosomal abnormalities incompatible with life—we figured that if he had to have something, at least he, and we, could live with Down syndrome.

But, hey, let's not give you the impression we had too much

character! In truth, our days were a roller coaster of anger, sadness, denial, resignation, more anger, more sadness, and exhaustion. It felt as though we lived in the hospital while our baby was examined in utero for a suspected hole in the heart and possible inability to swallow, and while he underwent six weeks of nonstress tests (they really should change the name of that one) because he seemed to be getting too big.

We just wanted him to "get born."

He *was* big. Nicolas burst into the world at 7:23 A.M. on March 3, 1998—almost nine and a half pounds of great big baby. Twelve hours later he was in an ambulance, on his way to a medical center that could examine him from stem to stern for every little and big abnormality expected of him. One day into life, my baby was fifty miles away from me. At least I got to have visitors any time of the day or night, because the nurses knew I was the mother who couldn't visit her own baby.

A child who requires such handling can become pretty intimidating in the minds of his parents. How could mere mortals like us ever hope to take care of Nicolas? When we first went to see him in the NICU (neonatal intensive care unit), he looked so helpless. The tape holding down the tubes to his nose left scars on his cheeks I can still see today. While nursing him those first days, I had to be careful to keep him plugged in to all his monitors. Doctors, nurses, and neonatal specialists became our temporary friends, giving us his day-to-day condition, telling us what he was like. It seemed they knew him better than we did.

Nicolas looked kind of out of place in the NICU, extra large among all the premature babies. He was the first baby you noticed when you walked in—like the bouncer at a bar. And after all that examining, it turned out that he *was* out of place. The doctors found none of the abnormalities they were looking for. We took him home after a week.

They forgot to circumcise him. Oops.

It has been five months now. Nicolas has big brown eyes like his sister, and everyone says he's the image of his dad. He's a little chow hound, never letting us forget when he's got a meal coming. It seems he's a night person, most animated at about 10 P.M., laughing and cooing and chatting.

He's a baby who happens to have Down syndrome. It's still there.

It's there when I see other babies who seem physically stronger, babies who smiled sooner. It's there when I know I have to hang around the house because the physical therapist or infant educator is coming. It's there when I notice that his eyes really are a bit wide-set, almond-shaped perhaps, and his nose is so tiny. And it's there most painfully when I remember how cruel the world can be to those who are "different." It will always be there, because it is.

Through Nicolas our family has come to realize that life isn't always easy. But we still are very blessed, and we know that this little boy with Down syndrome is himself a blessing. His life has put ours on a different path than we ever imagined, but here we are.

I can't pretend to have enough character to say that it's fine with us, that we're grateful for our son's extra chromosome—for the impact it will have on his life and ours. But I can say that these days we're seeing more of Nicolas and less of his Down syndrome. He is part of what our life is now.

So what kind of hope can I offer you?

Well, if you are finding out about your child's condition in utero, as we did, and you've chosen to let your child continue his life, whatever your reasons, I can tell you that you're doing a good thing. If there's life, there can be hope. For us, hope and encouragement have come from people and places that sometimes surprised us—and always sustained us. People knew we hurt, and they were there for us in many different ways. We did not seek out any other help before Nicolas was born. We did not call any of the many "friends of friends" who had children with Down syndrome. We wanted to meet our child first. That's what worked for us. But that's us.

What should you do?

I say read, read, read (but watch those copyright dates), ask questions, think, read some more, and then ask some more questions. Write about your feelings if you can't get them out any other way. Have a good cry whenever you need it. Find out what help is available for your little one and for you and apply for services— early intervention, medical assistance, conferences, support groups, and activities where you can listen, share, and learn with other parents.

My husband and I know what we envision for both of our children in their adulthood; we've even written it down. Remember that you really are the expert on your child, so make yourself heard regarding his needs and yours. And if you can't do that right now, take someone along to do it for you. Love your child now; make decisions for him for later.

And what do you need to know about yourself?

Mostly that you're stronger than you think. But probably not as strong as you wish you were, or feel you should be. I think that's okay. Through all of this, I find I'm still me, and we're still us. I'm still trying to lose those last ten baby pounds. My husband is still planning a million projects. My daughter still says the funniest things. Nicolas is not the center of our universe; he is just the newest member of it.

• • •

Gerry Anderson Arango, a college professor of education, lives in a Philadelphia suburb with her husband, Al, a social worker, and children, Courtney Isabella (1995) and Nicolas (1998).

2

HOW TO BE MY DAUGHTER'S FRIEND

by Melissa J. Himelein

*For the White Person Who Wants to Know How to Be
  My Friend
The first thing you must do is forget that I'm Black.
Second, you must never forget that I'm Black.*
                                          —Pat Parker

• • •

*If you want to be my daughter's friend, the first thing you must do
is forget that she has a limb deficiency.*

Despite several ultrasounds, we did not know of Emma's limb deficiency until her birth. After my final push, the obstetrician looked up and softly announced, "I need to tell you: This baby has no left forearm or hand." Her twin sister, McKenzie, born thirty minutes earlier, had already been whisked off to the neonatal intensive care unit because of unresponsiveness. Consequently, the news about Emma silenced an already tense delivery room.

Throughout the fitful night after the girls' birth, worry about McKenzie's health alternated with disturbing projections of Emma's future. I imagined aggressive preschool bullies hurling insults on the playground. Rude adolescent girls staring intently at my daughter getting dressed for seventh-grade gym class. Unrequited crushes on teenage boys looking only for Barbie.

Heading down this dark road, it was possible to flash through a lifetime of angst in a matter of hours. Only later did it occur to me that many of these snapshots were, in fact, remnants of the painful parts of my own development.

The morning brought reassurance about McKenzie's health (she would spend a week in the neonatal intensive care unit but recover completely) and a chance to turn our attention to Emma. My husband and I held, fed, and cooed at her, and she responded by nodding off contentedly. We had just started muddling through our first conversation about her arm when we were interrupted by the pediatrician's knock on our door.

Dr. Munson, whom we had never met before, is a fiftyish woman with a cheerful manner and bright smile. Ignoring the tears we were each wiping away, she plucked the sleeping Emma from her bassinet, holding her with the ease and confidence of someone who has been in the baby business a long time. After a brief examination and a quick adjustment of our botched swaddling job, she turned her attention toward us, asking, "How are you feeling about Emma's arm?"

I was surprised by the directness of the question but found myself glad for the invitation to vent. But how to give voice to my jumbled emotions, and to a complete stranger?

She gently prodded, "It's okay to grieve, you know. Parents need to grieve the lost image of a perfect child."

We protested that any grieving was not for us, but for Emma, who we felt sure would have a harder life as a result of her arm.

"Why?" challenged Dr. Munson.

"Because of all the things she won't be able to do," blurted Dale.

"Like what?"

"Like play the piano," he said. This answer surprised and touched me. Dale doesn't play the piano; I do. I hadn't even thought of musical instruments. With his words, I suddenly saw a parade of woodwinds, all requiring two hands to play.

"She'll play with one hand, or maybe with her feet," was the confident retort. "What else?"

"Well, how about the basics, like tying her shoes?" Dale continued.

"She'll find a way," the doctor shrugged, telling us an anecdote about a sixty-year-old relative who ties his shoes with his teeth. "These kids find ways to do everything."

I was worried about the social implications. Dr. Munson conceded that kids can tease, or worse, but asked if we were planning to live in the area for a long time. We were. "Once she finds a social group, no one will think much of it," she promised.

And then she concluded with a statement I've replayed many times: "The only thing this girl won't be able to do is wear her wedding ring on her left hand!"

What beautiful words. And uncanny wisdom. In one simple statement she had addressed our worst fear: that our child wouldn't be loved and appreciated.

I will be forever grateful that our first spoken words about Emma were punctuated by such an encouraging and optimistic point of view. Dr. Munson gave us our first brush with what I've come to call the "forget-I'm-disabled" perspective. It is the outlook embedded in the heartwarming tales of highly successful people with disabilities that appear in family magazines; I have a file full that I am saving should Emma ever doubt her potential.

It is also the sentiment expressed by friends or family members who say, "She's just like everyone else; don't treat her any differently," or, "She will succeed at anything she wants to do." When it comes to limb deficiencies, I have come to think of this as the "just-look-at-Jim-Abbott" viewpoint, named after the famous one-armed professional baseball pitcher who is so frequently mentioned as a shining example of thriving with a limb difference.

I love this outlook, and Emma, I'm certain, will benefit from this perspective as well. We plan to start off on the right foot (pun intended) by living it to the best of my, and her, abilities. And I fervently wish for all new parents in our situation the opportunity for a wise and thoughtful Dr. Munson.

If you want to be my daughter's friend ... Second, you must never forget that she has a limb deficiency.

At the time of this writing, our girls are eighteen months old, just enough time for us to have moved through a few stages of adjustment—and to have discovered another side to the story. I find that part of me has started to resent the glibness of the chipper predictions that Emma can do or be anything she wants. I understand their intent; we all want to look on the bright side. But cloudy days are a part of life, and to deny their existence strikes me as unhealthy.

Let's pause and look honestly at the world. Is it really so perfectly adapted for the one-armed? If so, why is it possible to find the book *One-Handed in a Two-Handed World,* which identifies a multitude of problem situations (and solutions, thankfully)? The book so overwhelmed my husband that he suggested we wait a few years to read it. Or why do we spend millions, maybe billions, researching and manufacturing prostheses? Clearly scientists have accepted that there are many tasks in life that are most efficiently performed with four limbs. And what prompted the development of the Paralympics? Limb-deficient athletes must recognize *some* disadvantage in competing against their able-bodied counterparts.

Physical tasks aside, I ask, even more frankly: Is society really so enlightened in regard to its acceptance of people with disabilities? How many Miss America contestants have had physical disabilities? Or prom queens, or fashion models, or *Playboy* centerfolds? Don't get me wrong—I most emphatically want none of these in my family—but such symbols do represent a prevailing standard of perfection.

My point is not to draw attention to the negative aspects of a disability. I do not intend to dwell on these, nor would I want others to do so. But just in case my daughter doesn't happen to be Jim Abbott, I want her peers and mine to take the time to understand that life may be a little harder for her. Statements that deny the inevitability of obstacles in Emma's path strike me as less than empathic, or maybe just dumb.

What does this mean for me in raising my daughter?

Forget disability. On a day-to-day basis, I won't worry about what Emma can or can't do in life. She has already amazed me with her adaptability, discovering many creative strategies to keep up with her sister through these early developmental stages. I figure she'll let us know the things she wants to do and we'll do our best to figure out how to make them happen.

But never forget. When times are tough, I want to be ready. I expect there will be some special parenting needs required of me, and I'll do my best to be prepared. If gymnastics and the flute are on Emma's desired-activities list, for example, I'll need more than the usual doses of parental supportiveness and reassurance—and ingenuity.

There will be social hurdles. Emma will be stared at upon occasion; she already is.

Forget disability. Lots of people with physical differences are stared at, from the very short, to the very tall, to the very beautiful. Staring is not necessarily negative. It can connote simple curiosity or interest, as it did when I spent a month in Ecuador as the only fair-haired and light-skinned person many of the locals had ever seen.

But never forget. I also recognize that most people prefer to live life blending in rather than standing out. Yes, I have become accustomed to, even comfortable with, the inevitable questions about Emma's arm, be they spoken by children or unspoken by adults. But how will Emma deal with it? Because I am an introvert myself, learning to smile at stares has stretched me. When I am alone now, I notice how lucky I am to be able to walk into a crowd and simply be another face.

In short, forget disability. I believe that, deep down, everyone has their disabilities; Emma's just happen to be more visible.

But never forget. Yes, everyone has their disabilities, *but* Emma's happen to be very visible.

What does this mean for people who want to be my daughter's friend?

Forget disability. Please treat Emma just like everyone else. Stare, smile, and offer advice—no more, no less.

But never forget. Don't pretend she isn't different. Before offering the next platitude, walk in her shoes for just a minute. And if she needs help tying those shoes, offer your assistance.

I like Pat Parker's lines so much because I think they suggest the challenge that lies ahead for me, and for Emma. I don't want her missing arm to become her identity, but I think it can and should be part of it. So far, she is a beautiful blond toddler with a grin that fills her face, a placid disposition that gives way to both fits of giggles and flashes of temper now and then, blue eyes that glisten like jewels in the sunlight, an obsession for picking up garbage in the great outdoors, an enthusiastic "bop" when the weasel goes pop, and a zest for Cheerios.

Oh, yes, and one arm that can't pick up a Cheerio. Please forget—but then remember—that last part.

● ● ●

Melissa J. Himelein, Ph.D., lives in Asheville, North Carolina, with her husband and two children, Emma (1997) and McKenzie (1997).

Melissa is an associate professor of psychology (clinical) at the University of North Carolina at Asheville. Her husband is a counseling psychologist in private practice. Melissa says, "I have no professional expertise in the area of disabilities, but, obviously, a strong personal interest."

3

LIFE IS GOOD

by Susan Sivola

Deep, abiding sadness is my constant companion, as is unending joy. Sadness for what will not be, and joy for what is—life and all the good things that can be shared, like love, happiness, friendship, and peace. There are days when sorrow weighs heavily and, thankfully, days when life seems quite typical. Typical. I no longer use the word "normal." What is normal? Normal has nothing to do with my life. I am the parent of a child with special needs.

At the age of five months, my precious daughter was diagnosed with lissencephaly, a congenital brain malformation that results in severe physical and cognitive disabilities along with a shortened life span. We were devastated to learn that our perfect child had an imperfect brain and much less than rosy prospects for her life. We coped in the usual ways: utter shock initially, but with support from family and friends and from our belief that God provides for all.

The Internet became our friend and lifeline as we diligently searched for information about lissencephaly and infantile spasms, the seizure disorder that frequently accompanies this condition. My support group exists on-line. I am truly grateful to have the opportunity through technology to be connected with other parents of children with my daughter's rare disorder. It has been a great comfort to know we are not alone. We figure that if someone else is out there doing this successfully, so can we!

Like many other parents, we have a horror story to tell about the physician we saw on diagnosis day. The pediatric neurologist told us not to bother to come back, because there was nothing they could do for us. He told us to take our daughter home and find another doctor to manage her seizures. At least we were told to take her home instead of to an institution!

Since then we have been fortunate to be involved with caring, helpful professionals who value our daughter's life. We had to search for a physician who fit that bill and were successful after seeking referrals from trusted friends and professionals. I have learned not to go to see someone without a referral from someone whose judgment I trust. It's important to us that our physician or therapist be someone who respects our right to make choices for our child—someone who will educate and guide, but who allows the final decision to be ours.

An excellent example of this process is the path we chose on our quest for seizure control. After trying three drugs that were unsuccessful in controlling Teri's infantile spasms—a nasty kind of seizure which causes regression—we carefully researched our options, discussed them with our physician, and then elected to go to Canada to obtain a non-FDA (U.S. Food and Drug Administration)-approved drug. Potentially risky business but, in our opinion, our daughter's best option. And it worked.

Everyone handles their emotions differently. I am a crier by nature, and right after Teri's diagnosis, I cried every day. I no longer cry every day, but I still have "crying days" when I am more susceptible to tears.

Things that can push me over the edge? Having to tell someone about Teri's diagnosis for the first time. Thinking about losing her. Unexpected acts of kindness—like the friend who, out of the blue, long after the crisis phase had passed, provided a meal for us; the security agent at the airport who, quite sincerely, said, "God bless her"; or the casual acquaintance who told me, "I am thinking of you."

I do not apologize for my tears. It is not my intent to make others uncomfortable, and I am sorry if I do. But perhaps it is important for others to realize that the issues we have to deal with can still be painful even though they are no longer new.

We have learned many life lessons in a relatively short period of time. Living one day at a time is the most significant of these life lessons. Trying to see too far into the future is scary; there are too many unknowns and, perhaps worse, too many "knowns."

Likewise, the past holds no comfort. My typical life disappeared when the doctor said, "Mom, we have a problem." I dreaded the first anniversary of D-day (diagnosis day) but, much to my relief, found that my anticipation of the day was far worse than the day itself.

We have learned not only to live one day at a time but to rejoice in the gift of that day.

We are not far into our journey with Teri Anne. We have come a long way in the adjustment/grieving process, but we still have far to go. Just when I think I am adjusting well to our new reality, I remember how much I hate having something to adjust to. Early on people would try to comfort me by saying, "Oh, you'll meet people and have experiences you never would have had otherwise." Quite true, but no real comfort when I did not want to be there in the first place!

An odd part of the adjustment process was rebonding with my daughter. The little girl I held for almost five months before her diagnosis is not the same one I have now. The same child, but not the same. We now have a whole new set of expectations for her and for us, a new definition of "okay." I love her dearly and would not trade her for the world. Still, I sometimes fight with myself to let go of what might have been and fully appreciate the beautiful child I have.

From the start of our journey with lissencephaly, one of my biggest concerns was for our oldest child, Scott, who is four and a half years older than Teri Anne. I am one of five children, and I so wanted Scott to have a sibling with whom he could play, fight, share experiences, and reminisce. When I became pregnant with Teri Anne, I was overjoyed to know my wish for him would come true.

And he does have a sibling, only not the way I had hoped. Grieving Scott's loss was as powerful as grieving my own. Scott, however, did not know he had anything to grieve. He does not feel cheated. He loves his sister, and she plainly adores him. He plays with her, sometimes, much to his father's dismay, jouncing her all around. She enjoys it. Scott assures me it will be okay that Teri will use a wheelchair, because kids in wheelchairs can do lots of things. He accepts Teri Anne for who she is, because there is nothing else to do! With sweet simplicity and wisdom beyond his years, he makes everything okay.

Okay. At first I could not see how anything could ever be okay again. I had spent years perfecting a technique to deal with life's obstacles. I'd just plow right through, knowing I would come out okay on the other side. Now it seemed there was no other side. It was a long time before some semblance of "okay" returned to my thinking.

Recently I spoke on the phone with an old high school friend. We spent some time reminiscing, catching up on each other's lives. At one point, she remarked, "So it sounds like life is good for you."

I could not reply. Good? How could she think our life was good? The trials we have had, the heartache and heartbreak? Wasn't she listening? My daughter has a devastating condition. It is not going to go away. It is not going to get any better. Life is not going to be easy. All sorts of issues await us. How can life be good?

Finally I stammered something out in reply. I don't recall exactly what.

But now, looking back on that conversation, I am grateful for her comment. I had lost sight of what makes life good. But she apparently recognized it in the way I talked about my family and our lives together.

Teri Anne is very much loved. She is well cared for. I believe she enjoys her life. Yes, life is good. As my husband so aptly said to me one evening, "You know, we are really lucky people." If I am successful as a parent, it will be because I do not lose sight of that.

Life is good. We are okay. You will be, too.

• • •

Susan Sivola lives in rural Iowa with her husband, Eddie, children Scott (1992) and Teri Anne (1996), two dogs, two cats, and a goldfish. Susan is a physical therapist who works part-time; Ed is a crane operator working in construction.

The Sivolas are actively involved in their church. Susan serves on the Early Access Interagency Council and has participated in several task forces aimed at improving services to families of children with special needs. She and another mother have established a local support group for parents and caregivers of kids with severe disabilities in which she and Ed are both active. She is also a member of the board of directors of the community health clinic where Scott and Teri Anne receive medical care.

As members of the Lissencephaly Network, the Sivolas are in regular contact with a number of other parents of kids with lissencephaly. Teri Anne is functioning at a level higher than her MRI (magnetic resonance imaging) suggests she should! (Nothing is impossible.) Preschool plans are for full inclusion. Teri Anne is not independently mobile and not generally able to take an active part in her activities of daily living. She is able to use switch devices including voice output switches to indicate choices and call for Mom. She also enjoys playing, especially with her brother.

4

HOPE FOR LITTLE HEARTS

by Lenore Cameron

My second son, Jeffrey, was born June 6, 1996. Everything went well. In fact, I went back to work four days later, kids and all, to our family-run delicatessen.

But Jeffrey was a very sleepy baby, and his breathing was fast. I had to wake him up in order to feed him. And when he did nurse, it was only for a couple of minutes. The pediatrician saw him twice over four days, but she was not concerned. She told us that it was normal infant breathing, and that he was just sleepy.

On the night of his second visit to the pediatrician, Jeffrey woke for his evening feeding, but he didn't nurse. He just lay there in my arms. The next day we went to the deli as usual. By 11 A.M., his breathing had become very labored, his nostrils flared with each breath, and his belly was sunken. I phoned the pediatrician, who said she wanted to see him right away. He went from the pediatrician's office to a local hospital, and from there, he was transferred by air ambulance to the intensive care unit (ICU) of an area children's medical center.

After doing tests, the pediatric cardiologist told us, "What he has is not what I thought it was. It's worse. You have three options, and none of them are good."

Jeffrey had hypoplastic left heart syndrome (HLHS), a congenital heart defect in which the left side of the heart is underdeveloped. Our three options were a heart transplant, surgery done in three stages, or "comfort care"—just making our child as comfortable as possible while waiting for him to die.

My husband and I were divided. I was willing to try anything, but my husband was afraid that we'd just lose him later, instead of now, when it would be even harder.

We talked with the doctors again. They told us that his quality of life was unknown, that he could be in and out of hospitals for the rest of his life, that his chance of surviving three open-heart surgeries was slim, and that the majority of parents chose the comfort-care option. It didn't sound as though there was any hope, and we took him home to die.

At home, I could see that he was hungry. Just because he was dying didn't mean he had to starve to death, I thought. So I expressed breast milk and fed him with a medicine dropper. For six days, I did this every time he would open his eyes—remember, he was a very sleepy baby.

As the days went on, and Jeffrey didn't die, I started to make some phone calls looking for a second opinion. My husband was very angry with me and did not want to discuss it. It was very painful for him to talk about. I knew that, but someone had to fight for Jeffrey. I patiently persuaded my husband that we should at least talk with the doctors from Boston, where the three-stage surgery is performed. After speaking with both a pediatric cardiologist and a cardiothoracic surgeon, Tim was finally convinced. He phoned me from the deli and said, "We're taking him in." When he came home, he walked up to me, gave me a hug, and said, "I'm sorry it took me so long."

On June 24, 1996, Jeffrey underwent stage I of the Norwood Procedure. He survived the surgery and was discharged on July 8. He had the second surgery the following January. In 2000, he is awaiting his third.

Our mischievous son is the result of a miracle because he made it through all the obstacles to his having the surgery in the first place! Shouldn't it have been easier? How many others haven't been as fortunate? Despite the success stories, medical opinions about prognosis remain controversial.

After talking with other parents of children with HLHS from all over the country, I have learned that the hopeless prognosis is not limited to us. I've also learned that different specialists have widely varying opinions on treating HLHS. But at the time of diagnosis, parents of a child with HLHS know nothing of all this. They entrust the lives of their children to experts and don't question what they are told. I was the same way initially. I figured these doctors were specialists. The idea of a second opinion never crossed my mind.

We also received no written information on HLHS. When I asked, I was told none was available. I have since obtained information on HLHS and have passed it along to doctors with the hope that they will pass it along to new parents.

After the miracle of Jeffrey's survival, I felt a need to help other parents who would be facing this nightmare diagnosis in the future. After learning there wasn't a support group for parents of children with congenital heart defects in Connecticut, Massachusetts, or Rhode Island, I started one. In March 1998, Little Hearts was born; four months later, the group had more than 50 families. Two years later, there were 175 families!

After our experiences with Jeffrey, I wondered how we could convince doctors to offer parents a more hopeful outlook. Then I had a brainstorm! How about taking a group picture of all these kids who had been born with HLHS?

So far, I've organized three get-togethers for parents with children with HLHS. Ten families came to the first one in 1997. In 1998, 18 families attended; in 1999, 43 families with HLHS children from all over New England joined us—with children ranging in age from two months to thirteen years. At these gatherings, I take a group shot of all our kids; we call it the "picture of hope."

What a testimony to quality of life these gatherings are! We parents watched all our children running around the playground, just being kids. Without looking at their name tags, you could not tell which child had had heart surgery! I have made more than seven hundred copies of the "pictures of hope" and have sent them to health care professionals all over. Recently I turned them into posters that now hang in clinics and hospitals.

My advice to other parents is this:

1. Ask questions until you're satisfied. Don't feel that you are "bothering" the professionals. It's their job to help you.
2. Always have pen and paper with you. Write down your questions and the doctor's replies. Take lots of notes.
3. Get a second opinion. Don't worry about hurting your doc-

tor's feelings. It's harmless and easy. Just have copies of the records forwarded to another doctor for an opinion.

Remember, you are your child's voice and advocate!

• • •

Lenore Cameron lives in Cromwell, Connecticut, with her husband, Timothy, and their two children, Matthew (1993) and Jeffrey (1996). Lenore worked at Aetna for thirteen years after graduating from high school. Tim worked for Northern Telecom for seven years after coming out of the Air Force. From 1988 through 1998, Tim and Lenore operated a delicatessen where they brought both children every day. Since its closing, Lenore has been a stay-at-home mom who devotes much of her time to helping other families and the growing support network.

Little Hearts is a support network of parents. It is not just for families with HLHS children. It is for families with children with all kinds of congenital heart defects, including those who have lost a child and parents expecting a child with a congenital heart defect. Visit on-line at: http//www.littlehearts.net.

5

HE HAS STARS IN HIS EYES

by Hope C. Thorpe

My husband and I were married three years before we had our first child. I had just turned twenty-five, and my husband was twenty-seven. When we found out that we were expecting, we were thrilled.

The first six months of the pregnancy went very well. I didn't have one concern in the world, not even a single day of morning sickness. At each monthly checkup, my doctor expressed his happiness with the way I was progressing.

Then everything changed. In the sixth month of my pregnancy, I was diagnosed with gestational diabetes, and my body started to produce antibodies that were attacking the baby's blood system. I had been affected by Rh incompatibility. Then we got the news of something "inconclusive" on the sonogram.

Since I suddenly had all these "problems," my doctor referred me to a specialist in a hospital an hour away from our home. Through all of the blood tests, sonograms, and various other tests, it wasn't until the eighth month of my pregnancy that the specialist told us there might be "something genetic going on." He did not give this condition a name or lead us to believe he suspected Down syndrome.

With all the uncertainty, the specialist decided it would be best for the baby to be delivered early. Labor was induced one month before my due date. Our son was born not breathing and had to be rushed into the neonatal intensive care unit. I was taken to my hospital room to recover.

About an hour later, two doctors walked into my room. Standing at the foot of my bed, they told me the baby showed signs of Down syndrome. They mentioned almond-shaped eyes, a large space between his first and second toes, low-placed ears, and "palmar creases"—straight lines traversing the palms of his hand.

"How crazy!" I thought. How could they make a diagnosis just by looking at him! Then they told me they had taken a sample of his blood to test his DNA (deoxyribonucleic acid).

I still had not seen our baby. After the doctors left my room, I called for a nurse. She wheeled me down to a room with seven incubators, a tiny baby in each one—each baby hooked up to IV solutions, monitors, oxygen, and other medical equipment. In the corner, I saw a puff of red hair attached to a beautiful baby—my little Anthony.

As I held him for the first time, I could see he had his daddy's hair and my cheeks. But I heard the doctors' words repeat themselves in my head: "Down syndrome, almond eyes, palmar crease."

I inspected him from top to bottom. Running through our family tree in my mind, I could see where he'd inherited each trait. This is just how he looks, I told myself. Nothing is wrong with him.

After Anthony had been home for two weeks I called the genetic specialist. I had convinced myself that Anthony was fine, and I expected good news. Then the doctor said the exact opposite of what I'd expected to hear. Anthony had Down syndrome. I felt the hope drain slowly from my heart. I remember crying without a sound.

At first I felt guilty. I wondered if I had done something wrong during the pregnancy. Then I felt sad, realizing that Anthony's disability would make his life more difficult. After a while, the guilt and sadness went away. I started to remember why we'd had a baby in the first place—because we wanted one!

We never asked for a perfect child. We just wanted to have a family together, and that's what we have. A baby with Down syndrome needs the same care as one without Down syndrome. We hold, bathe, play with, and, most of all, love Anthony just as we would love any child of ours.

What is different is our outlook on life. Having a baby with Down syndrome has enlightened our lives in many ways. We wake up in the morning to a baby who is smiling. We go to bed knowing our son is content. He has made me realize that we all should learn to slow down a bit and enjoy the things that we take for granted.

One of the things we learned about Down syndrome is that some people have white spots around the colored part of their eyes. Anthony has a cluster of them—we call them the stars in his eyes.

We believe Anthony's future is wide open. He will have the same opportunities as a child without a disability. In fact, Anthony may have more opportunities than he otherwise would have had. He has already met people he would not have met without his diagnosis. Our horizons have also been broadened. We know that whatever Anthony becomes will be a result of what we do with him and for him. But is this not the case with any child?

• • •

Hope and Jeffrey S. Thorpe live in upstate New York. Although Anthony (1997) was an only child when this essay was written, his parents hope for more children in the future. Hope works at a health insurance company; Jeffrey works at a lumber company.

6

LOOKING TOWARD THE FUTURE UNAFRAID

by Terrin Pelham

Ten little fingers, ten perfect toes, curly blond locks, and shiny blue eyes that look deep inside you. You couldn't possibly put into words what this newborn baby boy means in your life. After all, how can you put your very soul into words?

Suddenly the sound of shattering glass echoes in your head. Your heart sinks to the floor as the doctor describes Klinefelter syndrome and explains how chromosomes work. You cry. You look at your baby trying to see the difference between now and just ten minutes ago, before you knew.

You look at the doctor for a sign that he understands the heartache and fear he has just handed you. He smiles and tells you you can see a geneticist next week.

In the meantime, he tells you that even though XXY or Kline-felter syndrome is the most common genetic condition known to man, it is still one of the most underdiagnosed and misunderstood. He can tell you that boys with XXY may have learning disabilities, speech problems, and motor skill delays. These boys are called "late bloomers" as they may walk or talk a bit later than their peers.

He continues. At puberty, when the other boys are developing secondary sexual characteristics, your son may be delayed again. He will probably be tall and thin with sparse body and facial hair; he is likely to have small testes. Your son will probably not produce enough natural testosterone and will need regular injections or pills. He tells you that your son may experience breast tissue development but then emphasizes that only a few cases are so noticeable that surgery may be indicated.

You sit with your chin in your lap listening carefully. He begins to explain the effects of low, or no, testosterone, but then carefully reminds you that *your son* has an early diagnosis, so he can get that testosterone when he needs it and avoid many of the problems the doctor has just described. Then, just when you think you've heard the worst, he lowers his voice and tells you that your son will probably be sterile and unable to father children of his own. There is much more he could say—he pauses—but he wants you to get the rest of the information from the specialist, the genetics counselor. Before leaving, he advises you against going to the library to do your own research. What an odd prescription.

You go to the library immediately. For days you read. You quickly realize why your doctor had advised you not to do this. The outlook is grim. These studies are old, out-of-date, and, in many cases, just plain wrong, but, of course, you do not know this yet. You sit on the couch, book propped up in one hand, shining little angel of a baby boy cradled by the other.

Every so often you look up from the medical data to see the baby's shining blue eyes. They still touch your soul. His smile makes you stop what you're doing to try to remember what your life was like before he came. You think of all of your own imperfections and wonder if this child would love you the same if he knew them all. Of course he would, because this little boy has something adults seem to lose somewhere along life's trail. He still has the ability to love without condition. With that fact foremost in your mind, you close the dusty textbook, kiss your baby's cheek, and take a deep breath. Suddenly you know what you need to do.

You decide to give this child as much of yourself as he has already given to you. He loves you unconditionally; you will offer that kind of love to him. You hit the books again, but this time you are looking for ways to help him. You sift through the old studies and dig your way forward to the newer ones. You reread the classic textbook data and ask yourself if this is really what will be.

You realize the answer to your question lies with the men who have lived this life before your son. Before long, you are talking to dozens of men with XXY. Almost all were diagnosed later in life—some in puberty, but most in adulthood. You ask, "Would your life have been any different if your parents had known then what we know now?" And you hold your breath waiting for the answer.

The answer is a resounding, immediate "Yes!" You flash back to the textbooks in the library. Would those sad textbook cases have made it into the textbooks if the mothers of those boys had known? If they'd known what to do? If their doctors had known what to do?

Your task is clear: Listen to what these men are telling you and allow their stories and experience to help you help your son. They tell you to love your son and never doubt him; they tell you the pitfalls to watch for and how to help your son get over them; they tell you to listen more to your heart and your son, less to the school system. They tell you that you may need to educate your son's teachers. They remind you that no one will fight harder for your son than you will. They tell you to educate your doctor and everyone else who will play an important role in your son's life so your son can grow up in a better world. They tell you what a huge difference testosterone given at puberty would have made in their lives. They tell you to get a second medical opinion if you think the first one doesn't do your child justice. They tell you all this and so much more.

If anyone can write an owner's manual for your son, these men can. You realize that they have given you the ability to touch your child's soul as he has touched yours. You look to the future. You are not afraid.

• • •

Terrin lives with her husband, Les, and their two children (1987, 1996). She works as a travel agent during the day and a dispatcher at night. Terrin and Les also own and operate a computer bulletin board which houses Terrin's web site about XXY: http://www. tmoon.com/ks/ks.htm.

Terrin is also the owner of T.L.C. Create-a-Book, which makes personalized children's books. Terrin does all of the above work from home, which allows her to be with and raise her two boys. She dedicates her spare time to educating others about XXY in hopes of creating a better world for her son to live in, one that sees him as he will see himself—a wonderful human being.

7

TOO MUCH REALITY

by Pamela Simmons

The C-section went smoothly, and soon the doctor held Katherine up. There was just one brief cry, then silence. Although I couldn't see what was happening, I could sense the growing tension in the room.

The crash cart arrived, and doctors worked urgently to stabilize Katherine for transport to Children's Hospital. As they wheeled her to my bedside in Recovery, tubes and wires everywhere, I realized it might be the last time I would see her. I longed to scoop her up into my arms but could only reach out from my bed to touch her little arm inside the Isolette™. The paramedics placed a Polaroid picture on my gown as they wheeled her out, promising to do all they could.

Everything had happened so fast. I had expected to be cradling my newborn baby by now. Instead, I lay in Recovery overwhelmed by fear, grief, and disbelief. The pain was so sharp and deep it seemed more than I could possibly endure.

The next hours were heart-wrenching, not knowing whether she would make it or what was wrong. Thankfully, Katherine survived the night and, within days, became stable enough to be moved to a less critical nursery. But the questions remained. While doctors searched for answers, I strained to speed my own recovery in order to earn a trip to Children's Hospital where I would be able to hold my baby for the first time.

As I gingerly walked the halls of the maternity ward, I saw the other mothers gently holding their babies close. I wept as I passed the nursery full of healthy little babies. My arms were empty, my little bundle not so perfect.

I cried to God, "This pain is unbearable!" But I know He was with me, because somehow I did endure it. After crying and pouring my heart out to God, I regained courage and determination. If God trusted me to take care of His special child, I told myself, I was up to the task and would love her with all my heart.

Just days later we faced the first of many difficult decisions—whether to approve surgery to help with Katherine's diagnosis and, hopefully, determine appropriate treatment. It was almost unthinkable to consider putting her under anesthesia only days after she had been so close to death. But as she continued to struggle so much to breathe, eat, or move, we felt we had to take that risk.

Katherine handled the surgery well. Many tests and procedures later, the doctors assigned a very general diagnosis of arthrogryposis to describe her multiple joint contractures and muscle weakness—the cause of her restricted movement and, most likely, a contributing factor to her respiratory and swallowing difficulties. Doctors could not say if her other physical problems—cleft palate, dislocated hips, and softening of the trachea and larynx—were related. Since most of the test results were inconclusive, so was her prognosis.

Family, friends, and even people we'd never met were praying for Katherine. We were thankful for the support we felt through them and for each little bit of encouraging news. It was such a difficult and confusing time, both emotionally and spiritually.

I had long been a Christian. I relied on God to help me through each day and make sense out of life, but this was too much reality. All my neat little anecdotes about life now proved feeble. I clung to God to sustain me because I knew that only with His strength could I possibly survive.

I tried to have faith that God would answer my prayers to heal Katherine. At the same time, I knew that assuming that my faith would obligate God to heal my daughter was to reduce Him to nothing more than a genie.

I knew He loved me; I knew He grieved with me—but why didn't He do something? Just how did God fit into all this?

Years earlier, after a miscarriage, I had become very angry with

God. In the years since, I had come to realize that He was just as grieved about this painful world as I was. I also saw that He was able to use tragedy to help others. Because I was sure of His love and goodness, I struggled to make sense of it all, realizing His eternal perspective is much different from ours.

After four weeks in the hospital and training in CPR (cardiopulmonary resuscitation), physical therapy, tube feeding, and use of oxygen, apnea monitors, and suction machines, we were finally able to bring Katherine home. I desperately awaited that homecoming, longing to be able to see and hold her whenever I wanted. But I didn't realize how overwhelming her care would be, especially with an active three-year-old at home as well. The physical demands and emotional drain often seemed more than I could bear.

Most frustrating and disheartening was the emotional roller coaster ride driven by her physical health. For a while, she seemed to be improving and grew very alert and responsive. And in spite of her difficulties, she maintained the sweetest disposition and a most infectious smile! When she was doing well, I would cautiously allow myself to begin to dream of the future. But each time I did, she would soon be back in the hospital.

A total and complete physical healing was apparently not God's design—at least not then—because soon the bad times became more and more frequent. Finally we faced the choice of letting Katherine die or pursuing a tracheotomy and, possibly, long-term dependence on a respirator. I knew others had faced decisions like this. Perhaps I even believed I knew what I would do in such circumstances. But I had never really expected to face this decision. How could I stop short of doing all I could to save my child? But at the same time, how could I sentence her to possible "life imprisonment" tethered to a machine?

We went ahead with the surgery, and Katherine's care escalated. She was in the hospital five weeks while we learned how to manage the trache and ventilator in addition to her already full regimen of therapies, medication, tube feedings, and normal baby needs. When she came home again, I wasn't sure I could handle it all, but I was determined not to send her to a nursing home. Every day I felt as if I was running a marathon, often wondering if I was attempting the impossible. I struggled with guilt about my inability to spend much quality time with either of my daughters, not to mention a very stressed-out marriage. I questioned whether our choice was fair to Katherine, so restricted by the ventilator, or to her sister, now always second to Katherine's critical needs.

The stress was relentless, like being in emergency-response mode all day long. At any moment, Katherine's life could rest in my hands. Countless times she would go into respiratory distress. I would work frantically to clear her airway while trying to reassure her worried sister or, more often, explain why I couldn't get her juice right now!

My emotions were just as volatile. I struggled with bitterness toward others. For a time, I couldn't even go to the mall. I became so disgusted watching others deliberate over which color blouse to buy while I agonized over whether my daughter would see her first birthday, and, if so, what kind of life she would have. I poured out all my anger, pain, and frustration into letters addressed to God. I knew He was the only one big enough to handle the rawest of my emotions.

Today Katherine is halfway through her second year. Although the stress and demands still overwhelm me at times, experience, a routine, and nursing support have alleviated a lot of the pressure. Katherine is still on the ventilator, although we are beginning to try to wean her. She continues to be tube-fed, and her big sister has become skilled at flushing her feeding tube! Therapy has increased her range of motion tremendously, but crawling, walking, and talking are still distant goals. The future is unknown, yet we are hopeful. My questions related to prayer and faith persist, but I have also found a lot of comfort and peace in knowing God remains in control even when I don't understand and that His love for us reaches far beyond this life.

Fellow struggler, hang in there! Don't hesitate to question doctors or insist on what you know is best for your child. A good social worker is invaluable in identifying the best agencies to meet your child's needs. Persistence and frequent follow-up are the keys to securing that help. No one knows or cares for your child as you do.

•   •   •

Pamela Simmons lives with her husband, Bryan, and two daughters, Miranda (1994) and Katherine (1997), in Medina, Ohio.

Bryan works as a manager for a computer consulting firm in Cleveland. Pamela stays at home to care for the girls. Pamela and Bryan are working to form a network of parents of children on ventilators. Pamela says, "Bryan and I would like to thank our families and friends for serving as God's loving hands, sharing the burden when it becomes too heavy to bear alone."

8

AIDAN'S GIFT

by Valle Dwight

I think it's serendipitous that my second son's birthday is so close to Mother's Day. When Aidan arrived, I had already been a mother for more than three years. My first son, Timmy, a strong-willed, inquisitive boy, had taught my husband, Phil, and me many things—like how to survive on four hours' sleep, the best ways to navigate a tantrum, and how to hide vegetables in chili. But I don't think I came face to face with the true meaning of motherhood until Aidan entered our lives eighteen months ago.

It was the first day of spring when Phil and I checked into the hospital. Shortly thereafter, Aidan came into the world looking very much like his brother, howling, arms and legs flailing, a mop of wild red hair matted to his head. But when the midwife handed him to me, I looked right into his tiny face and stopped for just one instant. Hmmm, I remember thinking, his eyes look a little strange.

I quickly rejected that thought—no, everything's fine—and turned to Phil. We reveled in the afterglow of what had been an easy birth and talked about how lucky we were. We were filled with gratitude for the beautiful family we had created, and looked forward to getting home and starting our lives together.

Then the nurse arrived to tell us that she needed to send the baby to the nursery because he was a little cold and they wanted

This essay first appeared in *FamilyFun* magazine.

to warm him up. She took him away, and we began to call family and friends to share the good news about our eight-pound, thirteen-ounce newborn. But when Aidan still hadn't been returned an hour later, I had a nagging feeling that something was wrong. I didn't want to ruin the moment, or lend weight to my fears, so I said nothing to Phil.

"Oh, I'm Sure They Can Fix It"

The midwife arrived. She told us there was a possibility our baby had "chromosomal problems." I refused to let it sink in. Oh, a chromosomal problem, I thought. I'm sure they can fix it. Although my mind hadn't registered her meaning, my body must have because a chill ran right to my neck. Phil was silent.

Maybe one of us asked what she meant exactly. Maybe she spotted our look of obvious misunderstanding. So she spelled it out: "The nurse thinks he may have Down syndrome."

From where I sit now, I can divide my life into two parts. There's the time before we heard those words, and the time after. Before, we were probably like most people. We knew we were lucky. We were healthy. Our little boy, Timmy, was funny and strong and happy. We had jobs and a loving family. But until we were hit with those words, I don't think we had any idea how fragile luck can be.

I knew nothing about Down syndrome, but I had lots of frightening preconceptions. My first thought, even as I nursed my son in the hospital, was, "How will he get a job?" Right from the start, my instinct was to hold him tightly against a world that seemed irreversibly changed.

The Amnio We'd Passed On

I thought back on my uneventful pregnancy. Because I was over thirty-five, my doctor had advised me to have an amniocentesis. So I'd made an appointment for the prenatal tests that would determine whether my baby had a chromosomal abnormality or spina bifida. I got as far as the ultrasound. Just before the doctor started the test, I changed my mind. I told the doctor I didn't want to risk a miscarriage.

"Well, your chance is one in one hundred that you'll have a baby with Down syndrome," she said. "I've had ninety-nine other women in here this month and none of their babies had Down syndrome. You might be the one."

I had been ambivalent about the amnio from the start. Driving to the appointment, I'd told Phil that I didn't want to terminate the pregnancy no matter what the amnio revealed, and he'd agreed. We'd planned to have a second child, and there was no going back.

"Even if the baby has Down syndrome," I told the doctor, "I won't terminate the pregnancy, so what difference does it make?"

"Well, that's what everyone says," she told me. "But they change their minds when they get the test results."

I was offended by her flippant attitude toward my baby. "Well, I'm not changing mine." And we left, clutching the ultrasound photos of our beautiful baby.

Grieving for the Child We Had Expected

Now here I was five months later, holding my blue-eyed baby who suddenly seemed so distant. We took Aidan home and waited a week for the blood test that would tell us for sure whether the doctors' suspicions were correct. Meanwhile, we stared at him, wondering. We compared him to pictures of Timmy as a baby. And we went back and forth. Did he look the same or different? And were the differences we saw a result of Down syndrome, or because he was a different person? I kept thinking about the moment he was born, when I'd noticed something odd about his eyes.

By the time the results were in, I thought I'd resigned myself to the worst. But the news set me reeling. I cried for two days. I was grieving for the baby we had expected, the only one we thought we were prepared for.

Not One "I'm Sorry" Among Them

When the tears dried, I began the long learning process that will continue, I imagine, for the rest of my life. Having resolved to find out everything I could, I went on-line, I read books, I talked to people.

I was surprised to discover that everyone in the world, it seemed, was either related to, went to school with, or grew up next door to someone with Down syndrome. Everyone but me.

I discovered an Internet support group for parents, and at the urging of one of them, I posted a message announcing Aidan's birth. The fact that he had Down syndrome was understood. These parents wanted to know the truly important things, like our baby's height, weight, and hair color. Their questions put things into perspective for me.

Within days we had received more than fifty congratulatory notes—not one "I'm sorry" among them. Our spirits soared. Friends and family had been very supportive, but, let's face it, they knew as little about Down syndrome as we had. And they were all a little sad, too. But these other parents weren't sad at all. They felt that their children were a great gift, Down syndrome or no.

Letting Aidan Teach Us What We Need to Know

As I pored over the books and talked with these other parents, I found the factual side of Down syndrome fairly easy to piece together. Also called trisomy 21, it is caused when a person is born with three copies of chromosome 21, rather than the usual two. This extra chromosome, and all its associated genes, alters the development of body and brain. What this would mean for Aidan specifically would be hard to say, but he would be developmentally delayed to some degree (most people with Down syndrome fall in the moderate to mild range of mental retardation), and he would have low muscle tone. This would make it tougher for him to crawl, walk, and talk. The list of other potential problems was daunting: heart defects, hearing loss, vision problems, small airways that could make him prone to upper respiratory infections, and on and on.

In fact, it seemed that we spent the first few months of Aidan's life in the offices of endless medical specialists, most with titles longer than our baby's tiny body. By his first birthday, Aidan had seen a pediatric cardiologist, pulmonologist, ophthalmologist, audiologist, and orthopedist, to name just a few.

Of course, there was nothing in those reference books that could fully explain the other side of the story—the ups and downs of raising a child with Down syndrome in our society. That's what we've been learning from Aidan himself, and it's been a lesson filled with wonder. Aidan's life so far has been more complicated than Timmy's was. There are more ongoing appointments—weekly physical therapy, play group, and one-on-one sessions with a teacher. There have been challenging days and frustrating moments as we've all struggled to learn about each other.

But we've come to recognize that we've had trying times with Timmy, too—they've just been over different issues. Timmy never slept. Aidan goes to bed at 7:30 P.M. and wakes up laughing. Timmy threw tantrums to beat the band; Aidan definitely knows what he wants, but he's generally much less stubborn. We're learning, as all parents discover with the birth of their second child, that each child is different.

Rocking to "Itsy Bitsy Spider"

Aidan is actually more like other kids than he is different. He will learn to walk, talk, read, sing, and dance (you should see him rock to "Itsy Bitsy Spider"), although he will have to work harder than most kids to reach those milestones. And we will have to slow down and allow him the extra time. Beyond that, he will have skills, talents, and quirks all his own. He already does. He scoots around the house using his bottom, two hands, and one foot faster than any crawler I've seen. He can find his Barney doll no matter how well we've hidden it. And he's already using sign language, predating his eventual use of words.

When Aidan was newly born, "Down syndrome" was all I saw when I looked at him. But now I see that the syndrome is just a small part of who he is and what he will become. Aidan has shown us that contrary to stereotypes, kids with Down syndrome aren't always sweet angels. When he does get angry, he can throw a tantrum to rival his brother's. When he doesn't want to eat, he sweeps his vegetables off the table with a stubborn flourish. And he hustles away with a backward glance and devilish giggle when he knows he's put something in his mouth that he shouldn't. Like the rest of us, kids with Down syndrome have a range of personalities, moods, and temperaments.

The future for people with Down syndrome is brighter than it has ever been, and this makes me hopeful for my son's adulthood. Early intervention, medical advances, inclusive schools, and new therapies have meant that people with Down syndrome can live longer, achieve more, and contribute to their communities in meaningful ways. Most graduate from high school; many live independently, marry, and have jobs.

While I wondered on Aidan's first day of life how he would ever find a job, now I dream about the possibilities. Will he love the theater the way his father does? Maybe he'll want to work at a newspaper, as so many generations of my family have. Perhaps he'll be wiser than his parents and find work that actually makes money.

Still Lucky

It has been only a short time since Aidan came into our world. To a degree, we're still on an emotional roller coaster. We have days of unadulterated joy over what Aidan brings to our family. And we have more wistful days when we wish life were simpler, though these come less and less often. Sometimes I get sad about the might-have-beens, especially on the days when Timmy makes plans about things he and Aidan will do together, and I wonder which of those dreams will come true. Many days I feel guilty and unsure whether we're doing enough for Aidan. Would he be better off if we could afford this program, those vitamins, or that new therapy? And sometimes I get scared about what's down the road, especially when I think of the struggles he may face making friends in those horrible junior high years, or making his way in a culture that places such high value on convention and looks.

But I've long since realized that our luck did not run out the day he was born. Not at all. In many ways, our lives have been transformed. We have found loving support from people who used to be strangers. We look at the world differently and consider ourselves lucky to be able to. We have an appreciation for a slower pace; we take greater delight in each small step. And we have a newfound understanding of the preciousness of all people.

• • •

Valle Dwight, a freelance writer, lives in Florence, Massachusetts, with her husband, Phil, and children, Timmy (1993) and Aidan (1996).

9

THE FUTURE IS NOW

by Albert Freedman

The doctor, a pediatric neurologist, wore a bow tie, a furrowed brow, and a look of seriousness. After silently conducting a fifteen-minute examination of our six-month-old baby, the doctor suggested that my wife dress our son before sharing the results of his evaluation. Jack cooed and smiled as Anne pulled his shirt back over his head.

After some awkward small talk, the doctor described Jack's muscle weakness and his concerns about our baby's physical development. His words hung in the air for what felt like hours.

"It is very likely your baby has a neuromuscular disease. Because it is Friday afternoon, I would recommend he be admitted to our hospital on Monday, so we can run some tests. I can make arrangements for you to stay at the Ronald McDonald House."

A wave of dread passed through me. I felt surprised and angry at the suggestion that something was so wrong with Jack that we would be invited to stay at a Ronald McDonald House. We had noticed Jack was a rather floppy baby, not yet sitting up or rolling over, but we hadn't thought much of it.

My wife, Anne, began to cry. She immediately asked if Jack would die. "I cannot tell you what the future will hold," the doctor replied. "I need to see the test results to be certain of anything. It's possible I am wrong, but a neuromuscular disease is what I suspect."

We were able to schedule the diagnostic tests for Tuesday of the next week, and we took Jack home. And then we waited. And waited. And waited. Jack was our first child.

What would the future hold for our baby, and for us? For four very long days in November 1995, Anne and I were left to ponder that question. For four days, Anne and I took long walks together pushing Jack in his stroller. We talked about all of the possibilities for Jack's future. Maybe the doctor was wrong? But what if he was correct and our son did have a terrible disease?

As we walked down a long country road together one morning, Anne again raised the possibility that Jack could die, which stopped our conversation in its tracks. For a few frozen moments, we heard only the fallen leaves rustling under the wheels of Jack's stroller. We looked down at our little guy; he laughed as he saw both of our faces at once. We smiled back, hiding our fears. Losing our baby just didn't seem real. Jack was very much alive and happy, without a worry in the world.

As we waited, I realized I did not know anything about neuromuscular diseases. The only muscle disease I had heard of was muscular dystrophy. I thought about the children I had seen on the Jerry Lewis telethon and my stomach knotted—I wasn't ready to get too close to one of Jerry's Kids, much less be responsible for one. I wasn't ready to be the father of a child in a wheelchair. I didn't want our son to live an unhappy, limited, sad, and difficult life. I just wanted to play ball with him.

To me, not knowing was worse than knowing. Until the tests were completed, I didn't know if our child would live a normal life, live his life with a serious disability, or not live at all. All I knew was that I was scared.

The following Tuesday, after a series of tests, the doctors broke the news to us that Jack was indeed affected by a neuromuscular disease called spinal muscular atrophy, a disease for which there is no cure or treatment. The doctors told us that although Jack's cognitive development would not be compromised, he would be unable to remain physically healthy because of his weakened muscles. They told us our baby had about a year to live. They told us Jack would not suffer.

At the moment the doctors explained that babies with spinal muscular atrophy typically do not live longer than two years, I admit that I felt both shocked and relieved. I was shocked to hear Jack would die, but at the same time I felt relieved we would not be burdened with the awesome responsibility of caring for a child with a disability. Anne and I, along with our families, sat in silence as we absorbed this terrible news. For a few moments, we all looked at each other through our tears wondering what to say or do.

Finally, it was Jack himself who broke the silence. He wasn't happy about being cooped up in a little room with so many people. And he needed his diaper changed. And he was hungry. Within a few seconds, Jack reminded me that we were still his parents and he was counting on us to take care of him. I later came to realize that we would forever be Jack's parents, no matter what the future held.

During appointments with medical specialists during the next two weeks, we learned about CPR (cardiopulmonary resuscitation), monitors, respirators, and the decisions we would likely face. We learned things no parent should ever have to learn. We were told what would happen when our baby got sick. We were encouraged to make an appointment with a genetic specialist because of the very real possibility we could conceive another child with the same disease. The doctors were humane and honest and spent a great deal of time with the two of us, our families, and Jack. The doctors and nurses taught us everything they thought we should know about caring for Jack before taking him home.

But there was one important element missing from each of those medical consultations—hope. We didn't hear much about living with Jack from day to day. The doctors never mentioned the good days we would have together as a family. Looking back, I now realize it was Jack's job to teach us these important lessons. After all, doctors don't spend a lot of time with kids when they are well. Parents do that.

As I write this, more than four years have passed since we learned of Jack's illness. The doctors were right about Jack's diagnosis; he is severely affected by spinal muscular atrophy. He is too physically weak to sit up or walk, too weak to talk, and too weak to move his arms and legs very much. He has been hospitalized in the pediatric intensive care unit four times because of illnesses.

But four years later, Jack is very much alive. Amazingly, our son does not let any of his limitations discourage him. He's simply too busy and too determined to be discouraged about anything.

On most days, Jack's a very happy little boy who enjoys many of the same activities as other four-year-olds.

Despite his physical disability, a combination of technology and creativity allows Jack to experience a great deal of independence. Just after Jack's second birthday, he was fitted for a new power wheelchair. Before he turned three, he had learned to drive it. Now, a few months from his fourth birthday, Jack explores our home, the school campus where we live, museums, malls, and any wheelchair-friendly terrain. At this point, our greatest challenge is keeping up with Jack as he motors around. And like every other parent we know, we now have to use the word "no!"

For exercise, Jack swims daily with the help of a special flotation device. The water is therapeutic for the muscles, and Jack loves the increased mobility he experiences in the water. For learning and playing, Jack is the master of our home computer. With the help of a special trackball mouse and a switch, he is able to read stories, play games, learn his letters and numbers, and move from one program to another. Recently, Jack learned how to use communication software to "speak." By clicking on an icon or picture, Jack is able to tell us where he wants to go, what he wants to eat, the names of his friends, and lots more. He's thrilled to be able to "talk." Next year, if we are lucky, Jack will be able to go to school with the other children his age.

Although the reality of Jack's medical fragility is very much with us, our home has its own version of normalcy and routines. Jack's day typically includes some work and some play, three meals, visits with friends, a trip in the car, a bath, and bedtime stories. Like most families, we have our ups and downs. Our home is indeed filled with an unusual combination of children's books and toys, medical equipment, love, and uncertainty. Our family's rhythm is different from most, but it works for us. I've come to appreciate every smile, every newly learned computer game, every small stroke in the pool, and every new place Jack discovers while exploring in his chair. Each day we spend together as a family is truly a gift.

My feelings about our son's diagnosis have changed dramatically during the past four years. In retrospect, it's hard for me to believe I felt a sense of relief upon learning that our son would not live long. Now, when we receive mail from Jerry Lewis's organization, I welcome it. They do fine work. We are also active members of an organization called Families of Spinal Muscular Atrophy, a national group that supports kids like Jack and their families all around the world. To contribute to the cause, a couple of friends and I created the group's web site *(www.fsma.org)*. With so much about Jack's situation beyond my control, the web site project provides me with a constructive opportunity to do something proactive.

Looking back, the past four years have somehow brought more joy than sorrow, more triumph than defeat. No, I won't be able to play ball with my boy, and the loss of that dream still hurts every once in a while. But what Jack can do has become much more important to me than what he can't. My son is a happy, intelligent, hard-working little person of whom I am deeply proud.

The doctors now tell us they really don't know how long Jack will live. The researchers now tell us medical treatments may become available within our son's lifetime. Anything is possible, they say. Looking back, there was much wisdom in the words of the doctor who told us, "I cannot tell you what the future will hold."

It would be very easy for Anne and me to spend all of our time worrying and wondering about the future. But that wouldn't be fair to Jack. He needs us to be with him right now, in the present. He has places to go, people to see, and things to do. And so do we.

• • •

Al, Anne, and Jack Freedman live in Westtown, Pennsylvania. Al is a counseling psychologist who works with children, adolescents, and families at the Westtown School and in private practice. Al also supports children with special needs, and their families, through presentations and workshops at medical and educational conferences. Anne is a teacher who currently works full time taking care of Jack. Jack was born on April 23, 1995.

10

REDEFINING PERFECTION

by Carol Driver

"Special needs, handicapped, differently abled, disabled, exceptional, sick, chronically ill, and technology dependent—these are some of the terms you are going to hear people use to describe your son," the hospital social worker told us. She went on, "Some of these descriptions you will like better than others, and some you will despise, but you will, nonetheless, hear them from this day forward."

My husband and I walked away shaking our heads. What was she talking about? Lying in the incubator on the fifth floor of the hospital was a beautiful newborn baby boy, our little boy. He had been born with spina bifida and hydrocephalus, but what did that mean to us? All we knew was that he was our son and he was perfect in every way.

The doctors told us his head was large due to the buildup of cerebrospinal fluid in his skull. They gave us detailed information about the surgery they would perform to place a shunt in his ventricle. The shunt would act as a conduit to remove the excess fluid.

We listened and understood, but when we peered into that incubator his head looked perfectly fine to us. It was covered with soft brown hair that shimmered with red highlights. His nose was chiseled to perfection, and since he was born by cesarean, his face did not show any signs of the stress of being born. His skin was almost transparent and glowed with warmth. He looked like an angel sleeping on a cloud.

The doctors mentioned that he had clubfeet, but not to worry, future surgeries could repair them. Again, we examined the tiny, utterly perfect feet. Both had five miniature toes, each with its own tiny perfectly shaped toenail.

The doctors warned of other future problems including bladder and bowel incontinence. We could only think that all babies wear diapers; this was not our concern. All we saw when we looked at Dylan was our child, whom we loved. In our eyes, none of his imperfections or disabilities were visible.

As Dylan grew, new problems cropped up. As each challenge presented itself, we were again blind to the image others appeared to see. The muscles behind his dazzling hazel eyes were weak, but only in photos could we see that his eyes were "crossed." Somewhere deep in our brains we were aware of his problems, but our hearts only allowed us to see with love.

Several years have passed, and now when we look back at photos our vision is a little clearer. His head? Yes, it was large—very large. How could we not have noticed? But he has grown into it, and his magnificent hair covers the scars of many surgeries. His feet? Yes, they, too, were somewhat misshapen and, yes, surgery did correct them—to some extent anyway. Our son's beautiful hazel eyes were also fixed by surgery. Now everyone sees them the way we always did.

As for the social worker's list of descriptive terms for our son, we think she missed quite a few. We describe Dylan as a miracle, cute, very bright, brave, determined, happy, friendly, witty, active, silly, playful, a sports nut, and adorable. His sisters describe him as a loud and stinky brat, but they often admit that they love him. All of this sounds pretty perfect to us.

Is love blind, or have we redefined perfection?

• • •

Carol Driver lives in West Chester, Pennsylvania, with her husband, John, and children, Emily (1988), Allison (1991), and Dylan (1994). Carol is an office manager for a commercial real estate developer, a Brownie leader, and a "taxi driver" for her children's many activities. Dylan was born with spina bifida and hydrocephalus. He walks with the use of ankle-foot orthoses and a walker and is fed by a gastric tube. Dylan also suffers from serious respiratory complications, which have led to the need for a tracheostomy and mechanical ventilation while he sleeps. Says Carol, "He still looks perfect to us!"

11

GETTING TO KNOW MY SON

Karen Ciaccio

B.J. is beautiful. He has wispy blond hair, blue eyes, the beginning of freckles across his nose, and an impish grin that flashes across his face when his sister holds his hand. I love my son, and when I hear that little word "Mama" roll across his lips, my heart sings.

But it wasn't always like this. B.J. has Down syndrome, and when he was first born, before I really got to know him, I cried most of the time. I cried partly from the shock of just having had a child with Down syndrome and partly from the uncertainty of what the future would hold.

I cried when the doctor told me we were lucky B.J. didn't have a heart problem like many other kids with Down syndrome. I cried not out of relief, but out of disappointment. I was secretly hoping B.J. would have such a serious heart defect that he wouldn't live long, and then we wouldn't have to live with the pain of raising a mentally retarded child.

I cried, and I couldn't tell even my husband why. After all, if a child's own mother couldn't love him, who could?

Those were the early days, the first few weeks after B.J.'s birth, when doctors and specialists were coming and going most of the time. When I lived at the hospital, sleeping on waiting room recliners and eating what little food I could force down. Those were

This essay has been adapted, with permission, from the article "Learning to Love My Son" by Karen Ciaccio, originally published in *Liquorian* magazine in January 2000.

the days when a disconnected oxygen tube or a tangled heart monitor wire could reduce me to a flood of tears all over again.

I remember those days well. I remember the numbness I felt and the nurses' reassuring smiles. I remember looking into the incubator at a stranger and wondering what was wrong with me that I didn't feel closer to my own baby.

And then gradually, after several days of this self-doubt, I thought, "Maybe I can open up to these women nurses. They must have heard and seen it all before." So I told them how I was feeling.

They told me it wasn't uncommon for a mother to feel the way I did when her baby had been whisked away at birth for emergency care. There was nothing wrong with me, they said, and they reassured me that in time my son and I would bond—if I just gave it a chance. Thus began my long journey of getting to know my son.

Day after day, after our one-year-old was dropped off at Grandma's and my husband left for work, I would drive to the neonatal intensive care unit at the hospital. Day after day I would pour out my deepest feelings and darkest fears to those wonderful nurses who had become my friends.

One conversation in particular comes to mind, when the oldest nurse told me what a sweet little baby we had and that it wouldn't be as bad as I had imagined. I was especially down that day, and these words brought another flood of tears. I asked her how many years she had worked in neonatal intensive care. Her answer shocked me—she'd been working at the hospital more than twenty years. That was enough experience to give her credibility. I looked at my son and told him I would be there for him.

Through her encouragement, I learned how to hold B.J.—in spite of an IV (intravenous line), oxygen tube, and heart monitor wire trying to intimidate me. I gradually became more and more comfortable, and soon I was nursing him two to three times a day and bottle-feeding him the rest.

I started looking forward to my hospital visits. Sitting in the rocker, I gently stroked my son's little head and held his little hands—his tiny fingers barely able to grasp my pinky. I spoke softly to him, hoping he could hear me above the noise of the nursery. I told him that I loved him, and so did Daddy and his big sister, Stephanie, who had nicknamed him "Bubba." Soon we would be together as a family, I told him, like all other families who bring home a newborn from the hospital. I anxiously awaited the day he would no longer need his IV or oxygen.

And then, all too soon, the day came. "He's ready to go home," the doctor said. "He still needs oxygen, but you can handle that yourselves at home." Home! Away from the nurse's call light, and the security I had come to depend on?

We drove him to our apartment; he slept all the way. We got him settled into his new surroundings, belly lights, oxygen tank, and all. Then, as if my husband could sense my apprehension, he turned to me and suggested kindly, "Karen, why don't you go for a little walk? You look like you could use a break, and B.J.'s resting okay right now." I accepted his offer and went outside.

Now, three years later, I remember that walk as if it were yesterday. It was spring. The air was fresh and light, but my heart was heavy again. The sun was shining through the trees, but the tears in my eyes made it look like streaks of light. The joy I'd started to feel in the hospital was being weighed down by the new worries of being home on our own.

I walked slowly, not knowing where to go. I stopped to look at the leaves on the low-lying branch of a tree, and as I examined every leaf, a different concern came to mind. "What if the neighbor kids tease B.J. when he gets older? What if we get too old to take care of a forty-year-old son with Down syndrome? Who will take care of him then? What if B. J. develops one of the many other health problems associated with Down syndrome, like early Alzheimer's, or leukemia, or seizure disorders? What's our future going to be like, God? I love B.J., but I can't stand all the uncertainty of having a different kind of child."

And then the answer came. It was as if God were talking to me in that still small voice, but louder than He had ever spoken before: "Don't worry about tomorrow. No one knows the future. Even healthy kids can get sick and die at any time. Go day-by-day enjoying B.J. That's all that matters now anyway. You'll have the strength to deal with the problems when they come. But for now, you can relax and enjoy your son."

The answer hit me like a ton of bricks. I stopped and looked toward our apartment. I knew B.J. was sleeping, and I wanted to go back in and gaze into his crib at his little face and tiny hands, at his cute little nose and soft silky hair. I knew he was okay right then, and I just wanted to enjoy him. I would worry about tomorrow when it came—or, better yet, let God worry about it for me. And that's what I did.

That was three years ago. And now I can honestly say that life with B.J. has not been hard at all. In fact, our life is full of fun and blessings. B.J. is no longer "our son who has Down syndrome," but just "our son." We love B.J., and he loves us. Even if he cannot communicate with words as well as some, that impish grin and those big blue eyes tell it all. And that's good enough for me. He has had a few medical problems these last few years (asthma and seizures), but we've been able to deal with them.

It really does help to go day-by-day—even moment-by-moment when medical problems occur—but it's all been worth it. In fact, it has been downright beautiful.

● ● ●

Karen Ciaccio lives in Omaha, Nebraska, with her husband, Ben, and four children, Stephanie (1994), B.J. (1995), Catherine (1996), and Mary Beth (1999). Karen credits B.J.'s early intervention coordinator with helping the family find local resources. Karen is a stay-at-home mom who tries to keep up with all the latest research on Down syndrome and health issues. She says, "Our faith in God and belief that all human life is precious have made it easier to accept B.J.'s differences."

12

TRUST YOUR INSTINCTS

by Carol Gordon

We started out like so many other couples and waited to have our first child. When we had Rebecca, we realized that the center of our universe had changed, and it was a good thing. Not scary as we had feared, but a beautiful, life-altering experience. My immediate thought was, "That was great! Let's do it again!"

We did. Two years later I was pregnant again. I felt great! What could be better?

My blissfulness was short-lived. When I was five months pregnant, a midwife noticed that I was measuring abnormally small and requested an immediate ultrasound. I was blindsided! My terrific, typical pregnancy was not typical at all.

I was sent to a major medical center every two weeks for level II ultrasounds until, at six months, I was told to check into the hospital for the duration of my pregnancy. The fetus had a label—IUGR (Intrauterine growth retarded).

Our lives came crashing down around us. I had a two-year-old at home. My husband had just started a new job, and now I was going to be spending an undetermined amount of time away from my family—at what was supposed to be the happiest time of our lives. What had happened to our perfect plans?

Forty-six days later, my son was still not growing. No one had answers or knew what to do. Labor was induced, and forty-eight hours later, David came into this world at thirty-six weeks. He weighed three pounds, eleven ounces at birth. It took twenty days for him to reach four pounds and be allowed to come home. There were no balloons on the mailbox, no fanfare, no cigars, just my baby coming home.

We thought our troubles were over until we realized that David wasn't focusing or responding as our daughter had. The pediatrician cautioned me strongly to be patient, not to compare the two children. But as time went on, and David did not grow physically or developmentally, I asked to be referred to a specialist. Our pediatrician told me seeing a specialist now would be "a premature move."

Then my mother's intuition kicked in. Something definitely was not right, and I knew it. I went on a mission to find out why my child was not progressing normally. A speech therapist friend guided me through the referral process to Birth to Three, Connecticut's early intervention program. Self-referring my child was very difficult, but I figured that if I was wrong, the worst that would happen would be that I drove myself nuts for a while. More importantly, if I was right, David would be getting the therapies he needed rather than wasting valuable time.

The process was now in gear. I took David to a neurologist and geneticist. After five months of searching, David was diagnosed with a rare genetic disorder called Wolf-Hirschhorn syndrome. My way of handling this devastating news was to go on a fact-finding mission. I read articles until they were coming out my ears. Most were depressing and outdated. This was not the answer.

Finally, I called a parent-to-parent support group and was matched with a woman with a similar experience. What a relief to know I wasn't the only person with these feelings! I realized that I wasn't being overprotective or too assertive for questioning everything I did not feel comfortable with. I knew I was not out of line to be searching for an answer.

The support and guidance provided by Birth to Three has become an invaluable part of our lives. Having therapists that are more familiar with children with special needs made me feel there is a place for us. And there are people who understand.

We now know what we are dealing with, and with the assistance of Reach Out, Inc., our Birth to Three service provider, we have been able to start a support group for parents of children like David. We are learning to accept his limitations and rejoice in his progress and milestones, even though they are slow and few and far between. Being able to talk to someone who has walked this road already has made a big difference in our lives. There are great resources and caring people out there. Use them, reach out and talk to them. It will help you put your life in perspective.

My parting words to a parent who is experiencing a different-than-typical parenting experience are these: Don't give up the search, trust your instincts, and follow your child's lead. You will learn more from that child than he or she will learn from you.

• • •

Carol Gordon lives in North Haven, Connecticut, with her husband, Alan, and children, Rebecca (1991), David (1994), and Alexander (1998). David, four years old at the time of this writing, is verbal and mobile. He is still delayed but is making great progress. He adores his big sister, Rebecca, and has been adjusting well to being a big brother since Alexander's recent birth. Carol recently became a Community Resource Coordinator for the Children with Special Healthcare Needs program and an Advocate for Yale Family Connections, a network of resources for families of children with special needs.

13

IT'S OKAY TO HAVE HOPE

by Lynne Gregorio

Iplanned the births of my two boys to be twenty months apart, because I wanted them to have a lot in common and play together. I knew the first six months were going to be hard—caring for an infant *and* a toddler—but I figured once I survived that, I could enjoy watching Christopher and his younger brother, Austin, play together. My dream of what could have been was shattered when Austin's MRI (magnetic resonance imaging) report came back.

It started with a CT (computerized tomography) scan showing a large cyst in Austin's brain. At that point, however, the doctor gave us the impression it could be fixed by surgery, and he would be fine.

When the MRI report came in, I got the worst phone call of my life. We had just adjusted to the fact that Austin was going to have brain surgery and would probably need a shunt when the doctor called and told us, "Austin has multiloculated cysts, agenesis of the corpus callosum, and hypoplasia of the cerebellum."

I didn't understand any of these complicated medical terms. When I asked for a translation, the doctor told me, "It means the cysts are worse than we thought. Austin is missing one part of his brain, and another part is underdeveloped." Of course, to me, this sounded as though my son had almost no brain, would be severely disabled, and might even die. I got off the phone and cried.

Did the doctor explain to me that most of his brain was there, although compressed by the cysts? Did the doctor tell me that many people without a corpus callosum do just fine? Did the doctor tell me that because Austin was young, the brain could find other connections? Did he offer comfort, support, or any hope at all? No to all of the above. This man is no longer our doctor.

After Austin recovered from a month in the hospital and two major surgeries, I went into search mode. I needed to know what was wrong with my baby. I needed to know what I could expect.

But the doctors would not give me a prognosis because Austin was so young. I insisted I wasn't asking them to predict the future, that all I wanted was a realistic best- and worst-case scenario. They must have *some* idea, I said.

I asked them for articles to read. Articles were given to me, but the doctors said, "Only the worst cases are written about, so take these with a grain of salt." I still don't understand why only the worst cases are written about. If doctors are supposed to learn from research and case studies, don't they need to know the whole spectrum? I would read these articles and feel sick to my stomach. These kids had mental retardation, uncontrolled seizures, skeletal defects, heart and kidney problems, brain and central nervous system problems, eye problems—the list went on and on.

Still, as time went on, Austin seemed to be doing pretty well, all things considered. I waited for the doctors to notice, to validate the hope I was feeling inside. But most would not commit themselves. My neurosurgeon, however, said something very special to me. He told me, "Austin is going to be okay. I see a lot of kids that are not okay, but Austin has this gleam in his eyes. He will be all right." He was the first doctor to find something really positive to say, to give me hope.

Did I interpret his words to mean that Austin would be normal, that he wouldn't have any problems? No, of course not. I think doctors and therapists are afraid that we will generalize and come back yelling if things do not turn out right. I, too, saw that gleam in Austin's eyes, as had many others, but it meant so much for the neurosurgeon to say it. He gave me hope.

My therapist also gave me encouragement. She gave me an approximate time line for gross motor skills for "kids like Austin." She said most sit at nine to ten months, crawl at twelve to thirteen months, cruise at eighteen months, and walk at two years.

Did I interpret that to mean that this would be exactly what

Austin would do? No, but it really helped to have an idea of what we might expect.

At Austin's nine-month checkup, I was pleased with all the progress he had made. He was doing a lot of the little things that a baby needs to do before sitting, crawling, and standing. Austin had come a long way in the four months of therapy and was *almost* sitting.

But all the pediatrician saw was that he was not sitting well. He said, "Well, the gap is widening. That is not a good sign." I felt this was so inappropriate. He did not *listen* to me as I tried to tell him how far Austin had come and what the therapists were saying.

I would also like to take a moment to stress the importance of early intervention. Research suggests that children's brains are very pliable and have the ability to rewire themselves if they are given a lot of stimulation, especially during the first three years. These first years hold the windows of opportunity for our children, and we need to take advantage of them.

Last but not least, I would like to share with you my son's latest accomplishments. Austin started walking at eighteen months, and although he has mild ataxia (lack of muscle coordination), nothing slows him down. He keeps up with his brother and is trying to jump and to climb stairs without holding the railing. His motor skills are still delayed, but he does not let that hold him back.

Austin is also talking. His receptive language is on target for his age; his expressive language is delayed due to dyspraxia, a motor-planning speech problem. He is making great strides, and I truly believe that he will learn to compensate for his minor disabilities and lead a full and happy life.

My point is that you cannot predict a child's future development. Austin's brain is severely malformed, yet he is a smart and happy child who is doing remarkably well. Doctors may try to tell you to lower your expectations, but they don't always know. It's okay to have hope.

• • •

Lynne Gregorio lives in North Carolina with her husband, Joe, and their two children, Christopher (1994) and Austin (1996).

Their third child is due in June 2000. Lynne, who has a Ph.D. in mathematics education, teaches statistics at a local college. Joe is a program manager. For more on Austin, visit Lynne's web page at www.geocities.com/Heartland/Meadows/1199/.

14

I HAVE LEARNED . . .

by Eric C. Last

The birth of our third child was supposed to be a scheduled cesarean section, performed at the hospital where I practice.
However, several days before the appointed date, my wife began
labor, and her scheduled section turned into an urgent one. Not
long after the procedure began, our new baby, our Corrie, was
handed to me with the pediatrician's pronouncement, "Here's
your perfect baby girl." As I had done twice before, I cradled this
new life in my hands as tears of joy and thankfulness welled in my
eyes. Too quickly, the circulating nurse took our new angel from
me to be officially weighed and measured.

Not more than five minutes later, I felt a hand, gentle yet insistent, on my left shoulder. One of the nurses was there, whispering
to me that the pediatrician needed to speak to me. I thought to
myself that he was simply being a polite colleague, wanting to
wish us luck. Nothing could be wrong, I reasoned, because he had
used the words "perfect baby girl." But the look on his face when
I saw him waiting in the hallway told me that something had
changed.

"I can't be sure," he began haltingly, "but I'm concerned that
Corrie may have Down syndrome." He described "some things"

This essay is reprinted with permission of the American College of Physicians–
American Society of Internal Medicine. It appeared in the *Annals of Internal
Medicine* on January 15, 1996, vol. 124, no. 2, pp. 271–272.

that had him concerned, like very low muscle tone and a bother-some transverse crease on her palm. He told me about the tests that would be needed, the specialists who would be called.

I shook his hand and thanked him for his thoroughness. I then felt a real physical pain, the likes of which I had never experienced in my life. It began in my gut, went up through my chest, and ter-minated in a wave of nausea and tremulousness that seized my en-tire being. I was helped to a chair and given a cup of water while I waited for the obstetrician to complete his work.

Fifteen minutes later, the obstetrician emerged from the OR (operating room), looking drawn and shocked. Someone had told him of the events of the preceding minutes, and he immediately came to me and embraced me. Tears again welled up in my eyes, though now they were tears of grief and fear. Once composed, I asked how we were going to tell my wife. "That," he began slowly, "is something you are going to have to do." I tried in vain to get someone else, *anyone* else, to give her this piece of news, but all agreed it was best handled by me.

I walked slowly toward the recovery room, the obstetrician's arm around my flagging shoulders. I recalled the many times I had given bad news to patients—news of cancer diagnosed, cancer re-curred, AIDS, respiratory failure, any of the awful events that cause the body to fail. I wished I could be back in any of those sit-uations and not have to complete this task. I took a deep breath, entered the room, and held my wife's hand.

"There might be a problem," I said clumsily. "The pediatrician thinks Corrie might have Down syndrome." My wife squeezed my hand, grimaced, and turned her head away. Within minutes she was asleep again, momentarily escaping our new nightmare.

After spending a few moments in the delivery room lounge try-ing to summon some strength, I somehow made my way down-stairs to the doctors' lounge I had been in so many times before. I stared at the familiar phones, knowing I needed to pick one up and start dialing all the loved ones waiting anxiously to hear our good news. But the news I gave wouldn't be good. The hardest call was to our two older kids, telling them—with voice disguised as best I could—about their new sister, who was waiting to see them. I managed to complete the call, hung up the phone, and broke down once again.

I returned to the nursery, where a pediatric geneticist was present, clipboard-toting assistant at his side, to catalog all of Corrie's parts. He rattled off a list of anomalies indicative of the presence of an extra chromosome. Yet for each one, my brain jumped (ecstatically!) to another family member who had a similar trait. And with each, I became convinced that this was all an overreaction, doctors once again looking for things that weren't really there.

But there was also a small voice in the back of my head. I knew that I didn't want to believe that something so awful, so strange, could be wrong with our child. Yet I was starting to believe that they could be right.

The remainder of the first two days of Corrie's life were filled with new anxieties. There was difficulty obtaining blood for chromosome studies. Then there was the possibility of a cardiac problem, heralded by cyanosis whenever she cried. There were moments of solace, of comforting words and positive thoughts from colleagues, perspective-building words from the social worker.

But there was also a fellow physician who sank beneath insensitivity, gloatingly telling me how his wife had an amniocentesis with each pregnancy. "Don't you know you could have terminated if she'd had an amnio?" he asked.

Don't you realize, I thought, you are talking about my very real, very alive baby?

Each day I wandered the hallways of the hospital living each of Elisabeth Kübler-Ross's stages. Bargaining was the most interesting. I saw the pediatric ICU (intensive care unit) ambulance arrive from our affiliated teaching hospital and thought how much nicer it would be if Corrie had an acute, life-threatening problem, where her future would hinge on some miracle of diagnostic acumen or surgical prowess, where the odds might be heavily stacked against her, but where her life would be forever normal if the procedure were a success. Instead, we had the possibility of a future filled with unknowns, and that unknown void would stretch out for the rest of Corrie's life, and ours.

Beyond the shock and fear, the overriding feeling during that first week was that something very special had been stolen from us. There were little things that should have happened, but couldn't. The expectations of all the happy visits and handshakes in the hospital now turned into looks of sadness, expressions of condolence. There were the walks to the nursery, gazing at all of the newborns and staring at Corrie, trying to convince myself that she looked no different from the others. There was the traditional "surf and turf" dinner for new parents the night before discharge, when my wife and I went through the motions of enjoying ourselves, unable to hide our anxieties or sadness from each other.

One week after Corrie's birth, the geneticist called to say that the results were in and, yes, there were three number-21 chromosomes. But the real impact of that news didn't really hit until I saw the actual karyotype, with perfectly symmetrical rows of chromosome pairs except above the number 21, where an extra piece of genetic material lay waiting to change our family's life forever.

It is now a year since Corrie's birth, and our lives truly have been changed—changed in ways I could not have imagined twelve months ago. No longer do I think of words like "horror" and "fear" when I describe our situation or Corrie's life. I think of the beautiful images I have seen: the joyful expression on my wife's face that has replaced her dread, the sheer delight our older children get when Corrie responds to their play, the look Corrie gets when her daddy holds her (a look I'm convinced she reserves for me), and the incredible joy we all feel as she attains each milestone. I think of the progress she has made and of the staff of teachers and therapists who have cared for her, people who have, for me, defined the word "dedication."

And, yes, Corrie has changed the way I live, and so has changed the way I practice medicine. I have a new sense of appreciation for my truly ill patients and maybe a little less patience for those with trivial complaints. I have seen unbelievable coincidences in my practice, such as the friendship of a man I have cared for over the past six years whose family has adopted a series of children with Down syndrome, or the grandmother who came into my office bursting with pride two years before Corrie's birth telling me of her grandson's Bar Mitzvah—her grandson with Down syndrome. I have drawn strength from so many, including one person who was dying, who knew of our situation and who cared enough to ask.

But mostly I think I have learned about myself, and about love. And while we don't know what the future will hold for Corrie, I realize we can't predict this for anyone, even for ourselves. I realize that I have made certain foolish assumptions in my life. I took it as a given that my children would all go to school, would all attain some stature in the world that I used to know and took for granted. But that world is very different to me now, and I realize just how arrogant such assumptions really are. And because of that, I have learned to try to appreciate all that surrounds me, as often as I can, for there is truly so much to be amazed by and to be thankful for.

• • •

Eric is the father of three children, Farryl (1988), Harrison (1990), and Corrie (1994). He and his wife, Lauri, met while attending medical school. They live on Long Island, New York, in the town of North Bellmore. Eric is an internist in private practice in Wantagh, New York. His interests include medical education, medical ethics, and increasing the sensitivity of health care professionals to the needs of families of children with disabilities. He counts Farryl, Harrison, and Corrie among his personal heroes for their strength, love, and determination.

15

HARD CHOICES

by Laura Salomons

Two weeks away from my due date, my oldest son, Alec, was born via an emergency cesarean section. Although everything had seemed fine at a prenatal visit the day before, there had been a leak in my placenta. His oxygen supply had been so diminished that his brain sustained massive and irreversible damage.

The pain my husband and I experienced during Alec's first month of life was almost unbearable. We spent lots of time at the hospital, holding Alec and sobbing. When a loss like this occurs, the pain is so deep that you don't think that you'll ever get through it, but the human spirit is remarkable. Most of us survive—at least physically. Whether or not we recover our emotional well-being, not to mention learn and grow from such an experience, is another story.

During this crisis, nurses and doctors flooded us with information about our child's condition. Because these medical professionals were only human, they could not know all the answers; they could only guess the odds. As we dealt with this situation and the reality of the loss that we were facing, we had to decide how much hope to have. Soon after Alec was born, we realized that we had to come to terms with his condition and make life decisions based on realistic odds. In other words, we did not want to make decisions that would affect the rest of our lives based on the chances of a miracle with one-in-a-million odds.

Although we would have welcomed a miracle, and still would,

we finally let go of this hope. This letting go was painful, especially as our love for Alec grew daily, but I believe it has allowed us to heal more quickly and care for him better, because we did not spend our time and precious energy looking for the magic pill or person who would make things better. We continued to make decisions based on the reality of the situation. We used whatever energy we had left over to heal.

One of the hardest decisions we had to make was whether to care for Alec at home or to place him in a group care facility. This decision pitted our hearts against our intellect. We were his parents! Naturally, we wanted to care for him, to meet his basic needs, to comfort him, to provide him with any and all stimulation that might benefit him. The most unnatural, abnormal course of action would be to place him.

But we also knew that caring for him at home would consume our lives, probably to the exclusion of adequately caring for ourselves, as individuals and a couple, and for other children we might have. Furthermore, we knew that Alec's care would only become more difficult as he, and we, grew older. I also knew that funding for and availability of in-home assistance and respite care is never guaranteed and rarely consistent from year to year.

In the end, we decided to place Alec. If he developed more than predicted and his care became less consuming, we knew we could always change our minds and bring him home. We knew placing him was the more selfish decision, but we also knew that if we made it, the one life we had to live would probably be a healthier one, emotionally and physically. Fortunately, there was an appropriate facility nearby.

After placing Alec, we talked with social workers who work with families who have children with severe disabilities; we also visited some families who care for these children at home. Getting information about the in-home services that are available and seeing what families live through on a daily basis further convinced us that placing Alec was the right decision. What's also increased our comfort with the placement is the quality of his care. Given his basic medical problems, he's in relatively good physical health and smiles often. We manage Alec's care completely and take him home on a regular basis. What's key is that we have established a balance in our lives—a balance between going to work, being together, spending time with Alec, and, now, caring for our other children.

There are so many losses associated with this tragedy. First of all, Alec has lost the ability to experience all the wonders of life that we know of. But it comforts us to realize that he knows no other existence and is completely unaware of his loss.

As parents, we lost a healthy child and the chance to be a normal, conventional family. Many people have tried to comfort us on this point, exclaiming, "Who has a normal life?" Granted, many families have difficult situations to cope with at various times in their lives, but constantly grappling with the loss of hope and managing the medical and therapeutic care of a severely damaged child is a constant reminder of just how different our life is. Even now, after having two children who appear to be completely healthy, we are continually aware of this loss of normalcy.

The loss most affecting my everyday life is what I call the loss of carefree innocence—an outlook on life most of us have until we personally encounter tragedy. Until experiencing a major loss, most of us think of tragedy as happening to someone else. Since Alec's birth, I cannot comfortably assume things that most people expect—that a child will live long enough to graduate from high school or get married, or that any of us will be alive next year.

All of a sudden, because of what we experienced, we became aware of life's unpredictability and unfairness. We now know it *can* happen to us—and to anyone else. Our challenge is to live with that reality, while not allowing it to consume us or to color everything we do and every decision we make. We have had to learn to accept that tragedy and loss are a part of life, at the same time maintaining expectations that our lives will be happy and long.

The sadness associated with what might have been for Alec is constantly with us. Although we still cry over Alec's condition, these episodes are fewer and farther between. Soon after the tragedy, our sadness was accompanied by anger, resentment, and jealousy. I was angry that I had to cope with this traumatic situation while others seemed to have it so easy.

That anger has subsided now, but I believe it will never go away completely. What's important is learning to live with this emotion and not letting it interfere with my happiness.

Still, encountering families who have not experienced tragedy and loss can be difficult. This is not only because it reinforces how different I am, but also because I am wary of other people's reactions and thoughts regarding my situation. As I have tried to normalize my life, I have had to go through what I liken to a "coming-out" process, explaining and exhibiting my differences to the world and hoping for acceptance and support.

We've learned a great deal about life, people, and ourselves through Alec's tragedy. Alec has shown us what real strength and courage are, and he has taught us how to be better parents and better people. We are also able to recognize what's really important in life—things like health, being together, or just having a good day. It's somewhat ironic that tragedy brings newfound appreciation for life, only to have this appreciation overshadowed by sadness and anger that never completely disappear.

While we were consumed with healing and caring for Alec, I became pregnant with our second son, Adam. Although the pregnancy was a time of extreme stress, his healthy birth provided us with a new lease on life. We are now better able to appreciate and love Alec for what he is, rather than being overwhelmed by the sadness of what he is not.

The recovery process is ongoing. My husband and I have learned to live with the sadness and loss, as well as the anger. There is no doubt that we've grown stronger. We know that what life brings is uncertain and can be tragic, yet we have found meaning and happiness in life, in our relationship, and in all our children.

We know that the love we feel for each other and for our children, the strength Alec has given us, the inspiration we've received from Adam, and the joy we now experience with our third son, Dean, will provide a strong foundation for our future lives together.

• • •

Laura Salomons lives in Sharon, Massachusetts, with her husband, David Kantor. The couple has three sons, Alec (1994), Adam (1995), and Dean (1997). Alec has no practical use of his body due to cerebral palsy and receives all of his nutrition through a gastric tube. He is on various medications to help control seizures, constipation, reflux, aspiration, and vomiting.

Laura, currently a stay-at-home mother, has a master's in social work, and previously was executive director of the Children's League of Massachusetts, a state-level child welfare advocacy organization. David is a senior software engineer.

16

A TROPHY OF GRACE

by Leslie Neugent

It was another late night in the pediatric intensive care unit at Medical City in Dallas, Texas. It was my "shift," my turn to sit by the bedside of our six-month-old son.

This was J. J.'s tenth week in the unit, and his pale, motionless body was wearing down. His little arms and legs were tied down to the bed with Velcro to keep him from pulling out the ventilation tube that connected him to life support. The rhythmic sounds of his respirator droned on. Intimidating machines blinked and beeped, while ten IV (intravenous) bags surrounded his bed, pumping an endless supply of medicine through his body. We had been in this place so long that the get-well posters and cards sent by our family and friends were beginning to peel off the wall.

J. J. had been diagnosed with Down syndrome early in my pregnancy. My husband Chris and I took the news hard. We felt as though someone had died. Indeed someone had. The dream of another healthy son had died.

What would we do with a disabled child? Would he ever know and love us? Could we handle him? How would we deal with the cruelty our ignorant world would inevitably show him? Fears swirled through our heads faster than we could name them.

After his birth our devastation only grew. Not only would he be mentally retarded and look different. He also seemed to be losing the medical "lottery"—facing an endless number of life-threatening illnesses, some unusual even in babies with Down syndrome. Each new ailment came with no clear prognosis or cure.

Little J. J. was hospitalized every three weeks, like clockwork. By the time he was eight months old, he had weathered three rounds of pneumonia, two bouts of RSV (respiratory syncytial virus), two septic blood infections, congestive heart failure, numerous blood transfusions, and respiratory arrest. Any one of these could have killed him. Our nightmare seemed to have no end in sight.

In those wee hours of my hospital vigil, I sat holding J. J.'s tiny hands with my head resting on his bed . . . waiting. For what, I did not know. He was having a particularly rough day. On rough days the intensive care staff would call clergy to come and spend time with families. Given the long-term and critical nature of J. J.'s condition, Pastor Brian, the resident minister, made frequent visits to our room to offer a prayer and a hug.

But this night was different. On this night, Pastor Brian came into the room and changed my life.

This time he offered no prayers, no small talk, no hugs. He simply came in, walked quietly to the head of J. J.'s bed, and, in his beautiful Irish brogue, whispered, "J. J., you are a trophy of God's grace." Then he turned and left.

He said no more. He didn't have to. At that moment I truly came to appreciate the gift that J. J. was to us. His developmental delays, his medical difficulties, his "differentness" no longer seemed to matter.

The playing field had changed. There would be no more timetables or comparisons with other children, not even other children with Down syndrome. Our son was on his own mission. Our intellectually challenged, critically ill son was defying all medical odds. He was fighting for every breath we, the healthy majority, take for granted. And his fight came from a place deep inside. He battled with pure resilience of purpose. He would not give up. He had lessons to teach.

Dag Hammarskjöld once said that "we all come to earth with sealed orders." That night I came to realize that this little boy we had feared so greatly had his orders, his gifts to share, and his mark to make.

J. J. will soon celebrate his second birthday. Today he is a happy, mobile toddler, whose bright blue eyes and sweet smile melt hearts. Developmentally he is still significantly "behind." He still battles formidable medical challenges.

But J. J. continues to teach. On a daily basis, he humbly offers the gifts of compassion, patience, gratitude, peace, and unconditional love. J. J.'s gifts may never be quantified, may never earn money or win awards. But his gifts are trophies just the same.

• • •

Leslie, her husband, Chris, and their children, J. J. (1996) and Ryan (1994), live in McKinney, Texas. Leslie is currently a seminary student at Southern Methodist University's Perkins School of Theology in Dallas and is enrolled in a Clinical Pastoral Education (CPE) program at Children's Medical Center in Dallas. Chris is employed at Frito Lay, Inc., as vice president for the Wholesome Snack Division. Chris and Leslie are members of the Down Syndrome Guild of Dallas and are founding members of the Stonebridge United Methodist Church in McKinney. J. J. is a student at the Rise School of Dallas. He loves Barney and enjoys singing and listening to music.

17

GO AHEAD AND LOSE CONTROL

by Colleen Jesaitis

Be strong, they will tell you. It's what people told me repeatedly. Dictionaries offer a range of definitions for "strong." And strength is something I thought I had until my daughter, Carmen, was diagnosed with craniosynostosis, a condition in which the soft bones of the head close prematurely.

I cried when my husband, Chris, and I were told Carmen needed surgery to correct her skull defect. When Carmen's older sister, Veronica, asked why I was crying, the doctor responded, "Oh, she's just cleaning her glasses."

I cried when I asked my boss for the time off for Carmen's surgery, and she said, "Colleen, you need to be strong for your daughter."

I believed these well-intentioned people were right, and from then on, I held my tears until I was alone. I refused to be weak and let my emotions control me. I vowed to be strong and control my emotions.

A visit to a new pediatric neurosurgeon after our move to the Midwest revealed that Carmen's surgery had been only partially successful. She would need another operation.

This time I didn't cry in the doctor's office, and I didn't cry when I asked for the time off from work. I shrugged away any concern shown by Chris, my family, or my friends. I thought I was being so strong!

But while Carmen's skull reconstruction was being planned, our close little family started coming apart. Our individual efforts at being strong were desensitizing and separating us from each other. The silence was becoming destructive, and we each felt alone and afraid.

A week before her surgery, Carmen slipped getting out of the tub. We ran to her and surrounded her. In comforting her, we formed one big family hug and cried. Carmen was fine, but our common reaction made me realize how desperately we needed to allow ourselves to slip out of our strong silences to receive comfort from one another.

I understand now that letting our emotions show and sharing our sorrow with loved ones is precisely the way we become strong. Stoicism is often applauded as strength, but it is a pretense that harms us as individuals and can destroy us as families. Now that my family has learned this lesson, we continue to grow stronger.

For families just beginning the emotional struggle of an illness or disability, I offer this advice: Be honest with yourself and the ones you love. Share your feelings with your family and, especially, with the child in the center of the struggle. Our children instinctively sense when we are afraid, sad, happy, or worried. We can't hide our emotions from them, and our silence may make them confused or fearful.

• • •

Colleen Jesaitis lives in Kansas with her husband, Chris Lang, and children, Veronica (1991) and Carmen (1993). Carmen underwent skull surgeries in 1994 and 1998. For a long time, she had to wear a helmet during all her waking hours. Now she wears a helmet only when playing on the playground equipment, riding her bike, or participating in gym classes. After attending nursery school at a wonderful school for medically fragile children, Carmen began attending a regular public school when she entered kindergarten.

18

TALK TO ME

by Karen Scoggins

By the time my son turned two, it began occurring to me that he was not using words or communicating in any way. He had not uttered the words "Mama" or "Dada," nor did he respond when I called his name.

Finally, while riding in the car one night, he spotted some holiday lights and said, "Wow!" Everyone in the family was ecstatic; he had spoken! But I was an experienced mother, and I knew my two older children were communicating way before the age of two. I became consumed with the thought that my third child would never talk to me.

Other people's theories about my son's lack of speech ranged from rude to ridiculous. A few people told me I did too much for him; therefore, he did not need to speak. Someone else said he must be a genius like Einstein, who, I was assured, didn't speak a word until the age of three. Someone else proposed the theory that because he was the youngest child in the family, he could depend on his siblings to do the talking for him. Or maybe it was because he was a boy. I'll admit I accepted all of these theories, at least temporarily, at one time or another. But inside, I remained deeply concerned.

I started by consulting with my son's pediatrician. The doctor performed the standard hearing tests in his office and advised me to have him tested at a center for communication disorders as soon as possible.

Before I left the office, the doctor hinted that my son appeared to be autistic. I asked him to explain the condition and its causes.

He replied, "It's just bad luck."

I came home from that visit and frantically began searching for the word "autism" in medical dictionaries and on the computer. As I started to educate myself about this disorder, my heart sank and I began to feel numb. But although I could recognize the "red flags," such as my child's inability to communicate, I was not fully convinced.

My pursuit for answers grew more intense. My son underwent extensive hearing tests and passed with flying colors. This was something of a disappointment, because the possibility of partial or complete deafness seemed preferable to autism.

Finally, when my son was two years, three months, he had an appointment with a psychologist for a developmental evaluation. The three evaluation sessions did not go well, but I justified my child's difficulties by telling myself he could not "perform" under pressure.

When the test results arrived in the mail, it took me several days to open the envelope. The nine-page report confirmed my worst fears. Although the test results indicated age-appropriate motor skills, my son's overall behavioral functioning indicated severe autism.

I couldn't even say the word for a while. It was hard to digest such bad news about this child I had wanted so desperately that I'd spent months on complete bed rest during my pregnancy. I immediately went into overdrive to offer him the best possible early intervention and improve his quality of life.

With hard work and patience, my son is making progress. He is enrolled in a program for preverbal children four days a week. He is constantly progressing but still delayed. I know the road ahead is long, but I am hopeful.

I have come to accept the fact that my son has this disorder, and I treasure each step he takes. My goal as a mother is to make sure that all of my children are happy, healthy, and challenged. The goals for my child with autism are the same; it just requires a different set of parenting skills to achieve those goals.

• • •

Karen Scoggins lives outside Dallas, Texas, with her husband, Chip, and their three children, John (1989), Rachel (1993), and Jackson (1995). Chip is a financial lender and Karen is a stay-at-home mom. Jackson attends a private speech therapy program three days a week and preschool two days a week. He enjoys swimming and golfing with his family.

19

LEARNING TO COPE

by Melody Stebelton

"There's nothing wrong with that baby," my dad adamantly asserted.

Looking back I realize that the hardest thing about having a child with a disability is to admit to yourself and others that there is a problem.

"Dad, I don't think Garrett can hear very well," I pleaded for some understanding.

"Garrett. Garrett. Garrett," my dad said in a loud voice. Finally Garrett turned around. "See, he can hear just fine."

After three separate visits to our family doctor, he proclaimed that there was nothing wrong with Garrett and that I shouldn't be concerned he wasn't yet speaking. Hadn't he heard a thing I had said? Garrett's lack of speech was not my concern, and I had just about had it with no one listening to me. I let the doctor know this, too.

He looked at me and, in a disgusted tone of voice, imparted the best advice anyone could have given: "He's your child," he said. "If you want to take him to a specialist, go ahead."

So I did. And it turned out that Garrett did have trouble hearing—"severely to profoundly deaf," to be more precise.

After the diagnosis came the questions, lots of questions from lots of people. Some days I get tired of hearing the same questions repeatedly, but I imagine they will never go away. Most people ask questions out of a sense of concern or innocent curiosity; still, these are questions I would rather not have to answer.

I joined a support group soon after I found out about Garrett's hearing impairment. Boy, what a lifesaver that turned out to be. Support groups not only provide support, they also offer advice, encouragement, and helpful information about testing and resources. That old saying "been there, done that" holds a lot of water when you feel as though no one else knows what you're going through.

The leader of my support group, Mary, gave me good advice. The first thing she told me was that from time to time I might get depressed about my son's having a disability but that I should try not to beat myself up over it. She was right. A long time may go by without my getting upset about Garrett's deafness, but when it happens, I know that it's normal, and it's okay.

Mary also told us that a lot of people will tell us we have to accept the hand we were dealt, that there's something wrong with us if we don't. Mary told us to substitute the word "cope" for the word "accept." She said that learning to cope with a new situation is the only thing anyone can do.

Parents of a child with a disability would give anything for their child to be like everyone else. It's hard to watch other kids doing so easily what is so difficult for my child. It hurts to see other kids stare and leave my child out of activities. I usually step in and explain my son's disability in an attempt to help others feel more comfortable with him.

I believe my main job as a parent is to keep Garrett safe and bring him up to be an individual who can one day function independently in mainstream society.

I love my son for the person he is.

I've learned to roll with the punches. I see miracles in achievements that other parents think of as a typical development. I've learned that a child's smile is worth more than any treasure on earth. And most of all, I am so grateful that Garrett is mine.

• • •

Melody Stebelton lives in Lancaster, Ohio, with her husband, Shawn, and two sons, Garrett (1993) and Keith (1998), and a daughter, Darcy (1999).

20

AN EVOLUTION OF EMOTION

by Casey Cunningham

My son has *Down syndrome*. It was my first thought at his birth. The moment I looked into his eyes, I heard the words as though whispered from somewhere else, though no one in the room had spoken. *Down syndrome*. I knew it with certainty and dreaded the affirmation that would come later from the doctors and their tests.

Suddenly I looked into a total eclipse of my son's future. A permanent one, for if I remembered my high school biology, the difference lay encapsulated in every single cell in his body—an extra chromosome. I knew there could never be a cure for such a "defect," and the weight of that knowledge was almost unbearable. What I knew of Down syndrome was little, but none of it was good. Mental retardation. That was the one thing I knew for sure. My son would one day become an adult physically, but mentally his progress would be limited.

Nevertheless, I already loved this child. I loved him even before he was conceived, for I had longed for a child desperately. I cherished each moment I was pregnant and waived any tests that would have jeopardized the tiny life within me. Thus, my son had kept this secret until his birth.

As his father held him so proudly in that delivery room, I, too, kept the secret. His father would learn soon enough that a dark cloud loomed in our future; there was no need to point it out now. *We had a child.* He was beautiful; he was healthy; he looked just like my husband. Together, we would all find a way to deal with the Down syndrome aspect of this new little life.

My son *has* Down syndrome. It soon became a statement of fact. He *has* blond hair; he *has* blue eyes; he *has* Down syndrome.

Yes, the Down syndrome presented a challenge to us as parents determined to help him develop to his fullest potential. But aren't all parents similarly challenged? Don't we all want each of our children to develop to his or her fullest potential?

The differences lie in the way each child is challenged and, sometimes, in the timing—when and how the challenge is presented. My son's challenge was conveniently bundled up and labeled for us immediately, present from the moment of his conception. Almost from the start, we knew what we were dealing with.

And over time, I came to realize that our child was more like typical children than not, that life holds no guarantees for anyone, and that life's very unpredictable nature is what makes it so special. That what we truly love about each child is his or her *uniqueness,* not that which makes them just like every other child.

My *son* has Down syndrome. I have noticed that there now is a certain amount of pride in my voice when I say these words. I have learned that, contrary to my first fears, my son's future is very bright. What I initially saw as a total eclipse was caused by a lack of knowledge and vision.

The more I learned about Down syndrome, and about my own son's abilities, the more comfortable I became. I learned that as his parents, we have the ability to help him learn and achieve more than he would if we were simply to be bystanders. I have seen how hard he works to attain certain milestones, and it makes me so much more appreciative of his individual determination and strengths. My love for him is complete, and his Down syndrome has become an inseparable part of that love, just as it is an inseparable part of him. I am very proud of all that he has accomplished, and I take nothing for granted. I look forward to discovering what his future holds.

I'm often in the company of other moms who talk with pride about their children and all the things they are doing—something everyone expects of them. Now I join in. I talk about my son and all he is doing, even though this is something no one seems to expect. And with love, acceptance, and, yes, even pride, I add, "My son has Down syndrome."

• • •

Casey Cunningham lives in Towson, Maryland, with her husband, Jim Kirschner, and their son Junior (James William Kirschner, Jr.). Since Junior's birth in 1994, Casey has been active in the local Down syndrome parent support group and is currently completing her third year as president. She says her advice to new parents is always the same: Simply love your child for who he or she is. Don't worry about the future. Love and enjoy your child now, and the rest will fall into place.

21

BEYOND THE
DIAGNOSIS

by Mary Stephens

Our son Ian was born in March 1993. He was a full-term baby born with no complications. His pediatrician did note that Ian had some vague physical characteristics sometimes associated with genetic abnormalities; she also mentioned the possibility that he might have some learning difficulties. But since everything else seemed to be pretty normal, we easily dismissed the foreshadowing of the doctor's words.

When Ian was four months old, he had an intracranial bleed resulting from a shortage of vitamin K in his system. Thanks to the skills of some wonderful doctors, the blood clot in Ian's brain was removed with what we believed was a minimum of brain damage. He left the hospital about two weeks later. The doctors had been unable to determine why he had been depleted of vitamin K and all the other fat-soluble vitamins. Still, they expressed guarded optimism that with careful monitoring, he would be fine.

But when Ian was a year old, a metabolic specialist at Oregon Health Sciences University diagnosed him with infantile Refsum's disease (IRD), "a peroxisomal disorder that results in hearing and visual abnormalities, as well as low myelination of the brain." At that time Ian was not yet crawling, and a hearing test showed moderate hearing loss in one ear. Within a six-month period, his hearing loss plunged to the severe level—a ninety-decibel loss in both ears.

IRD is considered a fatal disease, but since it is a relatively "new" disease—first diagnosed only about twenty-five years ago—the life expectancy of affected individuals is open to debate.

If the objective reality of having a child diagnosed with a rare, incurable disease is profound, the subjective reality is overwhelming.

For starters, the time we spent waiting for test results was hellish. The doctors didn't exactly tell us what they were testing for; they used terms I didn't understand. I didn't know if they were going to tell me my son would be dead within weeks or perfectly normal.

Suddenly my life anxiously revolved around waiting for phone calls, consulting with specialists, and getting the much-dreaded test results. I remember feeling a great deal of animosity—which, even at the time, I knew to be irrational—toward "the doctors."

We've dealt with many wonderful doctors during the last six years, but at the time of Ian's diagnosis, I could see them only as the enemy. First "they"—the doctors, the enemy—told me my son would be blind or already was blind. Then "they" told me my son would be deaf or already was deaf. Finally "they" told me my son would die. I felt as though "they" were systematically stripping pieces of my son away from me.

Living with the diagnosis of IRD means learning everything we can about Ian's rare and remarkable illness. Try looking up "peroxisome" in the average dictionary; the closest thing you'll find is "hydrogen peroxide." After Ian's diagnosis, we pored over medical journals and searched the Internet in an attempt to demystify our son's prognosis.

Living with the diagnosis of IRD means discovering the world of the congenitally deaf-blind. Helen Keller, right? But where does one find an Annie Sullivan? Who will teach my child?

Living with the diagnosis of IRD means searching and advocating for an appropriate educational placement—interviewing school districts, preschool programs, and teachers, sifting until you find the gems. We discovered early intervention, went to IEP (individualized education program) meetings, learned the meaning of IDEA (Individuals with Disabilities Education Act) and lots of other acronyms.

It seems as though when you are handed a child with a rare disease, the rest of your life should fall into place; the little things shouldn't matter so much. Well, let me dispel that thought right now. Relationships go right on being relationships—with all the good days and all the bad ones. Money is still tight; days are still too short; the Cubs are never going to win the pennant but are always going to try.

Living with the diagnosis of IRD is not the same as living with Ian.

Living with Ian means waking up every morning to the sound of a child singing even though he hears very little. Living with Ian is watching his face light up when he puts his fingers in my mouth to verify through touch that I am his mom and receiving his very wet open-mouth kisses. My child is not a label, not a diagnosis. He's just sweet, happy little Ian.

I am not thinking about IRD when Ian is sitting in my lap, giggling over our turn-taking games. I am not thinking about educational politics when we are roughhousing in the living room. Ian is a child first and foremost. He needs what all children need—love, security, and encouragement.

That is the reality of our lives. In the years since Ian's birth, I've changed, some for the better and some for the worse. I know more about some things than I ever wanted to know, but I also know more about love—the love I feel for Ian and the love that he shows me.

• • •

Mary Stephens lives in North Carolina, where she has been working on a project to document the life story of a North Carolinian who lived from 1896 to 1999. Ian's father, John Harris, lives in Washington. Although they now live in separate states, Ian's parents communicate daily and continue to maintain a web page on IRD (http://www.pacifier.com/~mstephe/), which has put them in contact with many other families who have children with this condition. Ian attends school in Vancouver, Washington, with his one-on-one aide, Nancy Knox.

22

I AM A FATHER

by Christopher J. Beveridge

August 7, 1992, proved to be one of the greatest days of my life. Early that morning, James, the first of our three boys, was born in a small hospital in southern Illinois. I drove home from the hospital half delirious from lack of sleep, half pumped up with adrenaline—*I am a father!* I wondered if the people who saw me driving by could tell. I was certain they could see the incredible sense of pride I felt.

Maria's pregnancy had been relatively uncomplicated. We attended birthing classes together, read several books, and endlessly discussed our child-rearing plans. We weren't going to make the mistakes we had seen our friends make with disciplining, feeding, and taking care of their children. No, we were different.

James developed "normally" in terms of reaching the various milestones. He was a very responsive child who smiled early, rolled over at five months, and began walking and using a few words by his first birthday. All his early checkups revealed proper muscle tone and growth. As his father, I knew he was bound for greatness.

But his "normal" development was short-lived. Between the ages of twelve and eighteen months, his speech drastically tapered off. He was no longer using words he had spoken at twelve months. I wasn't concerned at the time, or perhaps I was too busy with my military career to be fully aware. I figured James was just developing in areas other than speech.

Then, while I was stationed in Colorado Springs, we got the first bad news. At James's eighteen-month checkup, the pediatrician told Maria that James was behind in his speech and some fine motor skills.

The pediatrician referred us to a developmental psychologist, who, in turn, recommended some early intervention programs to work on James's speech and other delays. I still wasn't concerned. I figured James was going through a phase he would soon outgrow. He didn't. Little did we know this was the first step on a journey down an endless road of diagnoses, misdiagnoses, rediagnoses, and frustration.

Along the way, we learned some important lessons the hard way. The first was to beware of well-intentioned educators. James had a preschool teacher with a tendency to think out loud. At one point, for example, after reading an article on obsessive-compulsive disorder, she suggested this "diagnosis" for James. She told us that some of his actions in the classroom and his insistence on order with certain objects were classic symptoms. During the time James was in her classroom, she made several other informal diagnoses based on her reading. Maria and I took everything she said very literally and spent hours researching and discussing each new diagnosis she came up with. Each time, we were left with more questions.

We also learned about the dangers of the "diagnosis rut." Because I am in the military, we have to move quite often; we've moved three times since James was born. Each move requires enrolling James in a new education program and a new course of therapy.

However, before James could start a new program, each state required an assessment by its own specialists. Often this "assessment process" consisted of an "expert" sitting down with Maria, who, during the course of the parent interview, would relate the diagnosis of the previous specialist. And voilà, with no direct observation or testing of James, this new expert would come to the same conclusion.

While the speed of this process helped us get James into new programs more quickly, it did not consider the possibility that the previous diagnosis might have been flawed or that James's situation might have improved or deteriorated since he was last tested.

The end result was that James's educational planning was based on data that was sometimes more than three years old.

But we learned from these experiences. During James's most recent assessment, we answered the parent screening questions but did not reveal the conclusions of previous assessments. The resulting assessment was much more thorough, and a different conclusion was reached; this time James was diagnosed with high-functioning autism instead of attention deficit disorder (ADD).

Naturally, we had mixed feelings about the outcome. However, Maria and I are convinced that this team of six specialists was able to see the "true" James over the course of his eight-hour assessment.

Actually, Maria had come to the conclusion that James fell along the autistic spectrum several months prior to his formal diagnosis. As a result, she was much more prepared for the team's conclusion. She had spent countless hours reading current literature and surfing the Internet, gathering as much information as possible. Through her research and careful observations of James, she was able to recognize the behavior patterns, learning characteristics, and speech patterns that indicated a form of autism.

We have learned the importance of advocacy. Maria's diligence and efforts have paid tremendous dividends. She knows James better than any expert could. She knows what he responds to, what he likes and dislikes, and which situations trigger poor behavior. More importantly, she has been able to point educators in the right direction with strategies for teaching James.

We have met with James's teacher, principal, special education teacher, and school psychologists. We have gone into each meeting knowing our parental rights and have been able to work with the educators to plan strategies for James's continuing education. Maria has filled a three-ring binder with information on autism, teaching techniques, inclusion in the classroom, James's most recent assessment and IEP (individualized education program), and a comprehensive list of available reference materials. By providing this information to James's teacher, principal, and school psychologist prior to the start of first grade, we hope to make sure everyone knows James from the outset. Agencies want to do the right thing; occasionally, we just have to remind them what the right thing is.

We have also learned some strategies for dealing with family and friends, each of whom seems to have his or her own ideas about what is "wrong" with James and how we should be dealing with the situation. Maria and I have learned not to let the words people say get in the way of the true love we know they feel for us.

"I don't know how you do it," our friends have said. "I don't know how I would cope if my child weren't normal." Others have told us, "I'm so thankful my children don't have any problems." Yes, these words hurt us. But we see that these same people love James and treat him as if he were no different from their own children. Their actions of love speak louder.

And sometimes our friends even say the right things. When I confided that James had been diagnosed with autism, one of my close friends gave the best possible response: "Well, I'm not going to tell you I'm sorry," he said, "because there's nothing to be sorry about."

Nothing to be sorry about, indeed. James is a wonderful child, and we are very proud of him. He has just learned to ride his bike without training wheels, likes to watch videos of his favorite train show, plays with his two younger brothers, and is incredibly adept on the computer. His reading comprehension skills are well above grade level. We work daily on his delayed social skills, and he is showing tremendous improvement. Because of James, we are more in tune with our other two boys. We are sensitive to their educational and social needs, and we marvel at each milestone they achieve.

There have been incredible emotional low points, but they fade quickly as we see James ride his bike by himself or read a birthday letter from his grandpa out loud. The pride I felt six years ago is reinforced daily. I am a father.

• • •

Chris Beveridge is a captain in the U.S. Army, stationed at the U.S. Army Recruiting Battalion Headquarters in Salt Lake City, Utah. He lives with his wife, Maria, and their three sons, James (1992), Logan (1995), and Davis (1997).

23

OUR JOURNEY

by Donna Cohen

To say that I was unprepared for Rachael's diagnosis would be a great understatement. That day I had taken my younger daughter to our new pediatrician for her six-month checkup. As we were leaving, I mentioned that my three-year-old, Rachael, was in a special needs preschool class, but I felt as though we should be doing more to help her learn to communicate.

Apparently trying to be reassuring, the pediatrician replied, "Well, autistic children often have problems with language."

Autistic? I was stunned! Nobody had ever used that word to refer to Rachael. In one of many reports, we'd seen a reference to a "pervasive developmental disorder," but we interpreted that phrase in very general terms. I truly thought the pediatrician, being relatively new to our family, had Rachael confused with another child. I asked her to check Rachael's record to be sure. She did. And, yes, that's what the record said.

I left the office to pick Rachael up at school, totally numb and still a bit doubtful that the pediatrician was correct. After all, Rachel had been evaluated by several professionals and had been in school for three months. Wouldn't somebody notice if she was autistic? Wouldn't they have told us?

When I arrived at Rachael's school, I asked to speak with her teacher and the speech and language specialist. Once all the children had left, I said, "I was just at the pediatrician's office. She said she thought Rachael was autistic."

I waited to hear them say, "Oh, no, she just has a language delay," or, "Absolutely not," but instead they both nodded.

Shocked again, I started to cry. "Why didn't you *tell* me?" I screamed. Both teachers were very supportive and calm, explaining that, as teachers, they were not allowed to make a diagnosis or disclose a diagnosis to a parent. In retrospect, I can respect their difficult position. But as a parent I was angered.

How to tell my husband, my mom, and my in-laws? This was so new and so raw I really didn't want to talk about it. In fact, I don't actually remember telling them. I do remember desperately wanting the pediatrician to be wrong. I immediately made an appointment with an autism specialist, waiting eight horrible weeks for the appointment. By the time the appointment date arrived, I had read up on autism, becoming deeply concerned and, in all honesty, terribly frightened. The books I read were not very optimistic. After a three-hour evaluation, the specialist concurred with our pediatrician. Rachael had autism.

Three and a half years have passed since that day. What a journey it has been. As I began to read more and more, I realized that I was not alone—other people had been in this situation before me. More importantly, I came to realize that there was action to be taken! We could not simply stand by and let things happen. We needed to intervene for the future of our child.

Various people had told us that we needed to be "advocates" for Rachael. At first we thought that meant speaking with the teachers and doing what we were told. In time, we discovered that we needed to do our own research, reach our own conclusions, make our own decisions as to what her needs were, and work with the school to get her the appropriate services. We've been very lucky to have a school system willing to listen to and respect our views.

Sometimes it is difficult taking Rachael out to public places. She becomes agitated, talks aloud to herself, repeats a video she has seen verbatim, or throws a tantrum for no obvious reason. People stare. A few make remarks. On some days, I try to educate the public, explaining her behavior in simple terms. Other days I'm just quietly annoyed at what feels like insensitivity.

Relatives and friends have been an incredible source of support for us. They have gone out of their way to make it possible for us to visit—putting breakables away and allowing us to bring a third person to help us with Rachael. We have been invited to weddings, cookouts, and other events. At times, when we hesitated to bring Rachael along, they encouraged us to let them know what adjustments could be made so we would feel comfortable including her. We found that the more information they had about Rachael, the more successful our visits would be.

Some days are easier than others. On the difficult days, I tell myself that life's an adventure and keep on going. On the good days, I think of all the wonderful gifts we've received through Rachael. We've made wonderful friends who also have children with special needs, people we probably would not have known otherwise. We have learned a lot about ourselves as we learn to speak for our daughter who cannot speak for herself. We have learned that it is okay to be scared, but it is not okay to allow that fear to paralyze us. Our younger daughter, now three, is already aware that people have different strengths and weaknesses. She is learning quickly about compassion and tolerance. She accepts and loves Rachael unconditionally.

We notice and appreciate moments that may escape other people's notice. Just recently six-year-old Rachael spontaneously said, "I love you, Mommy," as I was putting her to bed. I will never forget that moment and others like it. These are the best gifts of all.

• • •

Donna Cohen lives with her husband, Harold, and two daughters, Rachael and Naomi, in Windsor, Connecticut. Rachael (1992) attends an applied behavioral analysis educational program at school and is mainstreamed when appropriate. She loves music and gymnastics and is doing very well. Donna works part-time and regularly visits a nearby college to speak to education students about a parent's point of view, autism, and applied behavioral analysis.

24

WHAT TO SAY

by Sandra Assimotos-McElwee

Four years ago, my Sean was born with Down syndrome. After sharing the news with a few friends, I discovered that they all had the same reaction: they became upset and told me how sorry they felt. This type of response made me feel compelled to try to comfort them—at a time when I didn't have the emotional energy to take care of anyone besides our family and myself. After all, I had a new baby in the intensive care nursery. I was worried about him, but most of all, I knew I loved him, no matter what his diagnosis.

Then I thought, "Well, if this had happened to one of my friends, what would I have said?" I searched my memory and realized nobody had ever told me what the proper response should be.

So I asked. When I finally had time to do it, I talked to more than one hundred other parents of children with disabilities on the Internet, and I asked them what they wished people had said, or not said, to them. Here's what they told me.

What Not to Say to Parents of a Child with a Disability

- Avoid blanket statements that stereotype children with that specific diagnosis. Don't make any statement that starts with the words "They all . . ." Remember that every person with a disability is an individual.

- Avoid any statement conveying pity. Don't say, "I'm sorry," "what a shame," "how sad," or, "poor thing."
- Don't say, "It could have been worse." No matter what the diagnosis, at the time the parent probably feels that nothing could be worse.
- Avoid any statement that implies the parents may have been at fault. This is particularly true for children who have been diagnosed with autism, attention deficit disorder, or speech delays.
- Don't try to explain why God allowed this to happen. Avoid statements like, "God gives special children special parents." My husband and I believe God has a purpose for every life, but we don't believe in making blanket statements like these that put God into a tiny little box just to make us feel better.
- Avoid references to sainthood. Don't say, "I couldn't do it. You must be a saint." These statements imply that people with disabilities are so awful that only a saint could love them.

What to Say to Parents Who Have a Newborn with a Disability

- First of all, say, "Congratulations!" Yes, congratulations! It's fine to acknowledge that parents are feeling some grief, but they are new parents, after all. They went through nine months of pregnancy, labor, and delivery, and they have a new baby to show for it. They deserve to be congratulated.
- Compliment the child and the parents. We were thrilled when people asked to hold Sean or commented, "He looks just like his dad!"
- Remember that actions speak louder than words. When Sean was born, the actions of friends and relatives who actually *did something* made more of an impact than any words they could have spoken. Provide a meal, offer to baby-sit, take the time to learn about the child's disability by reading a book. Make concrete offers of help. Be available. The new parent won't have the time or energy to pursue you.

New parents of a child with a disability may need to help their friends learn how to respond properly. After all, this is new to them, too. After those first few difficult conversations with my friends following Sean's birth, we decided to tell the rest of our friends how we hoped they would respond to the news of his birth and his disability.

Sean's birth announcement included his vital statistics—nine pounds, three ounces; 21.5 inches long—but it also included this note:

Dear Family and Friends,

Sean is a very special baby, and this birth announcement can't possibly say it all. God has made Sean special and chosen us to be his parents, and we feel blessed.

Sean was born with Down syndrome. We wanted to give you time to adjust to the news, so you wouldn't feel the need to have an immediate response. We hope you will feel the same as we do—happy and proud. We would like you to see him as we do—as a beautiful baby boy. We also want you to treat him just like any other baby.

Congratulate us. We have a baby; we're a family now. This is not a sad moment. Please do not apologize; we aren't sorry. We are still gathering information about Down syndrome and probably won't be able to answer any questions for a while. In the meantime, we would like to encourage you to call us, and come see Sean. He sleeps, eats, cries, and dirties diapers—like every other baby. He's just got an extra chromosome.

• • •

Sandra Assimotos-McElwee was made aware of Down syndrome when Sean was born on October 6, 1993, during National Down Syndrome Awareness Month. He inspired her to make others aware of the incredible value of the lives of people with Down syndrome.

Sean lives with his mother, Sandra, and his father, Rick, in Rancho Santa Margarita, California. They lead a support group for parents of children with Down syndrome through Saddleback Church. Sandra also has a web site designed for parents with a prenatal diagnosis: (http://home1.gte.net/mcelwee.) Each week, she counsels pregnant parents on-line on the worth their baby holds and encourages them to continue their pregnancies.

25

"MOTHER SEEMS OVERLY CONCERNED"

by Caryle Seim

As we entered the hospital emergency room, I was almost screaming. I could feel my heart racing, my face flushing. "My baby cannot eat and cannot see, and I am not leaving here until I know why!" I declared.

I was at my wit's end. For nearly three weeks, my perfect new baby daughter could not stop crying when I fed her. When her huge dark eyes weren't filled with anguish, they stared at me blankly. Never following, never flinching. Something was terribly wrong, and I was either going to find out or jump off the roof. I could no longer bear her unexplainable pain and suffering.

Just three weeks earlier, Caitlyn had burst into my life with a lusty cry and Apgar scores of eight and nine. All appeared normal except for a hip dislocation over which the doctors expressed little concern. What I noticed immediately, besides a beautiful full head of red hair, were her long elegant fingers and toes. Actually, all of her was beautifully slender and long. She was perfect. A place for everything and everything in its place. I could hardly wait to get to know my wonderful baby girl! As I recovered from the necessary C-section, I tried to put aside my maternal concerns about her hip and enjoy the much-anticipated first days of my daughter's life.

After Caitlyn was fitted with a hip harness by an orthopedist, I was told that she should be seen by a neurologist to check her reflexes and head size, as her head circumference was above the ninety-fifth percentile. By now, however, the crying had begun.

She seemed to seize with pain every time she ate. Burping was forceful but brought her no relief. The absent darkness of her large eyes continued to haunt me. I told my friends that I felt she couldn't see me. The neurologist's exam and ultrasound revealed nothing out of the ordinary. She was a full-term, proportionally large baby with normal reflexes.

Despite the restrictiveness of the hip harness, which she wore twenty-four hours a day, she seemed content when she wasn't being fed. In spite of the reassurance of the doctors and friends, I felt anxious about the emerging pattern of feeding, crying, and vomiting. Sometimes it seemed as though more formula came up than went in. "If only she could talk," I'd thought, "then I'd know what hurts." The expression on her face after eating seemed to beg for relief. But from what?

At her first "new-baby" visit to the pediatrician, I explained how much discomfort and vomiting she continued to have—with no fever. Naturally, they tried to rule out colic and lactose intolerance by introducing soy milk products and smaller, more frequent feedings. But nothing changed until we found ourselves in that hospital emergency room. I could never begin to imagine what I was about to learn—and in such a roundabout manner.

The first emergency room doctor to see us began his patronizing assessment by watching me feed Caitlyn. I guess he had to make sure this first-time mom had acquired every nuance of successful feeding. After I passed that test, he examined Caitlyn more closely. He examined her ears, mouth, and nose, and then he came to her eyes. Without a moment's hesitation, he announced, "She has glaucoma! Why, just look at the size of her eyes! The pressures must be extremely high!"

As soon as an ophthalmologist evaluated her, I was told that without immediate surgery she could be completely blind in a matter of days. My heart began to grow heavy. On one hand, one of my concerns was validated—her eyes were not normal. But surgery? She was only three weeks old! The prospect of impending blindness put Caitlyn's digestive problems on the back burner. Now her sight became the main focus of my attention. I had to consent to one or more surgeries on her eyes and I had to do it immediately.

Only one surgery was required, and it was successfully performed two days later by one of only five hundred doctors in the world who specialize in the procedure. Time alone would tell how Caitlyn's optic nerve had responded to the extremely high optic pressures that occurred shortly after her birth. But how had this happened? What else might be wrong with my child? It was late that evening in the hospital that I first heard whispers of what might be afflicting my daughter.

The dark hall was full of hospital sounds: nurses rushing, IV (intravenous) poles clanging, and children whimpering. Long lines of youthful and fresh-looking residents streamed by the beds in the ward we were in. Finally the group reached us. Caitlyn's eyes were shielded and bandaged shut until morning, but there was much interest in her case. The questions began.

"Any history of infantile glaucoma in your family?"

"No."

"Diabetes?"

"No."

"Heart disease?"

"No."

"Long fingers and toes?"

"No, no, no!"

What were they getting at anyway? And why did they need to be interviewing me at three o'clock in the morning? I fumed silently.

Finally a young woman sat down with me and asked if I'd ever heard of Marfan syndrome. Did anyone in my family or Caitlyn's father's family have it? No, I had never heard of it, and I had no knowledge of a family history of it.

She explained that Marfan syndrome is a genetic disorder of the connective tissue, often affecting the eyes, heart, and joints. Characteristics of Marfan syndrome include tall stature, long digits (arachnodactyly), and poor vision (myopia).

Try as I might, I was having trouble calming the panic growing inside of me. What could it all mean? My heart was breaking. My beautiful, perfect baby girl was sick. It wasn't my imagination. I wanted it all to be a bad dream, a nightmare that I would awaken from, so I could get on with the happy life I had planned as Caitlyn's mom.

Days later we reported to cardiology for an echocardiogram. Unbeknownst to me, the mystery surrounding the vomiting and crying was about to be solved. In the course of examining and measuring Caitlyn's heart, I was told, the doctor had observed an "artifact" in back of her heart.

"Artifact?" I had never heard a human part referred to as an artifact. I could feel a numbness running into my fingers. I thought, if the news is too bad, I might just drop dead right here. "What kind of artifact?" I insisted. "What's an artifact?"

"Well, we can't say for sure, but we think it's her stomach."

Her stomach? I knew enough anatomy to know that this was the wrong cavity for her stomach. It wasn't my imagination. Her stomach had herniated, squeezing its way in back of the heart, through a hole next to her esophagus. During feeding, her stomach would fill half above the diaphragm, half below, causing her great discomfort until the stomach emptied. More tests were ordered. They concluded that the connective tissues closing the diaphragm around the esophagus had not closed completely so Caitlyn's stomach could slither from one cavity to the other at any time. Another immediate surgery was scheduled. This time, she was hospitalized for five long days. Fortunately, she didn't need a G-tube (gastrostomy tube) as we had anticipated, but she still required slow and patient feeding and burping for years afterward.

Caitlyn was nearly three months old before the two mysteries that faced us at her birth were solved. And these mysteries were solved only because I trusted my intuition and observations. I refused to be sent away without answers. And even though I've read in Caitlyn's chart that "mother seems overly concerned," it was this concern and love of my child that got me through those darkest hours.

Eventually Caitlyn, now six, was officially diagnosed with Marfan syndrome. Because of the undetected glaucoma, she has low vision and wears contact lenses and glasses. The surgeries that brought about the control of her optic pressures and relief to her tiny stomach required the precision and attention of angels and saints. We have since been through six other surgeries and a dozen exams under anesthesia—just to "keep things in order." Caitlyn is followed by no less than ten medical specialists, professional men and women who treat us with respect and dignity. And now, when this mother seems "overly concerned," doctors sit up and take notice.

My advice to other parents is to *trust yourself!* If you feel something is wrong with your child, you probably are right. If it feels serious, it probably is. Surround yourself with doctors, therapists, and teachers who are excellent listeners and who honor you as an important and intelligent member of an exceptional team of caregivers.

• • •

Caryle is the proud mother of Caitlyn Seim (1992). They live and play in sunny Atlanta, Georgia, where Caryle teaches at Cliff Valley School. Caitlyn enjoys playing the violin, being a Brownie Girl Scout, and attending school. When school is out, Caryle and Caitlyn relish exploring the pristine barrier islands of Georgia.

Caryle notes that people with Marfan syndrome can experience many or few of the syndrome's characteristics. Some of the most common include tall stature; long fingers and toes; nearsightedness (or ocular lens dislocation); heart problems, including mitral valve prolapse and aortic root dissection; scoliosis; and loose-jointedness. Few affected people have all the symptoms. Marfan syndrome sometimes goes undetected until young adulthood. In many cases these beautiful, tall, long-limbed people are encouraged to be athletically active. This can be a tragic mistake, because undetected and unmonitored, the heart problems associated with Marfan syndrome can lead to sudden death. For more information, contact the National Marfan Foundation (www.marfan.org or 1-800-8MARFAN).

26

SKIP THE GUILT

by Janice M. Block

Popular theory will have you believing that on your way to acceptance of your child's disability, you will go through various predictable stages. One of these stages is self-blame and guilt, particularly on the part of the mother. May I make a suggestion? Skip this stage completely, if at all possible!

My first daughter was very difficult to manage from the start. She had feeding problems, she had "colic," she seemed irritable most of the time, she didn't sleep well, and she had gastroesophageal reflux. And then she was very behind, developmentally. I was a well-prepared, well-informed mother who accepted this situation and never allowed myself to believe that I had done something to cause it. Sure, I had those moments when I thought, "Maybe I drank too much iced tea that summer or stood by the microwave too long." But these moments were fleeting. Most of the time, I chalked my daughter's problems up to fate, the luck of the draw, chance.

What I wanted at that time in my life was a baby. I hadn't specified a "perfect" baby, so I felt I had to accept what was given me. Still, I was exhausted from lack of sleep, frustrated by physicians who did not understand, and fearful about my child's future.

I always tried to remember that babies are sensitive creatures, and I tried not to let my baby pick up on my feelings of despair, disappointment, or sadness. As worried as I was about her slow development, whenever I interacted with her, I tried to show her how delighted and happy I was that she was in my life. Since I figured there wasn't much I could do to make her progress any faster, I could at least make her happy and build her self-esteem. It occurred to me early on that this would be important, as self-esteem would be crucial to someone going through life with disabilities.

As we went through one therapy session after another, it was very tempting to "overtherapize" her, to push her into making gains no matter what it took. But something else inside me said, "Wait a minute. This is who she is."

I had to learn the balance between helping her to do her best and forcing her to be someone she was not capable of being. This very hard lesson helped me to put myself in her shoes and think about how my actions could affect her self-esteem. I did not want her to sense that I felt disappointed in her and wished she could do or be more.

I watched other parents push, admiring their diligence as they searched for the best physicians and the best therapists. I also realized that these actions were therapeutic for them at a time when we all feel so helpless. I believe that those feelings of helplessness are the worst, especially in those early years of unanswered questions.

At the age of six, my daughter was diagnosed with Angelman syndrome, a rare genetic disorder. We have certainly traveled a difficult road with many challenges, but I'm proud to say I am the mother of a happy and secure young lady. And I continue to believe that having a good attitude can get you through those tough times.

The other day another parent of a child with Angelman syndrome asked me, "Isn't it nice to finally have a diagnosis?"

I agreed wholeheartedly, saying it was good finally to have an explanation for my child's behaviors.

"Yes," she agreed, "and to not attribute them to being a bad mother?"

"Oh, no!" I exclaimed. "I never went down that path!" And I think my child and family are happier for it.

• • •

Janice Block lives in Chapel Hill, North Carolina, with her husband, Jeffrey, and daughters, Allison (1991) and Leah (1997).

Allison attends public school in a severe-profound life skills class, with a partial inclusion program. Jeffrey works as a technical writer and training manager for a local software company.

Janice stays busy managing Allison's activities and therapies. She also does some child care and volunteer work. She adds, "It certainly takes a village to raise a child with Angelman syndrome, and we are very grateful to all the people who help Allison at home, at school, and in the community."

27

READINESS

by Cindy Daniel

I believe in readiness.

I planned for our first child, Connor, to be potty-trained at eighteen months old. Connor has always been a very bright child, but his "schedule" was not the same as mine. One whole year later than planned, he was potty-trained—and it happened over the course of two days. But I still had not figured out the readiness thing. At the time, I interpreted his success to mean that my parenting skills were improving. Looking back I realize he did it because he was finally ready to learn.

Our second child, Taylor, finally learned to crawl when he was almost two years old. What a wonderful accomplishment! It didn't matter to us that children half his age were running circles around him. We were thrilled that Taylor could get around by himself and get into whatever he wanted. (Wait. Did we actually want this?)

Now, as Taylor nears his seventh birthday, he is learning to walk independently with a walker. I couldn't be happier! Still, I must admit that I had moments of great doubt—moments that lasted for months. But Taylor acquired these skills when he was ready.

I don't believe only in readiness for children; I also believe in readiness for parents. That is, I believe that I will learn my lessons when I am truly ready to learn.

Taylor has cerebral palsy and several medical problems. I am thankful that when he came into our lives more than six years ago I didn't know all that our family would face. I wouldn't have been able to handle everything at once. I just wasn't ready. But I could handle one problem at a time. When I reflect on what has happened in Taylor's life, and, subsequently, in the life of our family, I find it amazing that we haven't all gone crazy. But we have found ourselves perfectly capable of handling one day and one challenge at a time.

A few years ago, I mentioned to my husband and our physical therapist that Taylor was getting too big for his stroller. He was three and a half years old and weighed more than thirty-six pounds, but he still couldn't walk. So I began searching for a bigger stroller. At that point, I never would have guessed we would end up purchasing a wheelchair.

I wasn't ready to consider this option. The very thought made me anxious and upset. What would other people think if they saw our little boy in a wheelchair? Buying a wheelchair seemed tantamount to admitting defeat in our struggle to help Taylor walk.

But after talking with another parent at Children's Hospital and Taylor's doctor, both my husband and I agreed that a wheelchair was the best option—for now.

Taylor has had his wheelchair for three years now, and it has been a blessing for all of us. Time—and taking things one day at a time—gave us a new perspective and acceptance we couldn't have imagined.

As I talk and listen to other parents on similar journeys, I become more and more convinced that children and parents need to be given time to be ready. Whether your child is learning to walk or talk, or whether you, as a parent, are dealing with doctor's reports or anxieties about your child's future, allow yourself and your child time. Knowing that readiness is essential to acquiring a skill or accepting a difficult situation will allow you to deal with frustrations that come along. Just because you or your child is not "ready" today doesn't mean that you won't be "ready" tomorrow.

"To every thing there is a season, and a time to every purpose under Heaven."

I believe in readiness.

• • •

Cindy Daniel lives in Sierra Vista, Arizona, with her husband, Scott, and children, Connor (1989), Taylor (1991), and Aidan

(1995). Scott is a chaplain for the U.S. Army, and Cindy is a part-time professor of communication. Cindy also writes a regular editorial for FIN Facts, *a statewide publication of the Family Information Network for families with young children who have special needs. The family home-schools Connor, who has attention deficit disorder, and Taylor, who has cerebral palsy.*

28

TURNING OBSTACLES INTO TRIUMPHS

by Diane Stonecipher

My readiness for a child and subsequent perfect pregnancy never hinted at what was to come—the difficult labor and the limp, quiet child vacuumed from my womb. In that instant, my life and the lives of many others changed forever.

I remember the next three and a half weeks as a collage—neonatal intensive care unit (NICU) physicians, tubes, machines, buzzers, alarms, first baths in a plastic tub instead of in our home, rocking chairs beside hospital cribs, breast pumps, shocked family and friends. I went through the motions as if in a trance. Even the full harvest moon seemed removed from the place in which I had landed.

My son was beautiful, just as I knew he would be. I ached to have him back inside my swollen belly, safe. The traumatic birth behind us, test results began drizzling in, hinting at our new future. There was well-meant encouragement in the dispensation of information from physicians, but as medical professionals ourselves, my husband and I recognized the implications. There is a vast gray area between no hope and false hope, but few seemed able to communicate anything between those extremes.

We brought our baby home to his nursery and settled in for what would be the longest year of our lives. No matter what we did, our child would not be comforted. He cried constantly, nursed incessantly, slept sporadically, and seemed completely terrified of his surroundings.

For every sense I had that his behaviors were extreme, people downplayed my feelings. All babies do this or that, they told me. Everyone could tell me a similar story with a happy ending.

But I could not ignore that my son's cries seemed pained, that he slept only three to four hours a day and nursed forty to fifty times. Magnetic resonance imaging (MRI) at two months confirmed our worst fears. I was exhausted, grief-stricken, hopeless and helpless, my own sadness magnified by the pain and despair of my beloved child.

Being a first-time mother can be tiring, puzzling, and isolating under the best circumstances. Being the parent of a child with disabilities extends the parameters beyond the place to which most people can relate. The tension created by this isolation exacerbates the all-consuming sadness.

You are tired beyond belief, but the night offers no reprieve. The day is broken up by the phone, the mail, the other parts of life that still demand your attention. The night is a dark, quiet version of the day, the time when you feel acutely alone. No one has answers, but the endless suggestions become almost painful to hear. People visit and then leave, saddened by how little they are able to help.

Friends and family both strengthen and strain you. Friends with children mourn the experiences you will be unable to share with them—days in the park, play groups, slumber parties, school sports. They feel guilty and relieved to have been spared your fate; these feelings make them uneasy.

In an odd way, I found more comfort from friends who didn't have children, as if they could empathize better without the emotional baggage of parenthood. Our own families were, and remain, in varying stages of denial. Seven years later, the degree of their denial is revealed by the degree to which they can accept our child, our life choices, and their potential role as members of the family.

It was particularly difficult to spend the tender days of my child's infancy without the expected closeness—gently rocking him to sleep, quietly nursing him, taking long walks with him bundled to my chest in a Snugli. Instead, there were doctors' appointments, medical tests, physical therapy, and medicines that did not go down with a spoonful of sugar. Every day was a painfully eviscerating rerun of the day before.

The "support system" was all around me, but it was so hard to know what I needed. My options were overlapping but all slightly off the mark. I did not find solace through support groups or through talking with "experienced" parents. I did not want to know the future. I could barely digest the present.

I did not want to know that the hardest parts were still to come. I especially winced at the inference that there might be some good in this—a growth of character and strength. I found my own fears in the stories of other parents, but I was not in a place where I could think about the future. I needed help with the business of getting through the day, through the next hour.

As time went on, the most consuming problem was fatigue—our son's and ours. It took almost a year to convince his physicians that he really wasn't sleeping. Finally, our reservations set aside by our desperate need for rest, we began sedating him at night. With a little more sleep, we began to see the future with some sanity, and he began to find windows of peace in his life. We were able to explore and define his boundaries and become aware of the comfort available within them. As he did the same, he was able to expand beyond the plateau where he had been stranded the past year.

It's been important for us to concentrate on what our son can do while respecting what he cannot do. I've learned that we should not feel traitorous for accepting the reality of a situation.

I am not a traitor to my son's being because I know that he will never walk, read a book, see a sunset, or be a husband or father. Instead we need to focus on the things he can enjoy—feeling safe, loved, and peaceful. That is not to say that I do not spend many days anguishing over the sheer difficulty of his struggle. But the other side of that is to witness an unfathomable courage, tenacity, and spirit. He accepts what is; this has helped the rest of us do the same.

Though our son is nonverbal, without any sight, quadriplegic, and profoundly developmentally impaired, we have learned to understand the way he communicates his needs. This has been an arduous and often frustrating process.

I believe that as you learn to trust your voice, you begin to hear your child's voice more clearly. I believe that if you listen, any child can find a way to "speak" to you. Listening to your child will carry you through crises with your child or avert them altogether.

It's important to realize that no matter how much you read and how many conferences you attend, there are still more unknowns than knowns. Do not feel obligated to do something simply because it is acceptable and/or standard procedure. You know your child; be open but not intimidated.

As your early grief subsides and you become accustomed to its diminished but resident level, there is much room for healing. Your old expectations become less important, and with the new ones in hand, you can move on with the business of living. For some people this takes a long time; for some, I suspect, it never happens. Some of it has to do with the nature of the disability, some with your support systems—familial, medical, financial, and spiritual. A lot of it has to do with your emotional capacity. It is not easy to run from something when you are living it every day.

We have had to do quite a bit of adapting. At first, we really believed that our own strength would enable us to go on without changing our life plans at all. That expectation was untrue and exhausting. We began to see that if we made adjustments to create the best world for our son, it would be the best world for us, too. We went on to have two more beautiful sons who are devoted and generous younger brothers. We changed where we lived, how we worked, and what we thought we would be doing. Seven years later, we are finding ourselves close to our original thoughts and dreams.

This is not to say that our challenges haven't been burdensome. This is not to say that there are no more days of harrowing fear and exhaustion, no things I desperately miss. We may not have done everything we planned, but in everything we have done and everywhere we have been, our boys have been with us. What once seemed impossible obstacles have become splendid triumphs.

• • •

Diane Stonecipher lives in Austin, Texas, with her husband, Bob, and sons, Luke (1991), Colin (1993), and Dylan (1995). Diane is a registered nurse who stays at home caring for Luke. Bob is a family practice physician who works in hospice care and as a consultant for medically fragile children in the school system. Luke was severely brain-injured at birth. His only volitional movement is of his left hand which he uses to play his music with a communication switch and tell his family he is hungry. He loves music, warm water, and the sounds of his brothers.

29

BEING KIP'S MOM

by Melody Grant

My son Kip was born on June 8, 1990. I was thrilled to have a son, a perfect complement to his two-year-old sister.

Later that day, my pediatrician asked my permission to conduct tests on Kip. He didn't mention any specific concerns, just said he'd noticed a few physical features he wanted to "check out"—a straight crease on the palm of one hand and a narrow chest.

He brought along another pediatrician, who was also a genetic specialist. This doctor would be filling in for my pediatrician over the weekend. The genetic specialist said he was sure Kip was fine, that he didn't see the need for any tests. I was torn but decided to consent to the tests, just to be sure.

When the two doctors left the room, a sick feeling started in the pit of my stomach. I just knew something was wrong with Kip. My husband and I agreed not to mention anything to our parents or friends until we had the test results.

My husband was sure Kip was fine. I was sure he wasn't. I remembered seeing a TV movie starring Tyne Daly as a mother of a son with Down syndrome, and I knew that was it. But I didn't share my thoughts with anyone. We took Kip home the next day and went into waiting mode.

Kip was a difficult baby right from the start. He did not suck well, and he gagged and spat up a lot during feeding. When Kip was four days old, I took him to the pediatrician for a checkup. He was very jaundiced and had lost weight. During that visit, the doctor told me the news—Kip had Down syndrome. It was a confirmation of what I already knew in my heart, but actually hearing the words took away that last bit of hope. My husband was called and came immediately to the doctor's office. As we cried and talked to the doctor about what this meant, the nurse offered to take Kip out of the room. I declined the offer. Kip was still my baby; I would hold him and take care of him.

Looking back, I have mixed feelings about Kip's early diagnosis. Kip did not have many of the usual physical characteristics and appeared relatively "normal"—so "normal" the genetic specialist had recommended not testing him. And sometimes I wish we'd had the time just to enjoy our son as a baby, not a baby with a label. On the other hand, it was good to know what was wrong, because Kip was a very sickly baby.

Driving home over the mountain pass, I remember thinking how easy it would be to drive off the edge and not have to deal with the pain I was feeling. I was just twenty-nine years old. Mine was a low-risk pregnancy. I hadn't even been tested for any possibility of birth defects. Then I told myself, "God wouldn't give us more than we can handle."

Telling my parents was the next hurdle. We visited, and I just blurted out, "Kip has Down syndrome."

"Then we'll just love him more," my mother replied matter-of-factly.

I don't know what I had expected from my parents, but knowing they would still love him was great reassurance.

That night I started reading the pamphlets and brochures the doctor had given me. They all seemed so negative and bleak. After a few minutes, I told my husband I didn't want to read any more. I didn't want preconceived expectations; I wanted to let Kip have every opportunity to be or do anything he wanted. My husband agreed. I never looked at those pamphlets again.

My husband told his parents the next day. They were very upset. My mother-in-law contacted a couple who had a daughter with Down syndrome and asked us to meet with them. My husband and I agreed we weren't ready for that yet. Again we felt we didn't want to lower our expectations for Kip by comparing him to someone else.

Next, we went to see the genetic specialist who had seen Kip at birth. After apologizing for having reassured me that Kip was fine, he discussed the type of Down syndrome Kip had, what it meant, and other factors. Another specialist, also at the meeting, told us it was okay not to make a big public announcement about Kip's condition, that we could let people find out gradually. She told us that the more normally Kip was treated, the more normal he would act. We have tried to follow that advice—insisting that Kip be treated like any other child.

I didn't realize how uneducated people were about disabilities, and I learned not to let people's remarks and reactions make me upset. Instead of getting angry with the cousin who asked if Kip "got this" because I didn't gain much weight during my pregnancy, I used her question as an opportunity to educate her about chromosomal abnormalities.

Still, I often asked why this happened to me, and sometimes it was really hard. One day a friend called, excited to tell me the news that she and her husband were adopting two healthy and perfect sisters. She added that they wouldn't take them if they weren't completely normal. I remember thinking, "Wouldn't we all like to have that choice?"

We didn't, but I realize I was chosen to be Kip's mom.

Over the years, I'd often prayed for patience, and then one day I realized God had answered my prayer by giving me Kip. My son would teach me.

Having Kip has had its ups and downs. Ensuring that he gets the proper education and other therapies has been very challenging. As parents, we've had to be "on top" of his education program and needs at all times. Even though I am an elementary teacher, I didn't know all the special education laws and loopholes. Support from parent organizations has been invaluable.

We've also had to struggle to get Kip the medical attention he needed. Our pediatrician seemed unconcerned with many of Kip's medical problems and reluctant to perform tests we requested. Leaving our longtime family doctor for another health care professional was a big decision but one that has been very beneficial to Kip. We've also been successful in trying somewhat unconventional therapies at times, such as using a natural herb treatment for constipation.

Raising Kip in a small town where everyone knows us, and him, has made him very accepted. Of course, I worry about Kip's future and how his continuing needs will affect the lives of his two sisters, but I also know we couldn't imagine life without his smiling face, warm hugs, and loving ways. I'm thankful that I was chosen to be Kip's mom.

• • •

Melody Grant lives in Boulder, Montana, with her husband, Earl, and children, Krista (1988), Kip (1990), and Kaley (1993). Melody is a third-grade teacher in the Boulder public schools, and Earl is a carpenter for a school district in a town thirty miles away. Boulder is in the Rocky Mountains of southwest Montana, thirty miles south of the capital city, Helena. The family enjoys biking, boating, fishing, hunting, skiing, horseback riding, and many other outdoor activities.

30

DREAMS

by Ann Waldrop

My husband and I were both twenty-eight years old when we decided to start a family. We blindly took that leap of faith together, and within three weeks of our decision, we had conceived. My husband was ecstatic. I was stunned it had happened so quickly and more than a little bit scared.

Some of the things I recall worrying about during my pregnancy were weight gain, eating a balanced diet, the pain of childbirth, the responsibility of being a parent, the inevitable changes to our lifestyle. I didn't dwell on the possibility of having a child who would be anything but happy and healthy. On the odd occasion that fears of having anything other than a perfectly healthy baby crept into my consciousness, I swiftly pushed them out of my mind. It was not something I thought I could handle, and I reassured myself that the odds were in my favor. Thousands of women had healthy babies every day. Why should I be any different?

My doctor decided to induce labor at thirty-six weeks into the pregnancy owing to concern over the lack of fetal growth. The most likely cause of the problem, she said, was a failing placenta.

Other possible causes? I insisted she tell me. I don't remember what any of them were, except one—a chromosome defect. But my doctor reassured me that I had none of the risk factors.

Our beautiful little girl was even smaller than the doctor had expected. She was so tiny, weighing less than four pounds. The next week was like a roller coaster ride. She seemed to do well at first, then developed difficulty feeding and breathing.

We expected tests on the placenta to explain what had happened, but the results came back normal. We waited, watching her endure more tests and wondering why this was happening. We were scared, but we tried our best to believe that the doctors would figure out what was wrong and make her better. Our daughter was so tiny, but so beautiful. It was almost inconceivable that anything could be seriously wrong. We picked out a name and painted her bedroom pink for her homecoming.

We got the diagnosis when Jesse was eight days old. The doctor told us she had a rare chromosome defect and asked if we knew what that meant.

We were stunned. My husband couldn't even speak.

I responded slowly. I said that I understood it was a type of birth defect, the kind that causes Down syndrome and some others. I asked the doctor if our daughter had Down syndrome, because she didn't look as though she did.

The doctor shook her head and said it was a much more serious condition.

There was silence in the room as my husband and I tried to grasp what we were being told. Rather than bombarding us with more information than we could absorb, the doctor waited quietly for us to ask a question.

I finally broke the silence, and asked the doctor if Jesse would live.

She responded affirmatively but said that she would be severely impaired.

We asked for more information, even though we didn't want to believe anything that we were being told. What did she mean by "impaired"?

This time, the doctor paused for a long time. When she spoke, she said our little girl would be severely mentally retarded, that she might never walk or talk. Although her voice was steady as she spoke, there were tears in her eyes. As first-time parents, we were completely unprepared for this news. After the doctor left, we held Jesse, cried, and told her how much we loved her.

We left the hospital and went to my mother's house. Somehow I managed to tell her what we had been told. She hugged us both, then held me while I sobbed.

My head was filled with images I had already developed for my daughter's future. Until then, I hadn't even realized that those images existed. As my mother told me how sorry she was, I went through the list of events that would never happen as I had imagined them—my daughter's first steps, her first day of school, high school graduation, college, marriage, children of her own. The simplest expectations for a first-time parent to have—now shattered.

My mother listened to me and then quietly said, "I know that thinking about all of those things is very painful right now, but you have to remember that those are your dreams, sweetheart, not hers. Jesse will have dreams of her own. They may not be like those of other children, but they will be her dreams, just the same."

Jesse is seven years old now. We are very thankful that she is able to do much more than we were told to expect when she was diagnosed. I will never forget my mother's words of comfort that night. I hope that my husband and I will always honor them by allowing all three of our children to cultivate and follow their own dreams.

● ● ●

Ann Waldrop lives in Ypsilanti, Michigan, with her husband, Eric, and their three children, Jesse (1991), Samantha (1993), and Tyler (1994). Jesse has cri du chat syndrome. She has fairly substantial cognitive deficits, moderate gross and fine motor delays, and severe speech deficits. She also has a sense of humor and is usually very social and happy despite some behavioral problems that have been very difficult to deal with.

Eric has his own business and Ann currently is a stay-at-home mother. She says, "Although Jesse presents us with challenges we never anticipated as parents, she has taught us many valuable lessons. Life with Jesse hasn't been what we expected, and many times it has been very difficult. Luckily for us, my husband is an eternal optimist, and even on the worst days, he helps me realize how lucky we are as a family to have each other."

31

HAVING EVERYTHING

by Jan T. Skoby

This boy has had two open-heart surgeries, has been confined in a full body cast for six months, has undergone bilateral eye surgery, has had pneumonia at least twice a year. This boy is in the hospital at least once a month, has to take three different medications every morning and night, still has spontaneous hip subluxation and a heart condition so severe he can't always run around with his friends without sweating profusely and feeling pain in his stomach. This boy is only seven years old. But this boy is happy.

What He Has

- a passion for all people;
- such sensitivity that he doesn't need to hear a spoken word to understand how someone is feeling;
- a nonjudgmental attitude toward all individuals;
- an eagerness to learn, and
- a passion for life.

What He Doesn't Have

- the ability to conceive that some people can be untrustworthy;
- the ability to conceive that not everyone will have his best interest at heart, and
- the ability to conceive that some people make decisions that are self-beneficial.

This boy sees only goodness in people. No matter what happens to him, no matter what pain others may inflict upon him, he will never see, feel, or conceive that it may have been intentional.

What He Has

- an extra twenty-first chromosome;
- a label;
- people in his life who see beyond that label, and
- people who love him for who he is—a sensitive, caring, beautiful, loving boy.

They say, "You have everything when you have your health." This boy certainly has changed the meaning of that phrase for me.

I now understand that you have everything when you have a positive outlook on life. I realize I have everything, because I am fortunate enough to share this boy's life. I am his mother.

Jump for the Moon!

You and I on a cool summer night
Walked the grass together in the still moonlight.
We were chasing fireflies running everywhere
Laughing and playing in the calm summer air.

I thought I, the teacher, must help you gain knowledge.
That night you taught me something I had not learned in college.
Although your verbal words at times are difficult to understand
You stopped running, said, "Mama," and reached for my hand.

You hopped up and down looking up at the sky
So I hopped with you, not understanding why.
I was not sure what you were trying to express
I just hopped with you, hoping eventually to guess.

You looked up to the sky and with a soft voice said, "moo."
I repeated what I thought you meant saying, "moo," too.
"No," you said abruptly, shaking your head.
I still was not sure what you thought you had said.

So again you took my hand, hopped, and said, "moo."
It was then that I realized you were trying to say "moon."
"Jump for the moon?" I asked. Your eyes opened wide.
You nodded your head yes as we stood side by side.

So there we were in the serene moonlight
Jumping for the moon with all our might.
We jumped and reached our hands to the sky
Trying to catch that moon—my son and I.

Amir, my little prince, I do believe it is true
An abundance of people will learn a great deal from you.
Even though you have challenges you still have to meet
You'll keep jumping for the moon, landing on your feet.

If you are now reading this brief little story,
Please take a moment and forget some of your worries.
If your life doesn't always proceed as you'd planned
Try jumping for the moon; on both feet you will land.

• • •

Jan Skoby lives in New Hampshire with her son, Amir (1990). Jan has held various positions in the human service field since 1989. She has worked in early childhood intervention since 1994. She is currently employed as a service coordinator for an early supports and services program in Amherst, New Hampshire. She is also actively involved in various volunteer programs including the Parent-to-Parent Program of New Hampshire and currently serves on the board of directors for the Education Intervention Network.

She writes as a hobby in order to share the experiences and lessons that Amir has brought into her life.

Amir has survived his third cardiac surgery, is no longer taking medication, and is a student at his local grade school. Amir's hobbies include tubing, boating and fishing with his grandfather, playing basketball, cooking, painting, swimming—and he continues to jump for the moon!

32

BE A PARENT FIRST

by Jo Anne Spencer

Being a parent is never easy. In this day and age, it can be a pretty frightening prospect, with gangs, drugs, and various other dangers to attract and influence kids. Kids don't come with directions, instruction manuals, unconditional money-back guarantees, or warranties. So how do you know what they need and how to take care of them? How do you become a good parent?

If you are one of the lucky ones, you had a good role model in your own mom and/or dad. If you weren't so lucky, you'll just have to muddle through and read, listen, and ask questions—a lot of them!

My theory on parenting is this: No one tells you what it's really like to have children—or they don't tell you the truth!

But how could they? Parenting skills are as individual as each parent and child. Parenting is a huge responsibility that should not be entered into without a great deal of thought to the commitment of time, love, and resources needed to complete the task. Even so, I have never experienced any greater joy—or sorrow.

Parenting a child with special needs is, at best, overwhelming. Overwhelming because on top of all the other normal parenting issues, the ones everyone expects, there are the special needs issues that no one ever expects or is prepared for—medical complications, educational setbacks, financial hardships.

We ask, "Where will I get the money to take care of this child? Will other people see the light and the promise of this child? Will he be labeled and overlooked? Will she make it through today? How many tomorrows do we have? What does the future hold?"

Come to think of it, on some level, these concerns may not be all that different from those of other parents. But I believe that having a child with special needs changes the way each of us views life. Our priorities change; what used to seem so important no longer seems like a big deal. Small victories—like the first independent movement of a limb—become monumental. Those little things other parents take for granted are so important to us.

Our role changes, too. We become doctor, therapist, nutritionist, and teacher to our children. And then, if we are not too exhausted by the end of the day, perhaps we get to be moms or dads.

But maybe not. Most moms and dads get to enjoy their children, but you may not allow yourself the luxury of just enjoying your child. You might feel you have to be constantly "doing" for your child, doing what it takes to help your child reach his or her fullest potential.

If that's you, I have one word for you. Stop!

It's okay to be just mom or dad. Sometimes it's even preferable—for you and, yes, especially for your child. Your child needs to feel your love and respect—that's right, respect—for who and what he or she is, regardless of what he or she can or can't do or can or can't be. Your child also needs down time, just as you do. Too much therapy can be as bad as not enough.

Sometimes just holding and hugging, speaking about how the day went, or just communicating through touch makes all the difference in the world. Sometimes a child's outlook, health, and motivation can change when that child knows he or she is loved. As a parent, you will also benefit from fond memories of closeness and relaxation instead of constantly overdoing and trying to utilize each waking moment in being a supermom or superdad. By all means, be an advocate, but be a mom or dad first!

• • •

Jo Ann Spencer is the mother of identical twin sons who were born seven and a half weeks early in September 1990. As a result of a somewhat rare condition referred to as twin-to-twin transfusion syndrome (TTTS), the boys have cerebral palsy, visual/perceptual issues, orthopedic involvement, learning disabilities, and global developmental delays. One of the twins required a kidney transplant, also as a result of TTTS, and received a kidney from his father at the age of eighteen months.

Jo Ann and her boys live in Tucson, Arizona, where she works part-time for Pilot Parents of Southern Arizona as coordinator of special projects. Pilot Parents is a support organization for families with children who have disabilities and is one of the two designated Parent Training and Information Centers in Arizona. Jo Ann runs Sibshops (support groups for siblings of children with special needs), writes and edits The Navigator, *Pilot Parents' quarterly newsletter, and provides one-to-one support for families who call looking for resources. She is on the board of the Individual Achievement Association, which provides conductive education, an alternative form of educational therapy for children with cerebral palsy, in the Tucson area. In her spare time she enjoys special needs tennis and other sports activities with her sons. They all enjoy gardening and outdoor activities. Jo Ann is a master gardener and volunteers at the Plant Clinic through the University of Arizona's Extension Garden Program. She has a B.A. in education from James Madison University in Virginia and an M.L.A. (Master in Landscape Architecture) from the University of Arizona in Tucson.*

33

THE PERFECT DAUGHTER

by Michael T. Bailey

On April 2, 1988, at seven o'clock in the morning our first child was born. It had not been an easy delivery. It ended in an emergency cesarean section. The delivery room was full of medical personnel shrouded in gowns and masks. Finally the doctor handed me the swaddled, red, and wrinkled bundle that was Eleanor Sumner Bailey. Only my wife, Jonna, heard him say the ominous words: "Get a pediatrician."

Like all expectant parents, we had thought long and hard about a name. We wanted this newborn girl child to have a somewhat unusual name that reflected strength and pride. My own love of history was satisfied by Eleanor of Aquitaine, the great medieval queen of France and England, mother of Richard the Lion Hearted. Jonna's feminism and passion for justice came to some extent from Eleanor Roosevelt and all she stands for. Eleanor, we decided, was the perfect name. She would be the perfect daughter.

"Your daughter has an extra chromosome. . . ."

These words came from the summoned pediatrician. I remember that he had no face—only a pair of dark eyes peering from the space between the surgical cap and mask.

"Your daughter has an extra chromosome. . . ."

I remember my first thought: "Oh! An extra chromosome. Smart kid. Chip off the old block." An extra *anything* seemed like a real advantage in this world.

"Your daughter has an extra chromosome. It's called Down

syndrome. If you are interested, we have some literature you can read before you leave the hospital."

The masked pediatrician finished his sentence. Abruptly he turned and left the room. Two nurses began to sob. I looked at Jonna. She looked at me.

Thus began our wrenching, happy, challenging, humanizing, angry, crusading, broadening, rejoicing, proud adventure in parenting a child with a developmental disability. Over the past ten years, we have learned that there is very little wrong with our daughter, but a great deal wrong with the culture into which she was born.

As for so many other families of children with disabilities, our first experience was in a "medical" environment. It took us a while to realize that the "medical" environment thinks about children with disabilities using a "medical" model—a model that teaches parents to think of their child as sick. Subtle and not-so-subtle messages tell parents to do everything they can to make their child more "normal."

Several years ago, on the advice of a medical professional, we went to see a specialist who dealt with issues of growth. We were concerned that Eleanor was too small, and we wanted to know what we could do to make her taller. In other words we wanted to subject her to growth hormones in an effort to make her look more "normal."

What we learned was that she was in the fiftieth percentile for girls her age with Down syndrome. How much more normal could she be?

Eleanor was not sick. She did not need to be made well. She was not broken. She did not need to be fixed. What she needed was a family that recognized that girls with Down syndrome are short. There was nothing *wrong* with her.

Gradually, it became clear that I needed to view Eleanor's life not from my own experiences and expectations but from hers. The question should not have been: "How can I make her taller?" The question should have been: "What can I do to help the world accept her for the person she is?"

Realizing how ignorant I used to be about developmental disabilities makes it easier to accept the ignorance and prejudice we encounter daily. Most of us have experienced "the look" our children get in the grocery store checkout line or the condescending pat on the head.

It may appear well-meaning, but it is the face of prejudice. Prejudice leads to discrimination, and people with developmental disabilities have lived with and suffered from discrimination for generations. If we parents do not take the lead in confronting these attitudes, prejudice and discrimination will be our children's future. I want it to end here. I want it to end with our family.

Each of us needs to believe sincerely that our children are people, first and foremost, that they can be valued members of the community. Inclusion begins at home. The world will not respect your child if you do not. Set an example by proudly taking your child wherever it is appropriate for children to go. Believe in your heart that you are the world's leading expert on the needs of your family and your child. Let nothing change that belief.

Parenting a "special needs child" inevitably means dealing with experts. Doctors, therapists, educators, agency staff members, government officials, members of the clergy, neighbors, relatives, and the postman may all feel the need to give you advice. Much of this information will be useful. But never let "experts" take your place. You need to have your own dream for the happiest and best possible life for your child. Do not let anyone turn you away from it.

I remember the first time I realized that I was depending on an "expert" who turned out to be completely ignorant.

When Eleanor was four we signed her up for a three-day-a-week summer Parks and Recreation program. We were assured that her "inclusion" with other children her age would be guaranteed by the presence of an "inclusion specialist."

When I arrived to pick Eleanor up at the end of the first week, I saw Eleanor and Sam, a little boy with cerebral palsy, with the inclusion specialist in the farthest corner of the playground—no other children in sight. Inside the school building, I heard the other kids happily singing songs. As I waited in the hall, I could hear Eleanor whining and complaining as she approached the door—behaving just like any other upset four-year-old who was being excluded from an activity in which she wanted to participate.

When the inclusion specialist saw me, she asked, in a very exasperated voice, "Well, what do you think?"

"What do I think about what?" I replied.

She answered, "It seems to me that Eleanor's Down syndrome has gotten quite a bit worse since Wednesday!"

Another extra chromosome! I wondered if I should call the faceless pediatrician and inform him of this latest development.

At that moment, I realized I knew more about inclusion than this person, whatever her education or experience. Since then, I've learned to disregard "expert advice" that does not conform to our family's dream for our daughter. Our family knows best. Experts are there to help us achieve our dreams. They are not there to dream for us.

Eleanor is now ten years old. She is in third grade in our neighborhood school. She is fully included in her classroom. She has a full-time educational assistant and lots of friends. Last week she got her reading "letter" for having read seventy-five hundred pages in the last four years.

Does she read at grade level? No. Does she read? Yes, and she is proud of it.

Eleanor has a great life, and we believe it will only get better. Our family has worked long and hard to close the huge developmental disabilities institution in Oregon. Now we are working to see that Eleanor will have the opportunity to direct her own services when she becomes an adult. We believe that Eleanor should have the right to make her own decisions as she grows—even a few bad ones. She has the right to privacy, and when she is an adult, she will have the right to intimate relationships. She has the right to dream her own dreams and live her own life.

Sometimes Eleanor makes us cry. More often, she makes us laugh. Her triumphs are ours.

In more ways than we imagined, Eleanor is the daughter we dreamed about before her birth. She has the inner strength of a queen and the compassion of a social visionary. She cares more for other people than anyone I have ever known. She has a great deal to offer the world and will make her own irreplaceable contributions to her country, her community, and her family. She is the perfect daughter we expected.

• • •

Michael Bailey lives in Oregon with his wife, Jonna Sumner Schuder, and daughters, Eleanor (1988) and Taylor (1990). Michael is statewide community organizer for Community Partnerships, a project of the Oregon Developmental Disabilities Council. He is a commissioner of the Oregon Disabilities Commission and a registered lobbyist. Jonna is a staff attorney at the Oregon Advocacy Center and specializes in the rights of persons with disabilities.

Taylor is in the Talented and Gifted Program at Hollyrood Grade School and loves chess, reading, and soccer. Eleanor attends the Laurelhurst School and enjoys soccer and swimming. She has testified before the Oregon legislature several times and counts Governor Kitzhaber among her friends. She is very opinionated and likes to say that "people like me are like everyone else."

34

SILVER LININGS AND EVERYDAY CLOTHES

by Joan Killough-Miller

Two pumpkin pies sat cooling on the counter the day before Thanksgiving, when a miracle occurred. My daughter, Hannah, walked across the kitchen floor. We watched in silence as she took a few lurching steps and froze in the middle, groping for something to hang onto. There was nowhere to go but forward. We applauded wildly as she came crashing into the kitchen counter, just below the pies.

Every child's first steps are special, but that Thanksgiving we felt truly blessed. Hannah has Angelman syndrome. Among children with Angelman syndrome, four is a pretty typical age to start walking.

When a child with special needs comes into your life, you are called on to express more thankfulness than the average person. You say things like, "She's so good natured," and "Thank goodness she's healthy and strong." You pull out these silver linings to put other people at ease, and sometimes, when the going gets rough, you wave them in front of your own eyes.

I am a mere apprentice at the kind of magic that turns tragedy into treasures. I mistrust the illusionists who pull miracles out of our worst nightmares. When I talk to a friend who is fighting cancer, or someone reeling from a bitter divorce, I am baffled when they start to talk about their blessings. Blessings? What kind of person finds blessings in that?

And yet, there are moments—fleeting moments—when I begin to understand. When the silver linings become our everyday clothes. Or, at least, when we try them on and find, to our great surprise, that they actually fit.

Last summer, at an Angelman syndrome convention, I had breakfast with a woman who told me about her son, who was just starting to walk at the age of eighteen. Stories like that used to make me cringe with pity and embarrassment. The image of a gangly teenager tottering on his first steps was just too much to bear. But that morning, in the coffee shop of a Seattle hotel, I asked the woman to wait while I went back to the buffet to fill my plate with melon balls and scrambled eggs. Then I settled in to savor her story. All day, it kept coming back to me, like a hundred-watt bulb on a pull chain. Each time it flashed on, I was flooded with the realization that anything is possible.

The real question is this: Would I trade that knowledge, and Hannah's hard-won victory walk across the kitchen, for a more ordinary Thanksgiving with the usual blessings?

I know what I am supposed to say. I hear it all the time. "I love her just the way she is. Given a choice, I wouldn't change a thing."

Well, I do love Hannah just the way she is. I admit I've had dreams about a genie who could wave his hand and take care of that little problem on her fifteenth chromosome.

But then I wake up. The real magic is right here, in the laughing, brown-eyed girl who set out across the kitchen floor with no guarantees. I marvel at the courage it took for her to put one foot in front of the other and step out into that open space. But then again, I think she just had her eyes on those pies.

● ● ●

Hannah (1989), now walks freely, although stairs are still somewhat daunting. She enjoys school, Girl Scouts, swimming, and music. She has recently started using some simple sign language to communicate, a milestone that brings much joy. She lives with her family in central Massachusetts.

Angelman syndrome is a little-known genetic disorder that results from a small deletion on chromosome 15. Early signs may include a small head size, seizures, and significant delays in motor and cognitive development. The most pronounced characteristic is the lack of spoken language. Other traits include an awkward gait, light-colored hair and eyes, and a happy demeanor with frequent laugher. More information is available by calling 1-800-IF-ANGEL.

35

RAISING ANSWERS

by Julia Shure

"**A**re they going to use a knife?" my daughter asks. "Is it going to be sharp?" And then, "They're not going to cut my leg!"

She's been hearing some talk about her upcoming surgery, and I realize that we'll have to be a little more careful, now that she's four, about how and what we say when she's in earshot.

I tell her that the doctor is going to straighten out her feet so it will be easier for her to walk and put her braces on.

"Will it hurt?" she asks. "Can I keep my socks on?"

Not that this is new. It's surgery number seven, and it's probably not the last. Nine months earlier she had scar tissue removed from the tethered nerves at the end of her spinal cord, and then had to lie on her back in the hospital for four days. We watched a marathon of Disney videos, and I held her hand at night.

A few seconds after she was born, we found out that she had spina bifida. This left her with weak legs, feet, and hips and difficulty with bowel and bladder control.

Like most children with spina bifida, she also has hydrocephalus, an abnormal buildup of fluid in the brain. It is controlled by a shunt, a valve attached to a plastic tube that drains the extra fluid from her brain to her abdomen. Surgeries two, three, and four were for shunt installation and replacements.

This time an orthopedic surgeon will unsnarl her left foot and stabilize both ankles with metal plates. Without braces, she stands completely on the outside of her left foot. But she walks—even if she limps a bit and can't go fast—and she jumps up and down on my bed. She tackles stairs with two hands. She tries to run and do all the same things as the other kids in her preschool.

The upcoming operation won't really fix her legs. Science cannot yet make muscles and nerves where there aren't any, or hook them up to the brain if they're not already attached. The doctors will give her flatter feet that don't turn in, but there won't be any miracle cure.

With the help of Celia's constant charm and unflagging enthusiasm for life, I'm learning to live with her condition. She has gifts that make up for all of this, I tell myself when sunk low by nagging, painful "whys" and "if onlys." My daughter is sweet and smart, loving and funny, I remind myself. It is a pleasure to be her mother.

She goes to birthday parties, swimming lessons, and a regular preschool. We take her camping. We try to treat her the same as our older daughter, not to make a big deal about her disability. This seems to be the best way to raise her in a world not yet ready for her—a world thirsty for miracles and high-tech cures but with little patience for a chronic, lifelong condition.

Now she's a cute little girl. What will life be like for her as a teenager or adult woman with a disability? How do we help pave her way without doing too much?

Denial, my defense mechanism of choice, runs thin when I'm faced with hospitals, school meetings, or Celia's questions. I'm waiting for the big one: "Why was I born with spina bifida?" I am trying to figure out how to answer.

I won't tell her she's special because she has a disability. I hate that word and its ramifications—special education, special shoes, special needs.

And I cringe when well-meaning people tell me there's a "special place in heaven" for her or that we were "chosen" to be special parents. I reply that there's a place on earth for her and that it needn't be so special. We want the same for her as we want for her sister—to grow up, to have friends and family, fun and work.

One friend, who has the benefit of strong Christian beliefs, tells her little boy who uses a wheelchair that when the angels brought him down from heaven, they cut his wings too much. She says the angels gave him to his parents because God knew they could love him more and better than anyone else. He loves this story and asks to hear it over and over.

A magazine article advises me to say something like: "We don't know why, but some children aren't born with all the parts they need, so you need to work harder. And we're going to help you." This will not fly with Celia; she will probably demand a more detailed explanation, which she will tailor to suit her needs.

One day last week she came home from preschool uncharacteristically quiet and somber. I kept trying to get her to talk about it, but she kept telling me she was okay and wanted to play in her room by herself. Later, she sat at the table and drew a picture of intersecting black lines. She said, "This is my scar on my back I got after I was born."

There was some weakness in her grip on the crayon, but there was power in her strokes. She was working it out. The next day she wrapped her stuffed bear in toilet paper and told me she had done the operation. "I've given him a shunt," she said.

Celia is not self-conscious about her appearance. She doesn't seem to envy her older sister's lithe, agile body. She'll don a pink tutu, put Kara's old ballet slippers over her braces, and turn slow, limping circles with arms overhead, humming the "Waltz of the Flowers" from *The Nutcracker*. At first, it made me sad to see those little shoes over the plastic braces and the feet that will never point. But then I thought, why not? She really likes herself in them, and there are too many unemployed dancers anyway. Why can't she just enjoy herself without my melodrama?

I believe she knows more than she lets on, more than she wants to talk about. A week after surgery last year, she said, "Well, I didn't die," even though she'd never heard anyone mention that possibility.

She was born with a generous, ebullient spirit and seems tuned in to a higher frequency. I've discarded the parenting manuals, and I take my cues from her about how to raise her. But I remain vigilant and protective, hoping our society won't squash her buoyant nature.

One day after summer school she came home upset that another child had been teasing her about her braces and the way she walks. Incensed, I immediately drove back to the school and talked to the teacher. The next day I talked to the class about spina bifida while Celia took her braces off and held them up. She then answered her friends' questions and took a bow.

Sure, she'll regret having a disability at times, but maybe she has it all figured out and doesn't need to know why. If she asks, I'll tell her that I'm glad she's our daughter and Kara's sister and that she came to us and nobody else. I'll tell her that we don't know why children get born with spina bifida, but I'd rather have her with spina bifida than not have her at all.

And someday I will tell her that she is my all-time best teacher. She's taught me that love and grief spring from the same well. That we can ride a river of grief and not drown in it, that it can wake us up. That we can savor the bittersweet fruit of life and become whole.

• • •

Julia Shure lives in northern California with her husband, Marc, and daughters, Celia and Kara. Celia, who was born with spina bifida in 1989, is now an active, articulate fourth-grader who enjoys books, music, swimming, horseback riding, and playing with her dog and cat.

36

DOUBLE WHAMMY

by Carolyn Carasea

April is Autism Awareness Month. But our family is aware of autism every month, every day, and every hour—doubly. Our lives changed irrevocably with the diagnosis of autism in our two young children.

Caryn was two when we first recognized she was more than shy. Her social and language development were delayed compared to other children her age. She was hypersensitive to light, sound, and touch. At night she would lie in her bed and bounce her feet off the wall until, exhausted, she would finally fall asleep. By two and a half, she'd stopped wanting to be held and avoided looking at our faces. We started looking for answers.

When she was three, a developmental pediatrician gave us the answer. Caryn had autism.

Autism. The very word seemed to crush the air out of my lungs. It evoked a mental picture of a silent child sitting on the floor banging her head against the wall.

The pediatrician stressed early intervention. Caryn had already completed a year of typical preschool. After the diagnosis, we were sent to a developmental preschool in an adjacent district. An excellent teacher worked with Caryn and with me. She taught me the most important rule of working with my child: Find Caryn's level of functioning and start there, rather than trying to get her to "perform" at the level I think she should be at. My husband, Jerry, and I agonized over Caryn's early struggles and constantly worked to help her. We began to make progress.

Then the other shoe dropped.

Our eighteen-month-old son, Matthew, stopped talking. Immediately we began speech therapy. By age two, not only had his speech failed to return, his behavior grew increasingly bizarre. He bounced on the trampoline for hours, ran in circles, and intermittently shrieked. He crushed bones in my thumb when he bit me. My face and neck constantly bore scratch marks from his clawing and pinching.

We went to a pediatric neurologist, who ordered a battery of medical tests—blood work, urine analysis, and an EEG (electroencephalogram). An afternoon in hell. Our toddler had to be restrained by five people, including us, to get blood. For the twenty-seven monitors to be attached to his head, he was wrapped in a sheet. I lay on the bed beside him and cried silently. I held him while they poured acetone over his hair to remove the monitors and gasped for air with him. Before we left the hospital that day, the doctor gave us the diagnosis with tears in his eyes: Matt had autism.

Jerry was angry. I was numb. It had never occurred to me that Matt might have autism, too. He and Caryn were so different! I cried through the long drive home. Jerry was uncharacteristically silent. The grief was equal to that I felt with the two miscarriages between my pregnancies with Caryn and Matt.

Soon we had two children in two different early intervention programs in two different outside communities. My life was a blur—driving Caryn and Matt to their programs, volunteering in each classroom, and working with both children at home. I read everything I could about autism, joined our local and national autism societies, and talked to other mothers of children with autism.

Autism consumed my days and haunted my nights. Even now it is very hard to admit how depressed I was. Every day was a struggle, and I felt as though I were drowning. Grief wrapped itself around my heart. Exhaustion so overwhelmed me that I sought medical help. I started on an antidepressant medication and sought counseling.

Time and therapy helped so much. I no longer felt the need to dump all my feelings of depression on Jerry. Jerry's constant support had been crucial, but I realized that he, too, had been suffering, keeping his grief to himself. A parent mentor group formed at our school. It has helped us all to have a forum for sharing our feelings and supporting each other.

It's been eight years since our daughter's diagnosis. Caryn is now eleven and entering the fifth grade, where she still receives some special tutoring and language therapies. Caryn is happy and blossoming. She tells me she doesn't have autism anymore; she asks when Matt's autism will go away, too. For the first time she is inviting friends over. She constantly asks questions as though trying to make up for her years of silence. Caryn loves to read and ride horseback. These days she will even let me hug her!

After six years of early intervention, Matt has come a long way, too. Now eight years old, Matt will be starting the second grade in a typical class where he will receive support, tutoring, and language therapy. With his dad's help, Matt's personal care skills continue to improve. He is starting to use some sentences, his shrieking is greatly diminished, and his attacks on me ended several years ago. He started reading at age four and continues to love books. Matt and Caryn have learned to play together. Occasionally he even gives me a great big smooch!

These days, Jerry is more patient with both children. An instrumental music teacher in a local high school, he also has become more patient with his students when they experience frustration in learning new skills. At some level, I know Jerry still feels cheated by not having typical children. It is hard for him to see the light at the end of the tunnel, and he worries about what will happen to our children when we're not around to care for them any longer. He also loves our children with an intensity that is beautiful to behold.

As for me, I have learned to accept my children as they are. I have learned to advocate for them. They never cease to amaze me, although I still grieve occasionally and am often tired. My children need intense parenting now and possibly forever. The "forever" part weighs heavily on me. I don't want my life defined by my children's disabilities, but I am still working to achieve a balance between their needs and my own.

With each draft of this essay, I became more honest in expressing my feelings. This was not easy. Some of these feelings are so painful. Jerry and I were devastated by the double whammy of our children's diagnoses. We suffer, but we also laugh, hope, and survive.

Our children still bounce—on their beds, on the trampoline, on their dad, and in our hearts. And we just bounce with them.

• • •

Carolyn Carasea lives with her husband, Jerry, and children, Caryn (1988) and Matthew (1991), in Clinton, Ohio. Carolyn volunteers in Matt's school working with children needing help in fine motor skills and co-edits a parent mentor newsletter for parents of children receiving special education services. She also participates in the Ohio Higher Education Partnership Project, a pilot program in which she speaks to college students in education and medicine about understanding and working with families who have children with disabilities.

37

WELCOME TO THE WORLD

by Nancy E. Holroyd

Leave it to a nurse to give birth during a change of shifts at the hospital—one group trying to leave, the other trying to ease into their work. Although there are double the usual number of medical personnel in the delivery room, it is deathly quiet, all of us looking at this baby together. After what seems like forever, she takes a breath. I look at her. She is beautiful.

There is no molding of her head. No bruising or swelling. She has short dark hair. I cannot believe her perfection. She is just *so* beautiful. And then she opens her eyes. *Oh, God, no,* I think. *Please close them.*

Suddenly the doctor and I are doing a surreal dance down her body. First the eyes, then the ears, then the back of her neck. Uncurling the tiny fingers to look at her palms. In unison, we travel from one body part to the next. Time held in abeyance. My brain is screaming. The room is silent. Waiting. Waiting for the doctor to tell me what I already know.

The unspoken thought forms, but does not slide past my lips. Finally, I break the silence. "Neal, does she have Down syndrome?"

His gentle reply: "You know the characteristics as well as I do, and she has a number of them. We'll do chromosomal studies."

Initially I coped by becoming very detached. I was, after all, a pediatric nurse. In a cool, clinical voice I told one of the nurses that I would get past this and be just fine. In the back of my mind,

I wondered if I would forever see this baby as a patient rather than as my child.

I didn't cry until "Black Thursday"—two days after Sheila's birth, when the postpartum hormones kicked in and started the tears flowing. I'd gone on a similar crying jag two days after the birth of my older daughter, too. But this time I used those tears.

Parents who give birth to a child with an obvious disability find themselves in the unique position of grieving for a childbearing loss at the same time they need to bond with their new infant. Some parents worry that they will never be able to bond with their baby, and then feel guilty that they are somehow missing a critical period for bonding. How *does* one bond under such circumstances?

- *Acknowledge your feelings, but try to be physically present with your baby.* Touch, stroke, and talk to your baby. But don't be too hard on yourself. The bond between parent and child is not irreparably shattered if this does not happen in the first few days of life.
- *Seek others who have been through this experience.* It can be reassuring to hear from others who have felt the same way you do. It's reassuring to know that others have gotten past these feelings of devastation.
- *Carefully choose the people you spend time with.* Surround yourself with people who can provide real love, hope, acceptance, nurturing, and privacy.
- *Read and write.* I read everything in sight and kept a journal. The reading provided me with information. The writing provided me with an outlet to react to everything I was reading.
- *Look for bonding opportunities in everyday activities.* Feeding times are a time to be with and bond with your baby. Or what new mother couldn't use a relaxing soak in the tub? But take the baby along. After soaping and rinsing the baby, maybe Dad can rub the baby with lotion and dress the baby while you enjoy some more time in the tub by yourself.
- *Take the time to nurture yourself.* You will have more left to give to your child and the others demanding your attention. Allow space for your relationship with your partner. It's easy to resent the other person's reactions if they are not the same as yours. It's easy to pull away from each other. But be for-

giving; you both must travel your own path through this difficult time.

My husband, Forrest, and I navigated the grief process in different ways. We spent varying lengths of time at the different stages. But in the end, I lost the most sleep worrying that Sheila would not survive long enough to have open-heart surgery. The possibility of losing Sheila soon became more frightening than the fact of her disability.

A few weeks after Sheila was born I had a dream. In the dream, I saw a small child at the bottom of a swimming pool. Before I could get there, I knew the baby was already dead. When I awoke, I felt more at peace than I had felt since Sheila's birth. I sensed that this dream was an expression of my grief at losing a "normal, healthy" child. This release gave me permission to love the baby we had. A bond had already started to form with the baby in my arms. Now there was nothing standing in the way of getting to know this child and welcoming her to the world.

• • •

Nancy Holroyd lives in Duanesburg, New York, with her husband, Forrest, and three daughters, Andrea (1985), Sheila (1987), and Colleen (1991). Sheila has been included in her local school from the time she entered kindergarten. Eleven years old at the time of this writing, she has become more insistent about when and where she wants to be included and when she wants to be pulled out of the classroom. Her parents and teachers are learning to respect her decisions.

38

"NORMAL" LIVES

by Karen L. Higginbotham

Our daughter, Alison, is a wonderful and beautiful child who gives us a great deal of joy. Alison is twelve years old and has multiple disabilities caused by having had infantile spasms, a rare seizure disorder, as a newborn.

Although doctors were very grim about Alison's prognosis, telling us she would not lead a normal life, she leads a life that is normal *for her*. Our family has made adjustments in many areas of our lives, but we all are living "normal" lives. Knowing this helped me to put our lives in perspective. I think this is the single most important realization I have had since Alison's birth.

Although professionals such as doctors, therapists, and teachers are important for Alison, I am also a professional. My profession is being Alison's mother, and I know her better than anyone. My thoughts and opinions matter and need to be taken into account regarding anything relating to Alison.

Alison requires maximum assistance with feeding, bathing, and dressing and is incontinent. Although nonverbal, she has learned to use some informal gestures to communicate some things to us (limitations in her fine motor skills prevent her from using sign language, and she is uninterested in using a communication device). She has cognitive disabilities that mean she needs more supervision than her younger brother, Dustin.

I'll be honest. At times, I do get overwhelmed with the amount of care she needs, but I realize this is a result of her disabilities, not her.

I still get teary-eyed when thinking of when Alison learned to walk short distances when she was six years old. We marvel at her every new accomplishment.

Alison receives special education through our public school system at our neighborhood school, two blocks from home—the same school Dustin attends. She has made her First Communion and attends Sunday Mass on a regular basis. She loves to swim and swing. She loves to go for rides in the van and has amazed us with her ability to know her way around town. She loves to go to the roller skating rink and have me push her in her wheelchair while I skate. Like most girls, she loves going shopping. She enjoys being around other children. She is curious about her surroundings and enjoys going new places.

Music has seemed to play a big part in her development. She "dances" by rocking back and forth. Her favorite performer is Alison Krauss, a bluegrass singer and fiddle player. In June 1998, we took Alison to one of Krauss's concerts, and Alison got to meet her favorite singer. It was so much fun to see how elated Alison was during this concert—she "danced" so hard that her father, Danny, had to hold her wheelchair down!

Having disabilities has not kept Alison from activities that she enjoys or from being part of our community. Alison is loved by many in our community. She enjoys life to the fullest. There have been times when I have had to fight some injustices concerning Alison, but I have also had to do that for Dustin.

Dustin has been a wonderful, loving brother to Alison. Sure, sometimes he gets annoyed about Alison's inability to do certain things. There also are times when he is jealous of Alison, but he soon realizes that he can do things Alison doesn't get to do, so his jealousy goes away quickly.

I realize that there are things that Alison may never do, and although I have learned not to expect her to do these things, I still hope that someday she will be able to.

It is my hope that she'll be able to speak someday, if only a few words. Many of my dreams involve Alison speaking. Recently I had a dream that Alison and I were shopping. Alison mumbled these few words at the sales clerk: "Is this outfit on sale?" I had to laugh and say, "She's her mother's daughter!"

Overall, the biggest challenge that I have faced is dealing with the bureaucracy of government assistance that helps us with

Alison's extraordinary needs. It can be very frustrating at times, but I have learned to be vocal. I have learned to speak up about Alison's needs—and the needs of other children with disabilities—to our elected officials.

With Alison at my side, I have had the opportunity to tell Alison's story to our elected officials in Washington and in our state capital and through the media. I might not always get the desired result; but if I don't speak up and complain, how will they understand her needs?

When speaking up for children with disabilities, I often think of the first time I saw Alison. At that moment, my thought was that maybe she would be a cheerleader one day. Alison has indeed become a cheerleader, but not for a football team; she has become a cheerleader for children with disabilities!

I have received a great deal of satisfaction from being Alison's mother. She has taught me a lot, not only about the needs of children with disabilities, but also about myself. She has given me strength I never knew I had. She has given me a great sense of pride. I am very proud that she is my daughter and that I am her mother.

Alison and other children with disabilities should be viewed as children first. Although she has some unique needs, her basic needs are the same as any child's—having a family who loves her and nurtures her, being part of our community, receiving an education, and having friends. She will always need a variety of supports and services, but none of us can live without assistance from others.

My dream for Alison is that she will reach her fullest potential. If she accomplishes that, she will have done far more with her life than most of the rest of us.

· · ·

Karen Higginbotham lives in Opelousas, Louisiana, with her husband, Danny, and their children, Alison (1988) and Dustin (1989). Danny works as a computer-aided draftsman for an engineering company. Karen volunteers as an advocate for children with disabilities. She has recently developed and maintains two web sites regarding grassroots legislative advocacy in Louisiana. She has been elected to serve on the board of directors of a family resource center that provides information and referral to families of children with disabilities. She also volunteers at a local cerebral palsy clinic.

39

FINDING OUR WAY

by Nate Terrell

When our daughter, Nicole, was first diagnosed with cerebral palsy, my wife, Anita, and I were consumed by fear and anxiety as we grappled with our shattered expectations for our first child's life. Although we longed to make meaningful contact with our beautiful little girl with wildly curly black hair, she seemed to take little or no interest in anything around her, including us. Often overwhelmed, we shut out the world and saved what little energy we had to take care of Nikki and ourselves.

During Nikki's second year, however, we began a transformation which has enabled us to let go of our fears for her future, connect deeply with her, and effectively stimulate her development. We have come to view Nikki as our teacher and have learned many important lessons from our intense involvement with her.

This process began when we realized that our anxiety about Nikki drained our energy and didn't help her or us in any way. We longed for a perspective which allowed us to celebrate rather than worry about her life.

Yet we were stuck. Stuck in the despair we experienced when Nikki seemed beyond our reach. Stuck in the fear that we would spend the rest of our lives taking care of her. Most importantly, stuck in an unknown territory where our attitudes and beliefs hadn't adapted to the landscape.

We finally reached a point where the pain became unbearable. We were left with no choice but to look within ourselves and try to change the beliefs and expectations that trapped us in fear and anxiety. After much self-examination, we decided that we had the capacity to make each day a happy one, regardless of Nikki's progress or level of independence.

We also realized that we could become more connected to and effective with Nikki if we were able to replace our fear and anxiety with happiness and peace of mind by letting go of any expectations we had for her. We were excited to discover that this new perspective opened the door for us to simply enjoy Nikki as she was, to encourage any efforts she made to do something new without worrying about whether or not those efforts would succeed.

We became increasingly able to pace ourselves according to Nikki's speed and pick up on her subtle, but highly significant, communication signals. When we responded to these signals and moved in tune with Nikki, we entered what we have come to call the "Nikki zone." Our ability to enter and remain in this unique place was dependent on our capacity to be completely present in the moment and join with Nikki in her world.

Nikki responded to our new attitude and approach to her with enthusiasm and became more animated and responsive in our presence. She clearly enjoyed the freedom she now had to explore the world on her own terms. Paradoxically, our ability to accept Nikki as she was appeared to motivate her to tackle new challenges.

Encouraged by Nikki's growing connection to us and confident that we could finally help her, Anita and I rearranged our work schedules so that we were able to provide her with extensive one-on-one attention, often up to twelve hours a day. We massaged her arms and legs to coax them into relaxation, made funny faces and sounds to get her attention, and placed favorite toys where she could reach for them. Fun for all was the only criterion by which we evaluated our activities.

Since Nikki loved it when we held her on her feet, we focused intently on helping her learn to stand on her own. Although she initially had great difficulty keeping her balance, she was tenacious in her efforts and eventually learned. At age three and a half, a year after learning to stand, she finally took her first halting steps. Nikki's intense look of determination at that moment, as she struggled to maintain her balance, will be forever etched in my mind.

Slowly but surely, Nikki has increased her mobility and come out of her protective shell to become highly attached to the people in her life who adore her as much as we do. This process has had many stops and starts. Nikki has gone through intense periods of development where she eagerly tackled new challenges such as drinking out of a cup by herself or walking up an incline behind our house. At other times, she has retreated into the safety of her own world and rebuffed our attempts to interact with her. When these periods occurred, we backed off and gave her the space she needed. When she was ready, she would nonchalantly do something new as if it had always been part of some secret plan.

Although we have benefited greatly from the guidance and help of a variety of experts, the key to our efforts with Nikki has been learning to trust and rely on our own instincts. The confidence we now feel contrasts sharply with desperate search for answers following Nikki's diagnosis when we rushed from expert to expert, searching for answers we now know did not exist. We have finally realized that no one can predict the course of Nikki's development or know for certain which treatment will be most effective. We can only experiment creatively and accept that Nikki is free to live her life on her own terms, doing what she knows is best for her at any given moment.

One of our most difficult challenges has been responding to the many people who imply to us that it is a terrible fate to have a child such as Nikki. For instance, Nikki's first pediatrician repeatedly told us how "tragic" it was that Nikki did not have the "unlimited potential" of most children. We replaced him with someone who could view us and Nikki without pity. Other people shook their heads sadly and said things such as, "At least she is pretty."

We have also been told by many friends that they could never cope with having a child like Nikki. This comment baffled us because we wonder what they would do instead of coping if they were in our shoes. We now realize that people say this sort of thing in an attempt to protect themselves from something they fear. Their reasoning seems to go like this: "If I am a member of the group that can't cope, perhaps I will be spared."

We respond to a world where many people feel uncomfortable

with Nikki and mistakenly judge her to be deficient by protecting her the best we can and taking every possible opportunity to model our unconditional acceptance of her. Unfortunately, we are not able to grab the world and shake it until all people like Nikki are viewed as inherently worthy and capable, regardless of their level of ability or achievement. But these people don't have to define our reality. We try to recognize that they, just like Nikki, are doing the best they can.

Today Nikki is an energetic and cheerful twelve-year-old who loves to roam around the house looking for something fun or noisy to play with, such as my guitar which she plucks with great intensity. She occasionally uses a few words, such as "more" when she wants something to eat. We feel fortunate to have her in an excellent private school where she basks in the attention of others who adore her as much as we do.

With Nikki as our teacher and guide, we have become happier, more peaceful, and better able to live fully in the present. When we stray off course and allow expectations or judgments to contaminate our relationships, our cure is to tune in to Nikki and allow her relentless goodwill to wash away whatever is preventing us from being at our best. We also experience a sense of purpose when we envision spending the rest of our lives taking care of her since we know we will always be involved in a venture into unknown territory.

Anita and I know we will face other challenges in the future, including making sure that Nikki's needs will always be met. But the hurdles we have overcome already have increased our trust in ourselves and each other. As a result, we face the future with a renewed sense of confidence.

We have no idea how far Nikki's adventure will take her—or us. We do know, however, that the quality of life's journey is much more important than the realization of specific achievements and that we can always count on the sparkle of Nikki's being to show us the way.

• • •

Nate Terrell, L.C.S.W., lives with his wife, Anita, and children, Nicole (1988) and Chelsea (1994), in Clementon, New Jersey. They continue to learn profound lessons from their work with

Nikki, who loves life and overcoming new challenges. Nikki is helped on her journey by her sister, who provides her with constant adoration and encouragement. Nate conducts workshops on working effectively with special needs children for parents and professionals. He is also a therapist at Family Counseling Service in Camden, New Jersey.

40

PARENT SUPPORT TO THE RESCUE

by Jennifer Titrud

Early in the third trimester of my pregnancy, I learned from a routine ultrasound that my baby had some intestinal problems that would require surgery immediately after birth. I prepared for the future as best I could. Friends, family, and my church rallied around. I toured the newborn intensive care unit and met with a genetic counselor, a neonatologist, and a pediatric surgeon. I took comfort in the feeling that I was in good hands at a major medical center.

When Laura was born, it was immediately apparent that the extent of her birth defects was much greater than we had expected. She was born with a cloacal anomaly (a malformation of the bowel, bladder, and reproductive organs), duodenal atresia (a narrowing in the small intestine), and a cleft in the soft palate.

Because of medical complications I experienced after her birth, Laura was two days old when I first saw her. I had been given Polaroid snapshots and my husband had described her appearance, but nothing can prepare a mother for the first look at a critically ill baby. She was not a pretty sight.

There were all those tubes, a ventilator, pumps, and monitors. She was swollen from head to toe with massive edema. But most of all, I was upset by the sight of her colostomy. It seemed so large in comparison to her body. It was a visible reminder that she had multiple birth defects. I knew that even after the ventilator and tubes were no longer needed, the colostomy would remain to remind us that many surgeries lay ahead.

Laura's experience in the neonatal intensive care unit (NICU) was stormy and included three surgeries and many complications. I survived those ten weeks by keeping busy with my two-year-old daughter, who desperately needed my attention. I also made daily trips to the hospital, spending hours learning new medical terminology and adding to my limited knowledge of the human anatomy.

When Laura finally came home from the NICU, it was a time of celebration and optimism. I felt the worst was behind me. Unfortunately, my high spirits quickly plummeted after a couple of days of dealing with a colicky baby who rarely slept, cried incessantly, and vomited up all the formula my husband and I painstakingly dripped into her feeding tube. As time went on, there were new problems and diagnoses. Laura was in and out of the hospital and in and out of the operating room. I felt as if we were on a roller coaster ride that would never end.

I survived by gritting my teeth and doing whatever had to be done. But this grin-and-bear-it attitude was taking its toll. My spirits were very low. I always expected the worst to happen; I was always afraid to get my hopes up. And I was starting to doubt my ability to handle Laura's special care needs.

Finally, I had to admit I needed something to pull me out of this depressed state. I remembered that a social worker at the hospital had given me the phone number of a Connecticut-based parent-to-parent support group called Parents Available to Help (PATH). I hadn't felt ready to talk with a stranger while Laura was in the NICU or when she first came home. But now I felt an urgent need to know that other people were going through this.

I called PATH and was put in touch with a mom who called herself a listener because her role was to listen to me and validate my feelings. As soon as I spoke with this mom, I felt an enormous flood of relief. Here was someone who could assure me from her personal experience that even my darkest feelings, such as anger toward my child, were normal. She listened to my problems and let them be important, often by saying little. For once, here was someone who didn't try to make everything better with familiar platitudes like, "It will all work out," or, "God doesn't give you more than you can bear."

Best of all, my listener (as I have come to call her) told me about her son, who'd had some of the same medical problems as Laura. He had undergone many surgeries and had several ahead of him, but he was a happy, active toddler. She impressed upon me how well children can adapt in spite of frequent hospitalizations and surgeries.

My listener never tried to solve my problems, although she often gave me helpful suggestions based on her personal experience. She couldn't take away my fears about the future, but our talks helped to speed my acceptance of the situation. Her reassurance gave me the self-confidence I needed to handle Laura's medical care and to trust my instincts.

Parent-to-parent support also helped me to deal with the sometimes clumsy and at other times downright inappropriate comments made by relatives, friends, and professionals. There was the oft-posed question about Laura's future reproductive and sexual life. Some asked how soon she could "get rid of" her colostomy. There was one well-intentioned friend who graced us with the story of his mother's colostomy and its foul smell. "I hope to God Laura doesn't need one when she grows up," was his punch line. There was a particularly arrogant physician who asked whether my facts came from "people or medical doctors."

But because I was talking regularly with a parent who had walked in my shoes, I didn't have to depend as much on the support of relatives, friends, and professionals. I still appreciated the kind words, meals, and offers of help that most people generously gave, but I was better able to shrug off the times that a professional rushed away without hearing my concerns or a friend stuck her foot in her mouth. A compassionate pediatrician once confided to me that he couldn't imagine how parents coped with their child's repeated hospitalizations and surgeries. He had treated thousands of children at a major medical center and spoken with thousands of distraught parents, but he knew that he had only an inkling of what it would be like if he had a sick child.

Parent-to-parent support also served as my gateway to information and resources related to my child's specific special needs. Through PATH, I was introduced to other support groups for parents whose children share similar medical conditions. I am now in contact with half a dozen support groups relevant to my daughter's several diagnoses.

PATH also put me in touch with parent training and advocacy groups and respite programs. At parent meetings, I met many knowledgeable parents whose suggestions and experience have been invaluable when I have questions. Perhaps I'm wondering how to approach the school system about a particular service I feel my daughter needs. Or I'm frustrated with my futile attempts to obtain reimbursement for hospital bills from my medical insurance carrier. No matter what the issue, I feel confident that one of the contacts I have made will have a helpful idea or know someone who has the answer.

The past ten years have brought many changes for me and for my family—most for the better. Laura did "get rid of" the colostomy but still has a urostomy, requires supplemental tube feedings at night, and faces more surgery in the future. I am active in parent-to-parent support, talking with parents and editing a newsletter.

The past ten years have also brought changes to parents of newly diagnosed children. These days, the Internet plays a growing role in parent support. Parents can arrive at the office of a medical specialist ready to discuss an abstract from a recent medical journal that they found on the Internet. Most support groups for specific disabilities have web sites, often with hotlinks to other resources. Discussion groups for specific disabilities on the Internet enable hundreds of people to share information about the latest treatments or provide tips for dealing with everyday problems.

My suggestion to parents who have recently learned that their child has a special health care need or disability is to contact a parent support group. Whether you are looking for someone who understands your emotional turmoil or are seeking access to information and services, a parent who has been there can meet your needs.

Even Laura has realized the value of peer support. She regularly attends the Pouch Patrol, a support group for children with ostomies or incontinence problems at Yale–New Haven Children's Hospital. She was eight years old when she attended her first meeting. On the way to the parking garage afterward, she said, "Mom, sometimes I get mad that I have all these medical problems, but now I know other kids have them, too."

• • •

Jennifer Titrud lives in Fairfield, Connecticut, with her husband, Blake, and their daughters, Emily (1986) and Laura (1988). Laura has undergone twenty-two procedures under general anesthesia and requires some special care each day. Despite this, she is a very active sixth-grader who enjoys bike riding and piano lessons.

Jennifer has provided parent-to-parent support for the past ten years through Parents Available to Help (PATH), a Connecticut-based parent support network, and has been the editor of PATH in Print, a PATH publication of personal stories and information, for the past eight years. She has also served as the parent liaison of the Greater Bridgeport Birth to Five Collaborative and a consultant in parent advocacy for Yale Family Connections, a network of resources for families of children with special needs.

41

UNCONDITIONALLY YOURS

by Elaine Tillman

By the time Brittany turned six months old, I knew something was wrong. Since her motor milestones were delayed, I consulted with a physical therapist, who promptly diagnosed her with cerebral palsy. I left his office in tears. The next week, a doctor confirmed the diagnosis, changing my life forever.

I started on a feverish search for information. I made phone call after phone call and wrote letter upon letter. Finally I visited a bookstore, and there it was in a medical book—"cerebral palsy: a disorder of movement and posture due to defect or lesion of the immature brain."

That moment of understanding was the most terrifying of my life. I sat in the middle of the bookstore floor sobbing. I could only imagine a "crippled child," a "handicapped child." My child had a disability.

I went through the next few months in a numb, mechanical state. The explanations to family and friends became so painful that I shut myself off from the outside world. Brittany was referred to a developmental center to receive therapies. I had never seen so many children in wheelchairs, with walkers, or wearing braces. I watched the other parents. They all seemed so at ease in this world I never knew existed.

My daily routine was quickly filled with medical appointments and a constant search for information that would help my family adjust. I visited libraries, therapists, and hospitals. Everything seemed changed. I even lost my name. Professionals called me "Mom." Some referred to my daughter as the "handicapped child." What happened to our identity as people? I remain grateful to those professionals who treated us as individuals and offered us support and kindness.

I went through the classic "Why me?" stuff. I was in deep grief. People meant well and tried to provide comfort. Especially in the beginning, many people told me to take care of myself and my own needs. I knew they were hurting for me, but I felt no one understood the depth of my pain. After a while, I started pulling away. I walked in two worlds.

The essence of my being unraveled. My sorrow, so intense at times, seemed impossible to reconcile with the routine of daily life. The romantic once-a-week "dates" with my husband turned into heartbreaking assessments of Brittany's extremely slow progress. Each date ended with one of us slowly catching the other's tears.

At first, my other children did not understand about Brittany's disability. But they quickly figured it out. My oldest son, Brandon, began to create adaptive ways to make ordinary activities work for Brittany. My youngest son, Daylon, was the go-getter, the teaser. He always had to make Brittany laugh.

Families living with disabilities must quickly develop survival skills to be able to live with the unknown. Our family, like so many others, faced a whirlwind of emotions. Healing is a lifelong process, and you need to give yourself time to grieve.

Making sense of the diagnosis is the first step toward acceptance, and my healing process began as a quest for knowledge. I read every available resource. I filed every available letter that came my way.

Support groups can also help. If you can't find a support group that meets your needs, you can start your own. Sharing practical advice and feelings with other parents helped me accept Brittany. I also learned that it is okay not to feel the way others expect you to feel. Our feelings, as intense as they may be, are normal and real.

Building and maintaining a care team depends on locating the most appropriate and beneficial resources for the family. Try to find a pediatrician who has experience treating children with disabilities. When looking into resources or programs, always speak to a program supervisor, documenting names and never taking no for an answer.

Being a parent of a child with a disability is not easy, nor is it easy to be a person with a disability. Focus on those things that can be controlled, and don't worry about the things you can't control. Sometimes you just won't have the energy to do anything extra even if it is important. Sometimes you just have to pull back and let some things go. That's okay, too.

Most of all, remember, you are not alone!

• • •

Elaine Tillman lives in Ash Grove, Missouri, with her husband, Charles, and their three children, Brandon (1983), Brittany (1986), and Daylon (1987). Charles owns his own wholesale plumbing supply company. Elaine is Community Resource Specialist for the Missouri Division of Developmental Disabilities and Mental Retardation.

Brittany is in a regular junior high school. She has done some modeling for a special products catalog. Her hobbies are collecting dolls and shoes. She enjoys writing letters, taking long walks in her jogger, going to flea markets, and shopping! Daylon is a sports fanatic who collects sports memorabilia and plays baseball. Brandon is a computer whiz who has his own web page. He loves to do woodworking and create ways to make things work for Brittany.

Charles is a board member of Special Kids Involved Publicly (SKIP), a local nonprofit organization. Elaine is active in finding resources for families in order to fill ordinary wishes for children with disabilities and coordinating her correspondence support group, From Our House to Yours.

The family lives in a rural area and enjoys camping, taking long walks, swimming, going to the lake, playing home video games, board games, and reading together.

42

I WISH. . .

by Barbara J. Ebenstein

I wish I had known that the intense sadness a parent experiences upon learning of a child's disability is called mourning.

For whom do we mourn when the child is alive? We mourn for lost hopes and possibilities. We mourn for the perfect child we imagined during the pregnancy.

For some parents, the death of this imagined child comes quickly—perhaps after only seven or eight months of pregnancy. The death is as sudden as the birth. An early diagnosis and prompt information on prognosis fling these parents into an intense mourning period from which they emerge with new strengths.

For other parents, the death of the imagined child comes gradually. There may be years of diagnostic testing to rule out one thing or check for another. These parents receive only bits and pieces of information. They have years to hold on to their image of the perfect child, and its death may cause them to experience a prolonged mourning period. This is the type of mourning I experienced as I received scattered bits of information about my daughter's diagnosis over a number of years. Only with time could I fit the pieces of information into a patchwork quilt and understand its pattern.

I wish I had known that it is all right to grieve over a living child. I wish I had mourned with my husband instead of by myself. I wish that friends and family had understood and given me the emotional support I needed.

I wish I had known that whatever form mourning takes, the intense sorrow eventually ends. I was sure that I would never laugh again. But there is a time when life triumphs over sorrow.

Risa was two when she took her first steps in the fitting room of a local children's store. I would have bought her a new dress sooner had I known that her delight in trying it on would propel her to take a few independent steps. I came to realize that life would still hold many happy times for my family and for me.

I wish I had known that a child's disabilities can affect the entire family in positive ways. When a child's disabilities demand parental attention, siblings are deprived of their fair share of their parents' time. Years ago, this deprivation was the excuse used to institutionalize the child with the disability.

But I have come to realize that the sacrifice of siblings is rewarded. Risa's siblings have learned perseverance, dedication, and responsibility through firsthand experience and example rather than moral lecture. They have learned to appreciate their own innate gifts and to be sensitive to the needs of others.

Years ago, the elementary school principal called to tell me my fifth-grade daughter had declined an opportunity to participate in the Student Leaders, a program that offered training and an assignment to work with younger children on the playground. But, the principal told me, despite her lack of participation in the official program, my daughter had assumed more responsibility for the little ones on her own initiative than any of the program's official participants. As a result, the principal delightedly informed me, my daughter would be made a Student Leader and receive an official hat.

I explained that my daughter needed no organized program or assignment, that her life had already trained and assigned her. Now, years later, she not only is a superb baby-sitter but has also earned a small fortune from it.

I wish I had understood the general tendency of others to identify the parent in terms of the child with the disability: "You know Barbara. She's the one with the child who . . ."

This limits the way the community perceives the family and cheats siblings of their proper recognition. I am still amazed when acquaintances think that all I am is the mother of a child with a disability. I should not have let the world see me or my family in that limited way. I am many things besides the mother of a child with a disability.

And I have *three* daughters.

Sarah, my oldest daughter, is the intellectual one. Sarah is an independent thinker who is a wonderful poet and actress. We have the same sense of humor, the same taste in theater, and the same responses to people. Mothering Sarah is sometimes like mothering myself. Sarah is the child of my mind.

Leanne, my middle daughter, is the emotional one. Leanne is intensely concerned about the feelings of others and is the expert baby-sitter. She is the most sensitive—and the one most easily hurt. But Leanne is also the bravest, the most daring and outgoing. Leanne is not afraid to take chances. Leanne is the child of my heart.

Risa, my youngest daughter, is the sweet one. Risa is gentle and affectionate. She adores all people and animals and cannot imagine them dangerous. A friend of mine referred to her as the personification of love. Even as Risa has brought me to the very brink of despair, she has taught me to slow down, to have patience, and to savor the small victories. Risa is the child of my soul.

Years ago, I told my older daughters that everything can be both good and bad. They asked me what was good about Risa's disabilities. After much thought, I told them that Risa can teach us many things. It is difficult to measure the human heart. We can measure someone's height or weight. But it is difficult to see into someone else's heart and gauge how much goodness lies there. Risa is a yardstick that allows us to make that measurement. Seeing how people respond to Risa helps us to assess the dimensions of their hearts.

Sarah and Leanne have many friends who come from different ethnic backgrounds and have varied interests and talents. Some dress distinctively. Some have dyed their hair bright colors. Every one of them has a truly good heart.

We have developed useful skills because of Risa's disabilities. I can silently yell at my children in public using a few choice American Sign Language signs. We all have learned to solve problems quickly and creatively. So we're out of applesauce? No problem! We'll just hide Risa's medication in a french fry!

Risa shows us that a sweet disposition can take you a long way in this world, that it is important to be gentle and kind, and that humor is always a good thing. She reminds us that it is okay to ask for help, and how nice it is just to cuddle a dog or touch something soft. She teaches us that more is not always better.

My family has certain values, such as individuality and social justice, and we are not easily distracted from what really counts by fads or trivia. Risa has helped all of us focus on the important things in life.

● ● ●

Barbara J. Ebenstein is an attorney who represents families in education and disability matters in New York and Connecticut. She is an adjunct associate professor at New York University, where she teaches a graduate course in education law. She often writes articles on special education and the law.

Barbara lives outside New York City with her husband, John E. Handelsman, M.D., director of Children's Orthopaedics at Schneider Children's Hospital of the Long Island Jewish Medical Center, and their three daughters, Sarah (1980), Leanne (1983), and Risa (1986).

43

SURVIVAL SKILLS 101

by Paula Holdeman

Remember the joy you felt when your doctor announced you were going to have a baby? Oh, the dreams and desires that followed. Then, in an instant, the hopes and dreams of nine months are shattered. The doctor sympathetically approaches your bedside after his initial examination of your baby and tells you something is wrong.

Everything after that is a blur, until reality slowly sifts in. You want to say, "Please just leave me alone, and let me grieve for the loss of my hopes and dreams. I can't handle this alone but I don't want your sympathy. Perhaps, in a few days, I'll want your support. And please don't tell me I must be strong. I don't want to be strong—not yet anyway. Doesn't anybody understand?"

Sound familiar? Those were some of my feelings eleven years ago after the birth of our fourth child and first son. Our three daughters were plagued with numerous birth defects, and we were so hoping for an uncomplicated child with relatively few health problems. Wrong! Our son, Michael, has had the most challenging problems of the four children. But through trial and error, I have learned to cope, survive, and persevere. Acceptance is an ongoing challenge for me because as each child grows, new challenges develop. Fortunately, I have learned some survival skills that I would like to share with you.

• <u>Survival Skill Number One</u>: *Determine your priorities.* With the support of my husband of twenty-five years, I have made a commitment to prioritize my energy, time, and ability. I call my priorities the "four F's"—family, faith, friends, and fraternities.

My *family* is always the top priority in my hectic schedule. As the parent of four children, I need to focus on their needs. Although all four of our children have different disabilities and health problems, I strive to see each one as an individual. I encourage them to excel in whatever they attempt and try to have the wisdom to retreat when things become too difficult for them. There are times when the needs of one child overshadow the needs of the others. I have tried to teach them that this is the way our life is. Even my husband knows this is our law of survival. His day, too, will come.

My *faith* has sustained me through tremendous trials, and I credit God for daily strength and wisdom. I believe everything I've been through and everything I've learned has had a purpose. When things get really tough, I live one moment at a time and leave the rest in God's hands. When it feels as though everything is falling apart, I remind myself that God can put it all back together again. Eventually. Whatever your faith is, it can help you to believe that Someone is in control.

My *friends* are another priority. I know from experience that it helps if you can befriend a network of people and develop techniques to draw upon their strengths when you need them. But a word of caution: Have the wisdom to use and not abuse these friendships. Don't ever allow your friends to feel you are taking advantage of them. To have friends, you must be a friend.

Finally, I try to give of my time to worthy *fraternities*. Parents of children with disabilities need outside interests. Focusing 100 percent of your time and energy on your child's needs is more stressful and draining than committing 90 percent to your child and 10 percent to an outside interest. I know it seems strange, but my children haven't changed me that much. I am still me. I still have goals and desires. Don't let your inner spark for life dwindle away.

• <u>Survival Skill Number Two:</u> *Don't sweat the small stuff.* Who cares if you didn't make the bed today? Just close the bedroom door. So what if the doctors want $50 a month toward the medical bills and you can only afford $20. What are they going to do—repossess your child? And guess what, most children won't complain about a store-bought birthday cake instead of a home-made one.

• Survival Skill Number Three: *KISS: Keep it simple, sweetheart.* Try to unclutter your life. Focus on your priorities, whatever they are. Don't try to be a supermom; we all know you can't do it all. And no one expects you to do it all. So don't be so hard on yourself when you can't.

• Survival Skill Number Four: *Let go of the guilt.* Whoever says, "What did you do wrong to have a baby like this?" should have to walk a mile in your shoes.

My time-honored response to that question is, "And what did you do to become such an idiot?" Okay, so maybe you're more tactful than I. Try responding with one from Ann Landers: "I'm surprised you would ask such an insensitive question." Whatever works for you. I learned a long time ago to stay away from that kind of person.

• Survival Skill Number Five: *Find someone else who has "walked the walk."* A spouse may offer you a shoulder to cry on, but he or she is carrying the same burdens as you. Your parents' hearts will break if you tell them about your overwhelming sadness. Other parents of children with disabilities are the greatest resource you can cultivate.

• • •

Paula Holdeman lives in Plentywood, Montana, with her husband, Paul, and children, Colleen (1975), Renae (1978), Gail (1981), and Michael (1986). Paula describes herself as a "survival specialist" who is happy to talk to parents of younger children with disabilities. "I realize you don't know me personally," she says, "but who cares? If you ever need to talk to someone who has been there, done that, and even bought the tee-shirt, feel free to call me."

44

A CHANGE OF PLANS

by Janis Cloakey

This was my second time around, and I thought I had planned for everything. I would have the new baby at the beginning of the summer, enjoy a few months at home with the baby and her two-and-a-half-year-old sister, Carol, and then, in the fall, go back to work as a part-time substitute schoolteacher. The kids would go to the day care center just down the street. Everything was in place.

In five minutes, it all changed. In fact, my whole life changed. I delivered Kristen Charlotte Cloakey at a well-known teaching hospital surrounded by the family physician who had delivered Carol at the same hospital, a nurse, and a few medical school students to whom we had given permission to observe. K.C. was a small baby, and the delivery was natural and easy. After one final push, she arrived in the doctor's hands. He announced that she was a girl. Suddenly there was a silence I shall never forget.

The head neonatologist was paged. His voice shaking, he said that judging by certain physical characteristics, it appeared that our daughter had a disability known as Down syndrome. Of course, further testing would need to be done. He left as quickly as he had come.

The events that followed are a blur to me today. Maybe it's better that way. The only thing I do recall is shaking my head and pinching myself to see if I was having a dream. Then I asked to see my daughter, because I wanted to nurse her. When they handed her to me, I was amazed and shocked by her beauty. Her color was a pretty pink and she looked so peaceful. I looked at all the physical features the neonatologist mentioned, but none of that seemed to matter.

After more tests, we took K.C. home and proceeded to live as normal a life as possible. I knew immediately I would not return to work. God has a funny way of directing our lives. I tearfully sent out birth announcements, writing in the upper left-hand corner of each card, "K.C. was born with Down syndrome. Please join us in celebration of our beautiful and special child." I received wonderful responses to that announcement.

Perhaps the hardest part of my life at that rather tumultuous time was running into casual acquaintances at the grocery store, the park, the mall, or other places and telling them what had happened. I remember how my stomach knotted up and my voice shook as I told them K.C. had a disability. It was hard for the people hearing the news, too. They didn't seem to know how to respond. As time passed, these conversations became easier.

Our family was blessed with a wonderful, caring family physician. As we were all under his care, we had a special relationship with him. K.C. was the first baby with Down syndrome he'd ever delivered. Someone told me later he stood outside the delivery room after the birth and cried. He brought me a dozen roses the next day, after we had found out K.C. had a heart defect. He never charged us for the delivery and services rendered the first year of K.C.'s life. He admitted freely there was a great deal he did not know about Down syndrome, but he always found a resource for us when we had questions.

Over the course of the next few years, K.C. endured two open-heart surgeries and numerous brief hospital stays for upper respiratory problems. I am happy to say she outgrew these problems over time and is now a happy, healthy, and *typical* teenager.

But I didn't become a *typical* parent. Money doesn't matter to me. Social position doesn't matter. Having the perfect home or perfect kids doesn't matter. This is what K.C. has done for me.

What matters is that I was there when K.C. took her first steps. I was there on her first day of school—she's been included in regular classrooms since first grade. And I plan on being there when she graduates from high school, when she finds her first job, and when she finds her first apartment.

In many ways, K.C. is my role model. She has a spirit and determination others would kill to have. I firmly believe that is what got her through her surgeries. She makes me laugh, and she gives love so unconditionally it takes my breath away. Her accomplishments may be insignificant to many, but they make me proud to be her parent. I am rich even though I am not wealthy; my life is full even though I don't have many material possessions.

K.C. also has had a profound effect on her three siblings. As I write this, Carol is almost sixteen and a not-so-typical teenager. She is caring and compassionate and loves to be with her younger sister. She did a number of reports in middle school on Down syndrome and even brought K.C. into her classroom to talk about her disability. Catherine, nine, is also a sensitive, nurturing child. She loves to play with K.C. and help her with her homework. Geo, now four, is the son I prayed for—though sometimes I have to wonder if I knew what I was asking for! He is full of energy and has learned many pranks and practical jokes from his sister. He has no idea K.C. is any different, although I'm sure the question will come up with him as it did with my other kids. And my answer will be the same: She is more alike than she is different.

My journey has been full of adventure—ups and downs, good times and bad. I am sure K.C.'s adulthood will present new challenges. Just writing this short essay was cathartic. Sometimes you have to see where you came from to really know how far you've come.

• • •

Janis Cloakey lives in Vancouver, Washington, with her husband, George, and their four children. George is a purchasing manager for an injection molding company. Janis is a stay-at-home mom with a custom sewing business. She says, "I have been blessed with a very supportive network of teachers, friends, neighbors, and family who have made our journey possible."

45

TIME

by Mary Jane Kitchens

Unlike many parents in this technological age, I had no idea of my daughter's problems until the moment she was born. I have tried to describe that moment many times since—my world crashing in on me, the disbelief and sorrow spinning through my mind, the pain and raw emotion . . . But how does one describe a moment like that? Words always fail me.

In the beginning, Mandy's disabilities and differences consumed my every waking moment. It was my first thought when I awoke each morning. My days were filled with tears, angry arguments with God, and guilt. Even though I knew I had done nothing to cause my daughter's disabilities, I somehow felt at fault. In bed at night, my mind would not stop spinning.

My family was very supportive, but I knew they couldn't fully understand what I was going through. My friends didn't know what to say to me. A few said things like, "God only gives special babies to special parents." I hated that. I didn't want to be "special," and I certainly didn't feel honored. Instead, I felt as though I were being punished, only I didn't know why. All I really wanted was for someone to "fix it." And no one could.

The main thing that helped me get through this difficult period was just loving and holding my child. The first twenty-four hours after she was born were a whirl of test after test—so many I barely got to see her. "Just let me bring her home," I begged my pediatrician.

I brought her home, and that was where the healing began. Day by day, little by little, I stopped noticing the differences and started noticing the wonderful things about my daughter. I simply cared for her and held her, and the rest fell into place. It wasn't overnight, but then it wasn't that way with my two "healthy" children either. Soon, after hearing her coo, seeing that smile, and watching those toes wiggle, I realized: "This is my child. She depends on me for everything, and I will be there for her. Not because I have to, but because I want to."

It also helped to talk to adults who were born with the same disabilities as my daughter. I saw that most were happy and well adjusted, living lives much like the rest of us. It gave me desperately needed hope.

Now as I watch Mandy grow and see the person she is becoming, I realize that she is going to be just fine. I see her determination, her talents, her coping mechanisms, and her ability to be happy, and I don't worry. Well, not too much—I am still her mother after all!

Today, I really don't even see my daughter's disabilities. At the store or park, when someone stares, it actually takes a minute for me to remember what they're looking at. And when it does come to me, it is no longer the "slap in the face" it once was. It's just another part of our life.

Time, more than anything, has lessened my load. Time is on your side, too. In time, you will learn what really matters—and what doesn't. You will learn that you *can* go on and that your child is a wonderful human being. You will learn to fight for what your child needs. You also will learn to let go when your child doesn't need you.

At the end of the day, you'll close your eyes and realize that you love your child—*this* child—more than life itself. And when you sleep, you will dream good dreams.

• • •

Mary Jane Kitchens is an office manager for an excavation company and a freelance writer. She lives in Ann Arbor, Michigan, with her husband, David, and children, Joshua (1988), Jacob (1991), and Amanda (1990). Mandy was born with VACTERL association, a number of congenital differences that are commonly

seen together; her upper extremities are most significantly af-
fected. Mandy's hobbies include Girl Scouting, horseback riding,
art, and ice skating.

   Mary Jane is a board member of Therapeutic Riding, Inc., in
Ann Arbor. David, who owns his own web design business, is the
web designer and webmaster for the VACTERL connection at
www.vacterconnection.org.

46

LESSONS FROM OUR LIFE WITH MATT

by Joyce Millard-Hoie and John Hoie

Mom's Turn

The day I left the pediatrician's office with our young son, not yet three years old, it was with the horrible realization that I had been overtaken by something I'd been running from for quite some time. I think I felt the same helplessness, panic, and terror that an animal about to be captured must feel. I clearly remember feeling I was trapped, that there was no avenue of escape. I remember wanting to rush home with my child where we felt safe in our day-to-day routine. As bizarre as this daily routine sometimes was, it was familiar enough to seem normal and had served to insulate us from reality.

Matt had turned our family life upside down, and all six of us were terribly stressed out. Daily we struggled to cope with a young child who was rigidly adherent to a precise way of doing things and who could not tolerate any deviation from his routine without displaying extreme behavior. As Matt grew older, I had increasingly narrowed our range of contact with the outside world, because it was simply too painful and exhausting to try to reconcile the needs of our child with the expectations of normal human interaction. In our manufactured reality, Matt was "easily upset," maybe "a bit spoiled"—but not autistic.

A formal medical diagnosis carries with it a range of assumptions, fears, and expectations. While it has a certain practical value in terms of making available various forms of treatment, medication, therapy, and educational programs, a medical diagnosis specifically focuses on describing a problem. A formal diagnosis has a very limited value in terms of raising a happy, healthy youngster who will develop his own unique and special capabilities.

In the years since that day, I have learned that it is creative, intuitive loving care and attention that will bring forth the best in your child and ultimately enrich your lives. If I could return to talk to myself on the day I left the doctor's office, I would tell myself the following things:

• *Don't project the current situation (problem or crisis) into the future.* Dire scenarios born of panic and desperation are negative influences and rob you of needed energy and creativity.

• *Listen to your "parent's intuition."* You will learn things about your child that no else can know with the same degree of depth and understanding. This kind of practical wisdom is a necessary and valuable tool for parenting your child.

• *Partnership and mutual support should be the basis on which you and your partner will parent your child.* Shared responsibility is the hallmark of good parenting and critically important for children with special needs. Both partners need time off to maintain physical and emotional well-being.

• *Early intervention is absolutely essential.* I subscribe to the "chaos theory" of parenting—"sensitive dependence on initial conditions." This is also known as the "butterfly effect," the idea that something as small as the movement of a butterfly's wings can affect global weather patterns. From this point of view, early, consistent, purposeful therapeutic intervention, provided by parents as well as clinicians, can yield enormous benefits. Small and seemingly inconsequential efforts to train and encourage your child can result in magnified positive outcomes.

• *Advocate for your child as a key member of the support team.* Lead, inform, educate, and listen to the professionals with whom you consult. I find it useful to think of professionals as hired consultants. Occasionally someone may have to be "fired," but the conscientious professionals who forge partnerships with us to provide the optimum interventions for our son receive my deepest respect and appreciation.

• *Plan ahead.* Visualize where you'll need to be in two years, and your goals and objectives will become clear to you. When we dreamed of sending our son to his neighborhood school, rather than a self-contained special education program, we were forced to objectively evaluate the situation. Picturing our son performing according to the expectations of a regular classroom made us take a good look at the specific skills needed and gave us new ways to measure his performance and progress.

• *Find practical ways to encourage your child's independence.* Ask yourself this question: "What part of this task could my child do for himself?" As essential as you are in the life of your child, you must prepare your son or daughter by building confidence and competence in basic responsibilities.

• *Celebrate and savor each accomplishment.* Operate on your child's timetable. Rejoice in the satisfaction that you and your child can experience with each achievement.

• *Teach your child good manners.* The basic rules of human civility apply to all, and children with disabilities are seldom granted any exemptions. Having good manners will ease the path of social acceptance for your child.

• *Acknowledge and support the contributions of siblings.* Brothers and sisters may experience feelings of sadness, anger, and frustration on a daily basis. Parents need to be forthcoming with information about the challenges families face in living with a child with a disability. There also needs to be an added emphasis on celebrating the special interests and achievements of each family member.

• *Reach out to other parents.* I can't forget the days of despair and endless worry I endured, and I know that my experience is probably not very different from that of other parents. Even if you don't feel you have anything substantial to contribute, join a parent support group; your presence will provide needed encouragement and inspiration to others.

Dad's Turn

It's important to accept the legitimacy of your own observations. Coming from a family background that emphasized achievement and the importance of the intellect, I found Matt's initial diagnosis of retardation earth-shattering. But after some reflection, I found myself disagreeing with that diagnosis. Obviously, there was something disturbingly different about our son, but I could sense the intelligence behind his ritualized actions.

As it turns out, I was right: Matt has autism, but not retardation. Whether that's more comforting is a matter of opinion. But the future of any human being is unknowable, even to experts in the developmental sciences.

It is important to view your child as a young human, with a variety of skills, abilities, desires, fears, and needs. There is a tendency to view your child primarily through the lens of his or her disability. And when you find your child acting in a more complex way, you're surprised.

For example, it took us a while to realize that Matt was embarrassed by his own uncontrollable tantrums. In turn, this caused him to experience feelings of unworthiness and depression. Some children with autism, and I suspect many children with retardation as well, are keenly aware of their differences. Part of the key to success is keeping them feeling good about themselves in the face of those differences.

Finally, I strongly suggest trying to let go of feelings of blame and guilt. The blame comes from trying to figure out which parent is responsible for the child's problem. Perceived genetic defects, an occasional glass of wine, even a "bad attitude" about the pregnancy can become reasons to blame yourself or your partner. Try to remember how draining and unproductive that is. The past is unchangeable.

Guilt often arises from antagonistic feelings toward your child. There is a natural tendency to resent the little intruder who has turned your life upside down. While you try to treat your child with love and gentleness, your inner voice may be screaming with rage. Perhaps worse is when you catch yourself wishing your child had never been born or would die quietly and let you off the hook. Try to remember that feelings are not evil. As long as you continue to treat your child with love and respect, these thoughts and feelings are no reasons for guilt.

—John Hoie

• • •

Joyce Millard-Hoie and John Hoie live in Phoenix, Arizona, and are the parents of four children. Their son Matt (1986) has autism. Matt has attended his neighborhood school, with support, since first grade and is an honor roll student. Matt's brother and sisters, Will, Marcy, and Marie, contribute in many ways to his success.

47

THE WOMAN IN THE PICTURE

by Carolyn Schimanski

In my house there is an 8x10 picture of me taken the day I got married. It's a close-up—just my face, looking somewhat seriously into the camera. When I am in a particularly melancholy frame of mind, looking at that picture makes me sad, for the woman in that picture is gone. Some days I mourn her loss, her innocence, her belief in fairy tales and Cinderella endings, her failure to understand the world's raw edges. I was twenty-three the day I got married; my husband Jim had just turned twenty-two. We knew so little about anything then.

Eleven months later, after an uneventful pregnancy and delivery, my daughter Maggie was born. She wasn't a planned child, and I don't think much else in my life has been planned since that day. When she was twelve hours old, as my husband peered into the nursery before leaving the hospital for the day, Maggie turned "navy blue"—Jim's words. He came running into my room yelling, "There's something wrong with the baby!" And my life changed forever.

Maggie spent ten days in intensive care while the doctors tried to figure out what had happened to her. I spent that time trying to figure out what had happened to me. I remember feeling as though I were in a bubble, moving through time and space, not quite connected to the world. Even the sunny, blue fall sky appeared alien to me.

This essay first appeared in *Exceptional Parent* magazine.

A casual observer could have watched me talking to doctors, spending time in the nursery, communicating with family and friends, never knowing that my personal reality had been tweaked slightly. I felt scared, panicked, and alone, but I operated like a supermom. In my heart, I knew that things would never be the same. I was convinced that I was the only one this had ever happened to.

How different I might have felt if I'd had another parent to talk to. Someone who could have helped me see that this does happen to other people and that they survive, persevere, even grow to become better people. I did not speak to another parent of a child with a disability until Maggie was about two and a half years old. When I walked into that support group meeting at Maggie's new preschool, I felt as though I had come home.

Here were the people who "got it"! Here were the other members of this bizarre club I had found myself drafted into! Here were the other supermoms who held their families together yet felt wounded inside. To this day, I hold these women close to my heart; they are the ones I call when I know no one else—no matter how well-meaning—could possibly understand.

I wish the woman in the photo could have left me less suddenly, less painfully. But the woman she left behind is smarter, wiser, and more confident. She knows her strengths and is comfortable with herself. She has tested the love of her family and friends and has found it to be strong and enduring. She knows there is little life can put in her path that she cannot face and conquer. She takes little for granted.

She feels sure that the only fairy tales are the ones that you write yourself. Most days she is happy to belong to an "exceptional family." Occasionally, she feels superior to other people who haven't been lucky enough to learn what she has.

So I have put that picture away in a drawer. It is difficult, and not really helpful, to remember who I was then. Reality is the future and my world as Maggie's mom. I wouldn't trade that for anything.

• • •

Carolyn Schimanski has lived her whole life in Delmar, New York, a small suburb of Albany. She and her husband, Jim, were high school classmates. They have three children, Maggie (1986), Katie (1991), and Tristan (1993).

Maggie has multiple disabilities, including mild cerebral palsy, moderate mental retardation, and pervasive developmental disorder, probably stemming from an unnamed chromosomal abnormality (extra material on chromosomes 11 and 13). She also has multiple abilities, including a fierce will, a loving personality, and passions for football, Rugrats, coloring, and her family.

Carolyn is the executive director of Parent to Parent of New York State.

48

CONGRATULATIONS!

by Jennifer M. Graham

Congratulations on the birth of your beautiful baby! Although you may not feel that this is a time to celebrate, try to remember that you are holding a precious, loving life in your arms, a child that will love you and teach you more than you can possibly imagine right now.

Our son, Mark, has Down syndrome. But to us, he is just Mark—a kid full of charm, self-confidence, and humor. Mark will be thirteen in a few weeks. It's hard to imagine now why I was so depressed and mourned the loss of my "perfect" baby for so long.

Of our four children, Mark is the kindest and funniest and, in many ways, has been the easiest and most rewarding to raise. But if someone had told me that thirteen years ago, I would have angrily rejected their prophecies. You see, I let my own fears overwhelm me. It took a year before I could finally see the bright, happy son who had come into our family. It took a year to open my soul, so I could hear and believe what so many people were telling me.

Reach out to other parents with special kids. They—and their kids—have a lot to teach you. And these are people who will uniquely understand and support you and your child throughout the years to come.

During Mark's first year of life, through a network of family and friends, I heard from strangers all over the United States, who wrote to share their stories of happy times with their own children with disabilities. Parents from local support groups invited us to their homes to meet their sons or daughters with Down syndrome. They were delightful kids, who greeted us warmly at the door, proudly showed off Special Olympics trophies, or—miracle of miracles—read to us from their favorite books. I began to feel glimmers of hope, but I continued to doubt that my child would reach such goals.

Our first years were very busy with early intervention programs. I attribute most of Mark's academic success today to these outstanding programs and to the dedicated teachers and therapists who worked with him. They always offered us what we needed most—hope. And Mark offered us the next best thing—his love and great big smile. His determination has always amazed us.

How did we move out of grief and back into life again?

Mark led us all the way. His first smile soothed my tattered, anxious soul. And soon, one day at a time, we learned not to limit our vision of his future.

There have been no "plateaus." Mark is still learning, still teaching us, and he now has big dreams for his future, just like our other kids. We have met the challenges of raising a son with developmental delays by believing in him.

Mark has always been part of the "regular" world. He attended early intervention programs, but he also went to our neighborhood nursery school. We wanted him to have "normal" speech and behavior to model. But we also wanted other kids in our community to play with him and get to know him as soon as possible so that they would better accept him when they were older. To many kids here, he's just Mark, no label attached.

We always pushed Mark just beyond where he was, making him crawl a little farther, reach a little further, or stand a little longer.

He had intensive speech therapy before he was even speaking intelligible words. We knew that if he could communicate well with other people, he would be better accepted by them. Speech was very slow to develop, and we relied on sign language for two years. His receptive language developed age appropriately, but it took him longer to respond verbally. Sign language gave us real communication. He picked it up quickly and was much less frustrated when he could tell us just what he needed or wanted.

Today, he speaks clearly in full sentences, and he has enough self-esteem to repeat himself if he is not understood. He has had parts in school plays, sings in the school chorus, and gives oral book reports in his (regular) fifth-grade class. He is also one of his school's official greeters, proudly welcoming community leaders to his school when they come to an assembly or play!

Last year Mark became the first student with mental retardation in our school district to be included in a regular classroom in a neighborhood school. He has learned things we never thought he would be able to grasp. He has made real friends who cheer him on at bowling parties or in playground games. He participates in every aspect of his school's programs, with a curriculum adapted to his needs.

Mark is a Boy Scout with a "regular" troop and works with the other boys to earn his badges. Scouting has been a wonderful social experience for him, proving to others, and to himself, how much he can do.

He has his own weekly paper route in our neighborhood. Counting money is a life skill he has to do independently and accurately. The job has been a great way to force him to count his own real money, make bank deposits, and assume responsibility— all done, of course, with some family and neighborly support!

Special Olympics is another important part of Mark's life, and he has won gold and silver medals in swimming, track, and roller skating. From ages five through eight, he played T-ball in our township recreation league; he now plays baseball in a Challenger Little League division. He throws and hits well; his fielding still needs a little work!

He serves as an acolyte in our church. And every time he lights the candles, someone in our congregation tells me, with tears in their eyes, how inspiring Mark is to them.

Forge friendships with all kinds of children. Your son or daughter will need both "typical" and "special" friends throughout his life. We all need a few true buddies we can be ourselves with, without the pressures of "being on" or worrying about whether we are accepted.

As more children are included in regular classrooms, contact and friendships with other kids with developmental delay are becoming harder to sustain. We have tried to keep Mark active in both "special" and "regular" activities, offering him a mix of friends.

As he becomes a teenager, those "special" friends are more likely to join him on social outings than are the other kids from school. As parents of a special child, you will need to be proactive in developing friendships. Don't wait for invitations; ask kids over for Friday night pizza or go bowling or swimming. Once kids know they can have fun with your child and the family, invitations from them are more likely to follow.

We have three other children. All four of our children have unique, special needs; Mark is just another one of the kids.

I remember how important it was for me to talk to people and how difficult it was to learn to live one day at a time. But in these early days, I ask you to listen to the voices of parents who have journeyed before you. So many of our fears were unfounded. And so many dreams—the dreams we thought had died when we "lost" our perfect child—have come true. Our lives have been blessed, energized, and made so much more meaningful by Mark.

Enjoy your baby's infancy. It will go by so quickly. In just a short time, you'll be looking out your window, watching him running through the sunshine in your back yard! And celebrating the blessings of this life.

• • •

Jennifer Graham writes about families of children with special needs from her home in Gwynedd Valley, Pennsylvania. She shares her life with her husband, Russ, and children, Emily (1981), Mark (1985), Carolyn (1988), and David (1990).

49

JOURNAL ENTRIES

Anonymous

Every day. It doesn't go away. The problem or the pain in its wake.

That's not quite true. Maybe two or three days a month I am able to get absorbed in something else, or my daughter connects, or I fool myself by ignoring how she is different, and I forget the major reality of our family life—my daughter has a developmental disability.

My beautiful, loving, gentle little girl cannot seem to grasp the ordinary to and fro of social interaction. Her auditory memory is precise, but beside the point. Tonight, her dad played "I've Been Working on the Railroad" on the piano. After hearing the first bar, she asked me, "Who's there?" I didn't know what she meant until I remembered that the doorbell at my dad's house plays that refrain. We visited him two years ago.

I am her interpreter. All the loose connections she verbalizes— off topic and whenever they occur to her—have some basis in past history. A story we read. An event at the zoo three years ago. Some are repeated chronically, not to be mistaken for chronologically. For example, she often repeats a little tidbit of information about one of my childhood pets, something I once shared with her and her twin sister. Out of the blue, perhaps a hundred times, she's said, "Mommy had a cat named Blackberry."

Asperger syndrome, sometimes called high-functioning autism. That's what they think it is. She dwells on topics, activities. Tunes people out. She has what might best be described as a social learning disorder. Kids with this disorder wish to be social, but at a fundamental level, they don't know how. Maybe this is where the occasional sobbing and tears come from.

She is a beautiful and usually happy child. Her dad hopes she'll be seen as aloof, perhaps mysterious. Maybe the other kids will sense her disability and, rather than targeting her for ridicule, will feel somewhat protective of her, or intrigued.

If you are a parent just coming to terms with the reality that somehow, at birth or before, something went wrong and your child will always be different, how do you cope? Do you become angry, deny it, argue with the experts, coddle your child, or just try to escape however you can? Maybe you try to find someone to talk to, but this person doesn't know your child well and thinks you're imagining the problems. You try to accept the reality but, at the same time, wonder what will happen if you challenge the experts and push your child to do a little more than they expect. Will she fail because you haven't protected her enough?

What we did was take turns. One day it would be my husband's turn not to function, the next day mine. I was lucky to have a great deal of support at my workplace. I asked for and got a leave of absence to arrange Ellen's intervention program.

Ironically, I'd just been hired to promote early intervention programs for young children. After I'd been through five child care settings in as many months, a colleague with young children took me aside and recommended an evaluation for my daughter. Both twins were accepted into the integrated preschool program at the center where I worked, and our insurance paid for private speech and language therapy.

Maybe your child has attention disorder or can't read or has cerebral palsy or autism that is further out on the spectrum than my daughter's. I'll never know how you feel or how you survive. You probably see me and think the same thing.

There are days when I just can't help feeling good anyway. Small successes mean a lot. I hope you think I'm strong. But I hope you will let me tell you that there are days when it's really hard. I know my daughter will never fit in.

Disability. Most people treat the topic like death. Since our daughter's diagnosis, they've been avoiding us.

My advice to people with typically developing kids is this: If you know someone who has a child with a disability, go ahead and talk about it once in a while. It's not catching. You don't even have to say much, just ask, "How is she doing? How are you doing?"

Maybe, if you're really close friends, you'll have to risk the discomfort of your friend sobbing in your Subaru. If so, just being there and listening really helps. But most days your friend is either going to tell you regular sweet, cute things her child did lately or, more than likely, she's going to enjoy the adult time and not really want to talk about kids or problems at all. Best of all, when your child goes to school, you'll be open to her friendships with kids who are different, and you'll continue to feel comfortable and matter-of-fact about people with disabilities.

Shortly after our daughter's diagnosis, my husband came home and told me about a lecture he'd attended. A physician, speaking about developmental disabilities, likened his baby's diagnosis of a hearing impairment to going on vacation but landing in bombed-out Beirut instead of on the long stretch of sandy beach you'd imagined.

The analogy made sense to me. I guess, for the sake of your child, you learn to go around the land mines the best you can. It's just that some of them do blow up in your face once in a while.

Just writing this helps me. I believe I'm coming to accept my daughter's disability. But I edge close to denial often. Back and forth, again and again. But no matter where I am on this spectrum, I love her just the same.

I wrote this essay a year after we were told our then four-year-old daughter had pervasive developmental disability. Seven years later I can say that it does get better with time. I stopped crying every day after I wrote this, but my husband and I are still up and down on that ladder of acceptance.

Still, we've gotten on with our lives and are active in our community. We're strong, diplomatic advocates for the needs of our daughter and her sibling. We talk about what it's like having a child with special needs. We moved to a new community when the twins were five, and we consciously chose new friends who are able to listen and support us when we need help.

•   •   •

The author of this essay wishes to remain anonymous to protect her daughter's privacy. Ellen (not her real name) was born in 1986 and now has ten years of social communication intervention under her belt. Like all teens, she doesn't want to be singled out as different. With the help of her many teachers and therapists and her twin sister, she has worked out a strategy to look and seem much like her typically developing peers.

50

DIFFERENT DREAMS

by Kim Kaster

I planned for my child. I loved him with all my heart even before he was born. I dreamed of baseball games, birthday party invitations, school days, family vacations, college, and, of course, all the things he could be when he grew up. Then one day the specialists told me that my perfect child was not so perfect. And my dreams died.

I actually felt as though I were experiencing a death in the family. So many different feelings came at me, so very hard and fast. Within the first few months of Zach's diagnosis, my emotions ranged from grief to resentment, from shock to frustration, from guilt to denial. And in between, I just felt numb.

I started gathering information about various therapies, food supplements, restricted diets, and other "miracle cures." I was sure one of these things would "fix" Zach (as if he were broken). Then his problems would just go away. At the same time, I denied that there was really anything wrong with him.

One day, on a family vacation, I became angry with my son. I was angry at him for not being "typical." I knew Zach's disability was not his fault, that I was being irrational. But I wanted to be like those other families I kept seeing. They seemed so relaxed and able to enjoy themselves. Why couldn't we be like that? I could not do this anymore! I certainly was not qualified to be a "special" mother to a "special" child. I felt totally inadequate and helpless.

Even while in the grip of these feelings, I believed them to be dysfunctional. The professionals in my life agreed. They tried to help me "snap out of it." I felt like a terrible mother and so very alone. It took me time to realize that all these feelings were part of a normal and healthy reaction to my child's diagnosis and disability. Most parents experience a similar range of emotions.

Once I realized that these emotions were normal—and that other parents felt them, too—I was then able to accept and understand them. It took me longer to realize that the feelings would always be with me at some level.

I thought I was over the grief. I felt I had moved on. Then one night as I sat with my son at a high school basketball game, the tears began to flow. My son will never play high school basketball, I thought. No matter that he might never have wanted to play, or that even without a disability his size might have kept him from playing.

At that moment, I realized that some degree of grief would always be a part of my life. I love Zach for who he is, but I also understand that emotions, both good and bad, go with the territory. Now when difficult thoughts and emotions creep into my life, I work my way through them with as little guilt as possible.

And my dreams for my son are not dead. They have just been altered. Zachary is allowed and encouraged to dream, too. I know my life with my son will be a roller coaster ride of emotions. But I am prepared and knowledgeable—strapped in and enjoying the ride.

• • •

Kim Kaster lives in Saline, Michigan, with her husband, Mike, and two sons, Zachary (1991) and Nicholas (1993). Kim serves as a facilitator of information to different groups on topics such as inclusion and community. She also serves on a variety of committees that deal with education. Zach has been diagnosed with autism and mental impairment brought on by an unbalanced chromosome translocation (1:8). He is an active child who enjoys riding his bike around the neighborhood and being involved in his community and school.

51

TRAVELING A DIFFERENT PATH

by Maureen S. Penton

I think the most difficult part of being the parent of a special needs child is not the struggles related to our children's health or education, but the realization that we must travel a different path to help them achieve their dreams—and our dreams for them.

One incident brought this into stark clarity for me. One evening, when my son was quite young, I sat in an auditorium watching my nephew on stage playing cello with a group of young musicians. I glanced over at my sister's face. She was beaming with pride at the accomplishment of her child. I began to cry quietly, knowing that I would never experience what she was feeling. When I told her why I was crying, she tried to placate me, as so many others have done, with the reassurance that my son would be fine. "It will just take time," she said soothingly.

She had no idea that my child would never be on that stage, that he would never be on the dean's list, that he would never be the doctor or lawyer or leader I had envisioned before his birth. I wish she had been able to tell me what I now know: that my child would prove himself in so many other ways.

My son is now thirteen and has just completed his first year of middle school. I have to admit to some nervousness at the beginning of that school year. I know how cruel and unfair kids can be at that age, and I was prepared for the day when he got off the bus in tears because he had been ridiculed because of who he was and what he looked like. But that day never came. In his own quiet and indomitable way, he overcame the prejudices.

So this is the first thing I would like to impart as a "veteran" parent: *We need to give our children the self-confidence and the tools to handle the real world.* As much as we would like to believe otherwise, we will not always be there when someone says something hurtful or cruel. We will not always be there when someone pushes our child or makes him the brunt of a joke. So we must arm our children with the weapons they need to fight the prejudice they will encounter.

My son and I role-play situations and discuss how to handle problems before they occur. I started doing this when he was quite young, discussing the proper behavior for a situation before we went into a store, restaurant, or theater. Then, in the car on the way, we played the game "What do you do if . . ." Then when various situations arose, he knew how to react—not because he could rationalize and come up with a solution, but because he already knew. In this way, he became a child people wanted to be around. He was polite and well behaved—traits that require no Einstein IQ.

Before my son started school, we discussed how to handle bullies. I made it quite plain that some people just don't know how to be nice and that we should never fight, unless there is absolutely no other way out of the situation. You see, my son has a rare genetic defect that causes him to grow very quickly, so he is much larger than other children his own age. When we talked about avoiding fights, I made it clear that this was for the protection of other children also. He knows that choosing to walk away or tell an adult is not a defeat. I have always told him the real winner in a fight is the one who chooses to walk away.

This leads me to another point I would like to make: *We need to help our children understand and embrace their differences.*

My son has been much bigger than his peers since the age of five. Most of the time, this has not been an issue, but there have been times that it bothered him. One time we went to a school carnival where there were rides for the children. My son was fascinated with the little cars that went around in a circle, but there was no way he could ever fit into them. It broke my heart to see him standing on the outside, watching the other children laughing and having fun.

So we talked about why it was good to be big. He could throw a bowling ball like a grownup, so he could knock down more pins. He could usually catch the rebounds in basketball and make more baskets. It didn't take long before he started to come up with more positives on his own. No, it wasn't the same as riding those little cars, but it helped him understand that he could do many other things. Now, years later, he is proud of his size and wears it like a blue ribbon.

The last thing I want to share is the value of support from other parents of kids like our own. My advice for novice parents is: *Don't try to do this alone.* Find someone who understands because they have been there. Finding others like myself has been the one thing that has helped me most as a parent. All the well-meaning words of encouragement from relatives and friends don't help us through the hard times as much as the advice or reassurance of another parent in the same boat.

The first few years of my son's life, I tried to handle things completely on my own. I fought battles with the medical community and advocated for my child in the educational arena. I was out there alone—the only person on earth who had to deal with these issues, or so I thought. Finally, by a stroke of fate or luck or whatever you might call it, I found a friend whose children had many of the same problems as my son. My first conversation with her was like talking with someone I had known all my life. I was no longer alone, flailing against the current. We could cry together, be angry together, and know that we each had someone else who knew what it felt like.

I don't know how many times I have picked up the phone after a particularly difficult day, called this friend, and just unloaded. Unlike others—those we affectionately call "the parents of Gerber babies"—we don't tell each other that everything will be okay; we don't say, "Oh, he will just outgrow it." We can commiserate, share good times and bad times, cry about things others might find trivial, and laugh at things most people would not find funny. But through it all, we are there for each other.

There are many support groups out there. You can find them through schools, community organizations, or word of mouth. But seek them out, and if one doesn't fit, keep trying them on until one clicks for you. I am a very independent person, and I didn't like admitting that I needed someone else. But the truth is that finding another parent like myself has saved my sanity and helped me become the parent I wanted to be.

Many years ago, my mother gave me a copy of an article she found in a magazine. Although it didn't make much of an impression on me at the time, I think of it often now. The writer described how we look at a rainbow, in awe of its magnificence and use of color. He suggested that we would never presume to make changes, to soften the hues or to enhance the curve. In this same vein, we can see our children as rainbows, each one different and unique, and we must appreciate them for who they are.

• • •

Maureen Penton lives in Omaha, Nebraska, with her son, Alex (1984), who was born with a rare genetic defect that can only be categorized as an overgrowth syndrome. However, his symptoms do not correspond with any of the named syndromes of this type. Alex's skeletal maturation has been four years in advance of his chronological age, making him very tall and quite heavy, although he is an active child. He has had some medical problems, mostly respiratory. He also has learning disabilities and has received special education services since the age of two. Maureen is active in local special education groups and is on the governing board of the Nebraska Parents Center.

$\backsim$

CHICKEN SOUP FOR THE SPECIAL FAMILY'S SOUL

by Carolyn Anderson

Homemade chicken soup never tasted so good as it did in the middle of winter when I was growing up in northeast Ohio. It was a true comfort food that warmed us all over during those cold winter nights. It was a healing elixir that seemed to soothe our symptoms during the harsh cold and flu season. No, it didn't cure all that ailed us, but it did make us feel just a little bit better.

Fifteen years ago, my son Kevin was born with very special health care needs. The difficult time right after his birth reminded me of the long, cold Ohio winters of my childhood, except that these nights were so much longer and so much colder. I realized how desperately I needed chicken soup again.

This recipe has been fifteen years in the making. Believe me, it's been changed many times. It didn't cure my son's illness, but it has offered me much comfort during some of my coldest and longest nights. I pray it will do the same for you.

Ingredients

• *Two cups of support.* It took me six months to hook up with the proper support group. Though it seemed like an eternity, it was time well spent. My sense of loneliness diminished as I talked with other parents. I found a sense of camaraderie as I talked openly to others who had the same fears and concerns. They had survived, even flourished; it made me realize that, in due time, I would do the same.

Ask your child's doctor, social worker, early intervention teacher, or parent coordinator for a local support group or a parent-to-parent match-up. There are national organizations that match parents of children with rare disorders across the country. I have been in contact with parents in Illinois, Pennsylvania, Colorado, and even Hong Kong. When it comes to our children, we all speak the same language.

• *Generous servings of information and resources.* Yes, it's true. Information is power. The more you know, the more you can prepare for what lies ahead. My son's neurologist told me not to look in medical books, that he would answer any questions we would have. The only problem was that we did not know enough to ask the right questions. My never-ending quest for information has paid off many times over. I have even been able to bring new information to the attention of medical professionals.

At one point I gave Kevin's pulmonologist information on two treatments that were currently in use throughout the country. After reviewing the information, the doctor agreed the treatments were most certainly worth trying. And as it turned out, these treatments have made a huge impact not only on Kevin's health, but also on the quality of his life.

Children's hospitals, especially if they are university affiliated, often will have a family resource center you can use. The Internet, today's information superhighway, is a wonderful resource for finding the most up-to-date information. And don't forget other parents. They are not only a wonderful source of support but also a wonderful source of useful information.

• *Dreams, dreams, and more dreams.* I have come to realize how important it is to have dreams for your child, and the earlier, the better. Kevin truly became a part of the family when I allowed him to have a future—something to which every child, no matter how severe his or her condition, has a right.

Kevin dreams of becoming a sports journalist. Will it happen? I think it will. But it really doesn't matter whether or not he actually reaches that goal. What matters is that he continues to work toward it. Therein lies the satisfaction. Therein lies hope.

• *Substantial amounts of perseverance.* Never say never. Don't take no for an answer. It is absolutely true—you do know your child better than anyone else, even though you may not believe it in the beginning.

One time I felt my son would benefit from some intensive vitamin therapy. My son's "conventional" doctor did not feel it would do any good. I did my homework, sought out a professional "preventive-medicine" doctor, and we went for it. In the end, Kevin benefited greatly. He put on six pounds, after not gaining weight for two years. His therapist also commented on his improved neck control and physical stamina. I refused to take no for an answer, and I was glad I did.

• *A dollop of tears.* Tears of sadness *and* tears of joy. In the beginning, it is only natural that your tears will reflect your feelings of disappointment, fear, and anger. However, as you begin to celebrate your child's achievements, those tears of joy will come just as easily. Both are important; both are a necessary part of the recipe.

• *A dash of humor.* Humor takes us away from the seriousness of the moment and helps us to maintain some sort of emotional stability.

I remember taking Kevin for his first flu shot shortly after he was diagnosed. As required by the inoculation protocol, the doctor read me a list of the shot's potential side effects. When he got to "temporary paralysis," I couldn't help but smile. Now, you have to understand that overall muscle weakness is a big part of Kevin's disorder. I interrupted the doctor and asked him if he thought we'd even notice. We both started laughing. This laughter broke up the intensity of the moment for both of us. In the years since, I have come to realize that laughter truly is one of the best medicines.

There you have it—my version of chicken soup. The important thing to remember is not the specific amounts of ingredients, but rather that it is homemade. You will add your own touch. You may add and subtract ingredients as you need them. You may need more at some phases of your family's life and less at others. Last but not least, don't forget to share your own version of the recipe with other parents. Maybe you can make someone's winter a little warmer and a little shorter.

Bon appetit!

• • •

Carolyn Anderson lives in Willoughby, Ohio, with her husband, James, and their sons, Brian (1978) and Kevin (1983). She has served on the Family Advisory Council at Rainbow Babies and Children's Hospital in Cleveland, edited the On This Journey *parent newsletter, and been a longtime member of the local early intervention county collaborative and its first parent coordinator. Currently she is working on the Higher Education Project in Ohio, a pilot program encouraging professionals and parents to co-instruct in the classroom.*

James teaches high school history. His unprecedented trivia knowledge has earned him the family title "Master of Useless Knowledge." Brian is a college sophomore, majoring in sociology, who aspires to be an FBI agent someday.

Kevin is now an honors student in high school. He wants to go on to college and become a sports journalist. He is hoping some of the Sports Illustrated *writers will be opting for early retirement in a few years. At one year of age, Kevin was diagnosed with spinal muscular atrophy.*

53

THE GREEN BIKE

by Sally Cash Ragsdale

Each morning before my nine-year-old son, Scott, gets on the school bus, he tells me he wants Santa to bring him a green bike for Christmas.

That might not strike most parents as a very significant occurrence, but when Scott was born, I wasn't sure he would ever be able to communicate his needs or wants, let alone ride a bike or distinguish green from other colors. Scott was born with Down syndrome, a genetic disorder occurring in approximately one in a thousand births and a leading cause of mental retardation.

At the time of Scott's birth, I knew nothing about Down syndrome, and I was very frightened. All my dreams and plans for this baby were replaced with fears and uncertainties. I went through all the stages of grief—denial, anger, guilt, and sadness—as I mourned the loss of the normal, healthy child I had anticipated.

How my emotions have changed since then! When I look at Scott now, I see joy, hope, compassion, and love.

My goals for Scott have changed as well. When he was a baby, I viewed his disability as a challenge. My goal then was to raise the brightest, most accomplished child with Down syndrome ever. I felt this was possible, because I knew that children with Down syndrome have a range of intellectual ability—from severe to mild mental retardation—and I knew that early intervention and ongoing education could contribute significantly to the intellectual and physical growth of these children.

Over the years, Scott and I have struggled together as he works at learning new skills and I work at not jumping in and doing it for him. When he finally achieves success, I am rewarded with his enthusiasm and pride. Each milestone has been a major accomplishment for both of us.

Scott is now learning to read and has mastered rudimentary arithmetic. He can write his name clearly—and has done so very skillfully on the two occasions that I have lost him in Kmart and the service desk had to page "Scott's mother"! He continually amazes me with his perception and memory.

So have I achieved my goal of raising the brightest, most accomplished child with Down syndrome ever? No. But I've done something even better. I have raised a kind, charming, loving child with a wonderful sense of humor, a smile that would touch any mother's heart, and a giggle that is absolutely contagious. Am I disappointed? Not on your life! I have been blessed beyond measure.

Scott has shown me that his similarities to other children far outweigh his differences. Children with Down syndrome feel the same emotions as other children. They love to participate in sports, read books, go to McDonald's, and play with friends. And they dream of getting green bikes for Christmas.

One of the most enduring and endearing, yet frustrating, traits of many children with Down syndrome is their stubbornness. I know this stubbornness can be an asset; I have never seen Scott give up on a task. But in this matter of the green bicycle, he perseveres just as resolutely. My attempts to convince Scott that a red bike would be just as much fun have failed. He is determined that his new bike must be green!

Nine years ago, I would never have believed that one of the greatest challenges I would face in raising Scott would be trying to find him just the right green bike!

• • •

Sally is married to Rex Ragsdale, M.D., a family practice physician, currently employed as vice president for medical affairs, Bayfront Medical Center, St. Petersburg, Florida. Sally has worked

in the health care industry for thirty years, most recently as a prac-
tice management consultant for a hospital services organization.
In 2000, the family moved to Florida from Evansville, Indiana.

Sally has four children: Jason Cash (1977), James "Scott" Cash
(1980), Douglas Cash (1982), and Marcus (1988). Scott also has
three stepbrothers and one stepsister.

"When Scott was two years old, I attended my first National
Down Syndrome Congress convention and became interested in
forming a local support group. I became the founder and Director
of UPS (United Parent Support) for Downs. The group served as a
resource for parents and professionals involved in the care of a
child or adult with Down syndrome. We met on a monthly basis,
provided counseling to new parents, and compiled a lending li-
brary of journals, publications, and books about Down syndrome
and raising a child with a disability. The group continued to pro-
vide these services until a few years ago when information and
resources became more readily available via the Internet. I still oc-
casionally receive telephone calls from new parents who just need
to talk."

54

THE JOURNEY

by Jillian K. Welch

I have lost my innocence. I know too much.

I'm writing as an "experienced parent." My husband, John, and I have spent the last sixteen years raising a son with multiple disabilities. Together, we made the decision not to have any more children, and we have no regrets now. David's multiple needs required all our energy.

Sometimes I feel burned out, other times, completely inspired. Mostly, I just deal with my role as the mother of a child who has had disabilities from birth.

Nobody asks for this, but the law of averages dictates it must happen to someone. I am one of the "chosen ones." Do I feel honored? Sometimes I do. I also feel cheated.

A custom-made book of guidelines would be helpful but impossible. Each child with disabilities is unique; each family will deal with so many different issues.

For us, dealing with David's medical needs has been like watching a line of dominoes tumble, one after another. It started with an emergency cesarean birth and tests showing that a blood clot had formed on the left side of David's brain about two weeks earlier. This, in turn, led to blocked ventricles, which, in turn, caused hydrocephalus. The hydrocephalus necessitated the insertion of a shunt, which led to all the follow-up surgeries that were necessary when one shunt after another failed to function correctly.

At six months, David saw his first ophthalmologist. "I'm not convinced he can see anything," the doctor announced.

At seventeen months, the orthopedic physician informed us that David had cerebral palsy.

Our latest medical discovery, diagnosed last summer, is that David has simple-partial seizure disorder and has had it for several years. We thought it was stomachaches with nausea. It turned out to be something more.

I could summarize the past sixteen years with a list of medical procedures, therapies, diagnoses, and conflicting bits of opinion and advice from innumerable specialists. But even that long list would omit so much—our many trips to the emergency room when shunts seemed to fail, the educational and classroom placement issues with which we've struggled, our difficulty in obtaining appropriate transportation to and from school, and, not least, the strain on our marriage. Just when we thought we'd solved one problem, another obstacle was likely to be thrown into our path.

This parenting business is scary. But as I've grown older and wiser, I have come to several conclusions.

First, I have concluded that our lives with our children are a journey. I've realized that it's too easy to become obsessed with worries about the future. I would tell new parents to try to slow down and enjoy the good times when they occur.

Second, I realize that I am a better person for having gone through this struggle. But I also know that my lost innocence was the price I paid for this enrichment as a human being. To make sense of my struggles, I needed to tell myself that this was a special experience reserved only for a small percentage of the population. But even now I still think, what if . . .

What if David had never had this hemorrhage in his brain? I wish I could know what he would have been like, what he might have accomplished if it were not for his disabilities. Yet I love him for who he is now—not for what he might have been.

I constantly remind myself that it's the journey that counts, not the destination. Sometimes it's a bumpy ride; other times it's very smooth. But it's always interesting. And most importantly, it's a journey that John, David, and I are taking together.

• • •

Jillian Welch lives with her husband, John, and son, David (1983), in Rochester, New York. Jillian enjoys reading, creative writing, poetry, art, and advocating for her son and other children with disabilities. John is a manufacturing engineer who enjoys golf, skiing, and spending time with his family.

David is legally blind, has cerebral palsy and a seizure disorder, and remains shunt dependent. In many ways a typical adolescent, his interests include current events, computers, music, swimming, bowling, and girl-watching.

55

THE RIDE

by Susan Helling

O ver coffee one afternoon I remember telling my best friend and confidant, "I'm all done grieving now. Man, am I glad that's over with. Now I can get on with my life."

This conversation occurred a few months after we were told our son, Ryan, then seven years old, had a degenerative neurological disorder. Little did I realize the path of grief was much longer and would turn into a roller coaster ride from which I couldn't disembark.

As I look back to those days, I wish someone had told me about what I now refer to as "the ride." There were many days when I was sure I would go crazy as I tried to cope with Ryan's diagnosis and an unknown future.

As a registered nurse, I'd had many opportunities to assist families who were experiencing grief due to the loss of a loved one or a medical crisis that changed their dreams and expectations. I knew a lot about the grief process and had clear opinions about how the process should go.

I knew something must be wrong with me since I wasn't feeling what the books said I should. I found myself continually looking for something that would address the turmoil of my emotional life. I often attended workshops, and when I saw a brochure for a seminar that addressed children's loss and grief and how their families coped, I remember thinking, "Finally, someone will give me the answers."

I don't know what answers I was expecting, but I left the seminar with a familiar feeling of letdown. I hadn't learned what I'd hoped for and I didn't feel okay as I wanted to. I still wondered why I didn't fit into the typical stages of grief I had studied during nursing school and why I couldn't reach a stage of resolution.

When I shared my feelings with my friend, she told me, "If you feel it, it is real and healthy, and that's all that matters." These words of validation helped me realize I probably was normal.

Over time I began to realize the ups and downs I was experiencing didn't fit into the typical stages of grief I had been taught. I started to understand that since my child was alive, the situation couldn't become resolved but, instead, had become a chronic state that could go on indefinitely. What was known about my son's condition changed frequently and unexpectedly, and each change brought a whole new set of problems.

That's why I think of the chronic grief process for parents of children with special needs as a roller coaster ride. Even though parents of typical children also have their ups and downs, I believe our track is quite different from theirs. For parents with typical children, the peaks, hills, and curves in the track are balanced with lots of straightaways. These parents spend more time at the top of the hills, relaxing and looking over the amusement park. They have time to enjoy successes before racing down the incline and on to the end of the track. They can climb off the ride at the end.

There are more hills on our tracks. The peaks seem higher and harder to reach, the inclines steeper, the curves sharper, the straightaways less frequent. It takes more energy to negotiate each curve and climb up the next hill before reaching a straightaway that allows us to coast for a while. Since there is no visible end to this ride, our fuel supply diminishes and the motor sometimes sputters.

On my own personal "ride," I often found myself wondering if I would have time to refuel before the next hill, and if there wasn't time, I wondered how I would get over the hill after negotiating all those curves. As the ride continued on and on, the hills seemed steeper and closer together. The car felt as though it might careen completely off the track. With no end in sight, I had no opportunity to get off the ride. I was exhausted and wondered if I might be going crazy.

Parents who travel endlessly on "the ride" often find themselves isolated and not in control of their lives for extended periods of time. The emotional ups and downs encountered on a monthly, weekly, daily, or even hourly basis often go unrecognized. Consequently, important issues are frequently misunderstood and many times are not addressed at all.

After I had unwittingly been given a ticket to ride, I waited for the day I would feel better so I could get on with my life. I now realize life wasn't something to wait for; rather, what counted was what I made of each day. This realization came after I had some time to heal, gave myself lots of self-care, and found the courage to accept the help of others.

A form of self-care I find helpful is our state-funded respite care program. This program allocates money so families who have children with disabilities can pay the provider of their choice to stay with the child while the parents take a break. Respite services can act as a cushion when the ride gets rough and provide an opportunity for you to have time for yourself. If this service is available, I'd encourage all parents to take advantage of it.

Should no formal respite program be available, I'd suggest working out an arrangement with family or friends. This might be as easy as accepting someone's offer to help. Initially, I found it very difficult to say yes to offers of help. I've since come to believe that people offer assistance out of genuine kindness and concern, and my acceptance of these offers to help brings satisfaction to them as well as relief for me.

When times are tough and I can't get away from the house, I make an effort to find time for self-care. For me, this might mean spending a few minutes in a hot bath with the door locked. I've also learned to talk to my family before I have reached the end of my rope. This is sometimes as simple as telling them I need a few minutes to myself before dealing with their problems, or as complex as sharing my innermost feelings with a confidant in order to unburden myself and lighten my load.

I believe another very important part of self-care is to ask yourself, "What part of this problem is mine to own?" Many times I found myself trying to do too much. There were many times someone else could easily have done tasks I took on myself if I had relinquished some control.

Even though this sounds easy to do, it's not. When the rest of life is careening out of control, it is easier to hang on to tasks that award a feeling of control. It requires determination and practice to let go of those things that aren't your responsibility or that can easily be delegated. This must be coupled with the ability to say no and a willingness to deal with your own sense of guilt after doing so. From experience, I can say I've found the person to whom I say no is usually less upset about it than I am.

Another important form of assistance is available from other parents who have children with special needs. For me, a local support group afforded opportunities to share concerns and make contact with other parents who had children with special needs. In addition to support, I was able to glean information and benefit from their expertise and experience.

As I have watched Ryan grow into a wonderful young man, now almost seventeen years old, I realize how far I've ridden on my roller coaster ride. In spite of, and maybe because of the tough times, I have gained renewed appreciation for life's joys. I also understand that parenting a child with disabilities requires a cycle of adjustments that will continue throughout life.

As a part of learning to care for myself, I have learned to refuel my tank frequently through the help of family, friends, and community resources. Although it did not come easily, sharing the burden has lightened my load considerably.

I still listen to parents of children without disabilities talk of everyday problems and find myself thinking how simple their lives sound. However, I know my life has become easier as well. And although my "ride" is far from over, I am now able to reach the peaks more easily and find myself enjoying the view from the top more often.

• • •

Susan Helling lives in Aberdeen, South Dakota, with her husband, Tom, and two children, Bekka (1978) and Ryan (1981). Bekka was diagnosed with leukemia at age sixteen and successfully completed two and a half years of chemotherapy; she is still in remission and doing well. Ryan has a form of leukodystrophy, a degenerative neurological condition that destroys the myelin sheath, or the cushion around the nerves.

Susan is a registered nurse who has worked on the obstetrics unit of a local hospital since 1979. She is coordinator of the

Aberdeen Area Family Support Program, which provides service coordination and financial assistance for families from a seven-county area who have children with developmental disabilities living at home.

56

THE RUDEST AWAKENING

by Robert A. Naseef

Swept away by the electricity of the moment, my heart pounded with excitement as I held my son's soft, delicate body next to my heart. He was all I had dreamed he would be in those first instants of life as our eyes met and locked onto each other for the first time. Visions of the future danced in my mind's eye—playing baseball, building model airplanes together, having a warm, close relationship.

And that's the direction we seemed to be headed during the first eighteen months of Tariq's life. He rolled over, raised his head, began creeping, then crawling, cruising, triumphantly walking, and then proudly communicating with words.

Then Tariq got an ear infection and the train went off the track. His life—and mine—have never been the same.

All of a sudden, the exciting time when every day seemed to bring a new accomplishment was gone. I lived my life in a fog. Tariq stopped talking, stopped playing normally, and began flapping his arms in a strange repetitive manner.

Eventually, after years of early intervention, my boy was diagnosed with autism and mental retardation. That hit me like a brick in the face. It was a confusing and bewildering time. I didn't know which end was up. I felt a grief beyond words—as if someone had died—but my child was very much alive. He still looked like the Tariq I loved so much, a totally normal-looking child. Were my eyes deceiving me?

Portions of this essay first appeared in *Exceptional Parent* magazine.

The feelings did not come in distinct phases. They were entwined and blurred, but there seemed to be some pattern. Elisabeth Kübler-Ross first articulated the stages of grief as denial or shock, anger, bargaining, depression or sorrow, and, finally, acceptance or coping.

Unfortunately, not everyone who uses these terms understands them. When presented dogmatically, these ideas are not helpful to parents who are struggling to cope. As with any theory, there is a wide range in the way people react in everyday life. Real sorrow is not predictable.

A parent in this situation may find that his or her emotions are in turmoil, running a gamut of reactions, including fear, shock, anger, guilt, sadness, and shame. Body, mind, and spirit reel from the impact. Worst of all, you find you have no control over the way you feel. Grief may hit you when you least expect it—during a Christmas shopping trip, for example, as you buy baby toys for a nine-year-old; that's a time I remember.

Often the grief can be for ourselves—that our lives as parents did not turn out the way we expected. Our child may be happy and content, but we still struggle to let go of the dreams we had and create new ones, to accept and enjoy the child we actually have.

Indeed, I have come to realize that this is the struggle of all parents, even those of typical children. Who ever turned out to be the perfect parent of the perfect child? But when your child is so far from the norm, your very identity is challenged. While our friends are coaching T-ball or attending dance recitals, we may be learning sign language or giving injections.

My inner transformation was reflected in my dreams.

When I first knew something was wrong but couldn't accept the severity of Tariq's problem, I would dream at night of the way I interacted with Tariq during the day, doing things that his early intervention therapists recommended. I would imitate his repetitive movements, like flapping my arms when he flapped his. When I would do this during the day, Tariq would usually notice me, stop what he was doing, give me a little smile, and then go back to what he was doing.

But in my recurring dream, Tariq would look at me intently while I was mirroring his behavior, and then slowly form a word or two. My heart beating faster, I would rejoice and hug him.

The next morning, I would wake up feeling renewed and ready to keep working to make the dream come true. I tape-recorded his grunts and babbling and listened to the tapes later searching for progress or meaning. At times, I thought I heard some meaningful sounds but never any words.

Eventually I began awaking exhausted and overwhelmed, realizing the dream was not coming true. It was hard to endure the fading of my hopes.

It was also hard to see that all my hard work wasn't getting results. I steadfastly refused to believe that I had no control over my child's condition. Throughout my life, whenever I had worked hard at something, I had succeeded. I'd also been taught that when people were sick, save for a fatal illness, they got better. How could I think otherwise?

Daytimes with Tariq were exhausting. A moment's inattention, and he could run into traffic. He rarely slept through the night. Tariq's special needs seemed endless. I was constantly tired, and I was becoming increasingly aware that my love and hard work weren't enough. With few relaxing moments during the day, my dreams provided a welcome respite.

In a dream around the time of Tariq's eighth birthday, my boy spoke to me in sentences. I was overjoyed, but as the dream continued, I woke up within the dream knowing that Tariq had not spoken. The next morning, relieved, I began to accept Tariq as he was. I realized I could still love him. I didn't have to keep pushing him or myself. Through my dreams, my mind had let me know that having a "normal" son was an unreachable dream. I finally exhaled so many frustrations and took in my first breath of serenity.

A few years later, in a new dream, Tariq looked at me intently with his big brown eyes, told me that he loved me, felt my love, and knew I had done everything possible for him. He told me that he was happy and wanted me to be happy, too. Then he began playing with his tongue and making unintelligible noises, seemingly unaware of my presence. I felt sorrow and longing for what could have been. If only he could have continued talking.

But when I woke up, I had the definite sense that I had moved a little further on my journey. Tariq, with his limitations, was a part of me, and I was a fuller, deeper person despite the loss. I had survived and healed and was different now.

Tariq continues to be a catalyst for a life fuller, deeper, and more loving than I ever imagined. Some of my greatest joys and deepest sorrows have been in the moments he and I have shared. His disability is so severe, but his soul, his inner essence, is totally normal. Without speaking a word, he has taught the little boy in me to speak. In this way, he is with me at every moment. He has positive and negative emotions and has taught me to see them readily in myself and others. In a world that has valued reason and intellect above emotion, children like Tariq teach us to look inside ourselves. As a thoughtful father told me recently, they are not "children of a lesser God."

But my struggle to accept Tariq's fate was something nobody in my life could understand at the time. Although I have raged over how lonely it was, that was nobody's fault.

What can help you get through this kind of struggle? When people ask how you are and want to hear the real answer. When someone asks how they can help and really wants to. Meeting people who have been through it. Meeting people who can find value in your child just as he or she is in the moment. Kind words and the time to heal your broken heart.

Joy and sorrow may be our soul mates. As Kahlil Gibran wrote in *The Prophet,* "Your joy is your sorrow unmasked. . . . The deeper that sorrow carves into your being, the more joy you can contain."

The sorrow, although unwelcome, can be a pathway to an unconditional love that grows from a realization of the intrinsic beauty of each child's existence. We parents of children with disabilities can feel fine about ourselves when we grasp this and give up superficial achievement-based values. For Tariq, as for most children with disabilities, there has been no miracle, despite all my striving and wishes. I was powerless to change him, but he has changed me so much that I have no idea who I would be without him. I am okay without the baseball and the model airplanes. I did get a close, warm relationship with my son—and a touch of wisdom. No way would I give that up. Still, there are times that I won't deny wishing we could sit down and really talk.

• • •

Robert A. Naseef, Ph.D., is a psychologist who lives in the Philadelphia area with his wife, colleague, and best friend, Cindy. Their blended family includes three daughters, Antoinette (1981), Kara (1991), and Zoe (1993), and a son, Tariq (1979). Tariq, who has autism and mental retardation, lives at the Devereux Foundation's Kanner Center in nearby West Chester, Pennsylvania.

The story of Naseef's journey with Tariq and his work with families of children with special needs is told in his book Special Children, Challenged Parents: The Struggles and Rewards of Raising a Child with a Disability *(Birch Lane Press/Carol Publishing Group, 1997). A paperback version will be issued in the near future.*

57

GET OVER IT!

by Jo Ann Simons

When my son, Jon, was born with Down syndrome twenty years ago, I wish someone had told me what he told me recently: "Get over it!" I realize now that I wasted tears, and I wasted time. Of course, some period of mourning was inevitable, but I wish I had known how good it would be.

I wish I had known that twenty years later I would be worrying about college, drinking and driving, teenage sexual relationships, and sibling rivalry. I wish I had known that I would not be worrying about him crossing his midline or his mean length of utterance. I wish I had known that he would express his views on world events (for example, he told me he thought President Clinton's sex life was a private matter) or that he would confront the Holocaust.

Recently Jon has been seizing every opportunity to assert his independence. I don't mean the little stuff like making his breakfast, taking his medications, and paying his bills. I mean the big stuff. He resents my meddling and his sister's bossiness; he is embarrassed by his father's silliness. He is a teenager on the brink of leaving home. While he may be living under our roof for a few more months, he has been trying to separate emotionally for quite some time.

I remember one day last year when he walked out the front door and into the car of a classmate for a ride to school at 7:30 A.M. He told us he had plans after school to study in the cafeteria and that he would be getting on the bus at 4:30 P.M. to ride to the basketball game since he is the manager. He informed me he'd need a ride home from school at 10 P.M. For those of you not able to do the math, this came out to fourteen and a half hours from the time I told him to "have a good day" until I heard from him next. To be sure, he has done this before, but that did not stop me from wondering whether he had made it to the bus, whether he had money, whether he would eat anything, and whether he would be on the bus when it returned.

Another day when I called home from work to see if anybody was home, I listened to the messages and heard Jon's voice: "Well, I missed the bus. I guess I'm going to walk home." Click.

I called back an hour later, and Jon answered the phone. When I asked him how he got home he said, "Sawyer's dad."

"You mean Sawyer from the basketball team?" I asked.

"Yes."

That was when I told him how proud I was of his independence, but that it also was hard for me to watch him grow up and let him go.

Then, just as any modern teenager would do, he told me, "You need to get over it."

• • •

Jo Ann Simons is executive director of the East Middlesex chapter of ARC, the national organization of and for people with mental retardation, in Reading, Massachusetts. From 1999 until 2002, she is serving as president of the National Down Syndrome Congress. She was on the board of directors of Special Olympics International from 1989 to 1995.

Jo Ann lives in Swampscott, Massachusetts, with her husband, Chet Derr, an engineer at General Electric, and Jonathan (1979) and Emily (1983). Jonathan has inspired Jo Ann's commitment to persons with disabilities and Emily reminds her that being typical is special, too.

58

MISSION OF LOVE

by Trena Tremblay

Welcome to the journey of a lifetime. You will be receiving a wonderful education, but your diploma will not be the kind you can hang on the wall. Rather, it will be one you will come to know in your heart every time you reach a milestone. You will have not a single graduation day, but many, as you and your precious child grow together—discovering and achieving many wonderful accomplishments you might in the past have taken for granted.

Never, ever forget that you have been chosen for this very special journey. It matters not what the challenges may be; what matters is that you open your heart to this child. For as difficult as things may get, you will discover that this soul, wrapped in this precious little package, has much to give and volumes to teach you about yourself—if you are willing to learn.

Each of us is uniquely and wonderfully made. We all have abilities and disabilities. We all come in different packages. Some of us carry our beauty on the outside, some on the inside. We may find ourselves in a society that values the wrappings much more than the contents of the package. For in our busy and fast-paced society, it takes less time and much less effort to create a beautiful and appealing package. True beauty requires much more effort, time, and commitment, but as you will come to understand, such things are the treasures of the heart.

You can make a difference in this crazy world. Your little person has come to show you how. Our children are not here to accomplish what most others can do! I believe they are here for a far more important task—to remind us how fragile, delicate, vulnerable, precious, and very significant each of us is. They are here to remind us of what we really need to make this life worthwhile.

Still, your journey will not be an easy one. You will need to find special tools to aid you on your quest. Just as you would not consider taking a long trip in a vehicle with flat tires, you cannot hope to make this journey with improper information and a negative attitude.

Focus on your child's abilities, not his disabilities. Begin today! Seek out those who will support you in doing that. Such people can be hard to find. Even the professionals may need some redirection from you.

Do not give up in any area until you have exhausted all possibilities. You will come to know your child best—much better than the professionals. If you can't find the support your child needs, consider creating, developing, or starting it yourself. When all your efforts seem to be wasting potential learning time for your child, regroup, refocus, and redefine priorities.

Always keep your child's self-esteem, socialization with peers, independence, community involvement, and dignity and quality of life as your top priorities. This list of priorities should be the same for any child, with or without disabilities. What will be different will be that you will have to work harder to earn these things for your child. You must be an active and aggressive advocate.

Twenty-one years ago, I read a sign in a pediatrician's office: "Parenting is the most difficult job you will ever have."

All these years later I can say this: To read this sign is easy. To comprehend it . . . is perplexing. To walk it . . . is horrendous. To survive it . . . is a test of the human spirit, a lesson in perseverance, a trip into the twilight zone, and a miracle!

To look back on it is awesome!

• • •

Trena Tremblay lives in Bristol, Connecticut, with her husband, Henry, and their sons, Brian (1977) and Adam (1980). Trena has her own home-based business as a licensed day care provider with experience in caring for children with special needs. Henry is in the tool and die trade. Brian attends a day program that is supported by a local ARC. Adam is pursuing a career in architecture.

Trena and Henry, along with other families that include young adults with special needs, have created Vision Star, Inc., a nonprofit corporation. They plan to build appropriate, affordable, supported housing for challenged individuals as an alternative to living with their parents indefinitely. As of 2000, the group is seeking funds to purchase land.

59

WELCOME TO HOLLAND

by Emily Perl Kingsley

I am often asked to describe the experience of raising a child with a disability—to try to help people who have not shared this unique experience to understand it, to imagine how it would feel. It's like this. . . .

When you're going to have a baby, it's like planning a fabulous vacation trip—to Italy. You buy a bunch of guide books and make your wonderful plans. The Coliseum. Michelangelo's David. The gondolas in Venice. You may learn some handy phrases in Italian. It's all very exciting.

After months of eager anticipation, the day finally arrives. You pack your bags and off you go. Several hours later, the plane lands. The stewardess comes in and says, "Welcome to Holland."

"*Holland??*" you say. "What do you mean Holland? I signed up for Italy! I'm supposed to be in Italy. All my life I've dreamed of going to Italy."

But there's been a change in the flight plan. They've landed in Holland and there you must stay.

The important thing is that they haven't taken you to a horrible, disgusting, filthy place full of pestilence, famine, and disease. It's just a different place.

So you must go out and buy new guide books. And you must learn a whole new language. And you will meet a whole new group of people you would never have met.

It's just a *different* place. It's slower-paced than Italy, less flashy than Italy. But after you've been there for a while and you catch your breath, you look around. . . . And you begin to notice that Holland has windmills . . . and Holland has tulips. Holland even has Rembrandts.

But everyone you know is busy coming and going from Italy . . . and they're all bragging about what a wonderful time they had there. And for the rest of your life, you will say, "Yes, that's where I was supposed to go. That's what I had planned."

And the pain of that will never, ever, ever, ever go away . . . because the loss of that dream is a very significant loss.

But . . . if you spend your life mourning the fact that you didn't get to Italy, you may never be free to enjoy the very special, the very lovely things . . . about Holland.

•　•　•

Emily Perl Kingsley has been writing scripts for Sesame Street *for thirty years. Much of her work on the show has focused on enhancing the understanding and acceptance of people with disabilities. Emily is the mother of Jason Kingsley (1974) and served as the dictation typist for Jason's and Mitchell Levitz's book* Count Us In: Growing Up with Down Syndrome *(published by Harcourt Brace in 1994). Emily lives in Briarcliff Manor, New York.*

Emily's essay has been read by parents throughout the world since it was first published in 1987. We are honored that she has given us permission to include it in this book.

60

WE LET THEM LEAD US

by Nathan and Louise J. Elbaum

Tolstoy begins *Anna Karenina* with the statement, "All happy families are alike; each unhappy family is unhappy in its own way."

We have often felt our family is the exception to that rule. Twenty-eight years ago, we could little have guessed that we would have two sons with fragile X syndrome—the syndrome was not understood as a genetic condition until our sons were six and nine years old. Yet, with the support of family, friends, and many other good people, we have treasured the gifts our sons have brought to our life. While some of our dreams for our sons have been abandoned, our new dreams continue to amuse, delight, and captivate us. Our children give back to us in many ways, some tangible—like taking us out to dinner on special and not-so-special occasions—others more fleeting. Yes, we have a happy family, but it is happy in its own way.

Mike was born in 1970. He was six weeks premature, and the doctors attributed his fussiness and slow development to his prematurity. We were told he might be slow catching up to his peers and that we should "relax and enjoy him." We did, but that did not stop us from entering him in a special education program when he was three. We thought that with a little extra boost, he would catch up in time to enter kindergarten with his peers.

We were right and wrong about that. His special education teachers felt that, since he was not very verbal and was not entirely caught up, he should remain in their special school. We compromised with half-day kindergarten and half-day special education. Needless to say, daily contact with peers who were very verbal and who did not depend on teachers to intervene gave Mike's speech a giant boost. But it soon became clear that there was something different about how Mike learns.

When Mike was three and a half, his brother, Philip, was born. Philip was a full-term baby. When the doctor examined him he said, "This one is perfect; enjoy him." We know he meant to be reassuring, but we heard, "Mike is imperfect; how can you enjoy him?"

As it became clear that Philip, too, was slow to develop, we intensified our search for explanations. We had the Feingold Diet summer, during which we ruled out artificial colors and flavors as the cause of the boys' learning difficulties. We did biochemical tests, saw psychologists and psychiatrists, and had a genetic evaluation. We got conflicting suggestions—You aren't expecting enough; you are expecting too much.

We were told our sons needed lots of structure. We learned that we do not have a structured life and that we weren't comfortable trying to have one. So we continued to trust our gut feelings and learn from our sons about who they were, how they learn, and what we could expect from them.

The road has not always been easy, and we have not always been astute. After three years of having Philip learn to count from one to four with one-to-one correspondence, it occurred to us that we had better abandon that goal and find another way to give him the math skills he needed to ride his beloved bus. He quickly learned to find forty-five cents in combinations of nickels, dimes, and quarters. It is amazing what will happen when you stop nagging and start motivating.

Knowing that it is important to interact in one's community, we have always chosen to have our sons be educated with and spend time with their age peers, when possible. This has required some creativity. For example, Philip, who attended five different schools in two years owing to school district decisions, often had to have his peer time after school or at summer camp.

Adulthood brought new challenges. For Mike, adulthood meant independence. With support from a group of friends, former teachers, neighbors, and the assistant to the trust officer at the bank, we found and bought a house for Mike, fixed it up, and furnished it. Understanding that this was a big step toward independence, Mike became more and more reluctant as the moving date approached. It took considerable firmness to insist that Mike pick a moving date and then stick to it. But once the move was completed, Mike was so pleased with himself that he was ready to open new horizons. The very next day he asked whether we thought he might someday get married! We answered that we thought it was possible, but that we also thought it would be wise to try going out with a girl first.

We've learned that Mike enjoys, even needs, his own space, the freedom to talk back to his television without feeling embarrassed. Mike writes his own checks to pay his rent, his electric and phone bills, and his newspaper and magazine subscriptions. He has a credit card that he uses responsibly. He does his own shopping and cooking, mows his lawn, and shovels his walk.

Unlike Mike, Philip has no problem having people around. He enjoys living with his parents and has no plans to move out. Since he is pretty independent and fun to be with, that's fine with us. Unlike Mike, Philip cannot maintain a checkbook independently. But he has social skills his brother has never dreamed of. He goes out to dinner with coworkers. He organizes family outings to movies, sporting events, and musical evenings at the coffee shop where he works.

Philip constantly stretches our horizons. He has dragged us to enough University of Wisconsin basketball games to make us fans. He has taken his mother on a wilderness horse packing trip and plans to take her sea kayaking this summer. He always has some event to anticipate and is willing to risk trying new things.

We feel very lucky.

Our adult sons have lives that satisfy them. They welcome us into their lives and greatly enrich ours. They do not tie us down or keep us from doing other things. When we have traveled to Europe, Mike has moved in with Philip. Together, the boys take good care of themselves, get to their jobs, plan their dinners, or go out and share their interest in sports—though often glued to separate TV sets. When we return, we find the house in order, garbage properly disposed of, dishes and laundry done.

Of course, we would have been pleased to have sons who graduated from college, who went into the Peace Corps, who completed graduate studies. We had dreamed that our children would lead us on a vicarious intellectual and moral journey as we cheered them on in their accomplishments. Theirs was not the journey we had planned. But still we let them lead us. We like to think that as they have challenged us to be creative with our lives, we continue to challenge them to do a little more and try new things in theirs.

• • •

Nathan and Louise J. Elbaum live in Madison, Wisconsin, with their son Philip (1973). Mike (1970) lives in his own house about half a mile away. Nathan was born in Warsaw, Poland, and came to the United States when he was twenty-two. Now retired, Nathan spent most of his adult life working for public assistance agencies, first in New York City and later for the State of Wisconsin. Louise has a master's degree in social work and has done doctoral work in the Neurosciences Training Program at the University of Wisconsin–Madison. She is coordinator of the Great Lakes Regional Genetics Group, a network of clinical geneticists and public health administrators. Mike works in the production kitchen and the Lakeside Cafeteria in the Memorial Union at the University of Wisconsin. Philip works at a local coffee shop and at St. Mary's Surgery and Care Center.

61

WHEN MY DAUGHTER BECAME BLIND

by Mary McHugh

When she was six, my daughter began wetting her bed again after four years of being dry at night. At first, I thought it was because she had started first grade in a new school and was nervous about the move. But when she began regularly falling asleep during the day, I knew something was wrong.

The pediatrician confirmed my fears. Kyle had diabetes.

I knew nothing about this disease. Nobody on either side of the family had ever had it, as far as I knew. Like most people who know very little about diabetes, I assumed it would be controlled by insulin and wasn't really a big problem. I was so wrong.

There are much better methods of monitoring blood sugar levels now, but thirty-two years ago, things were different. Aside from the severe insulin reactions that could render her unconscious because of low blood sugar, Kyle was also in danger of going into a coma if her blood sugar soared to high levels.

Still, Kyle's specialist minimized the possible side effects of diabetes—blindness, kidney failure, amputations, congestive heart disease, and strokes. I didn't want to know about the terrible things that could happen to her anyway. I wanted to believe she could lead a perfectly "normal" life. Kyle had an illness that could kill her, but aside from that, everything was just fine. I had the act of denial down to an art form.

While Kyle was a child, it was relatively easy for her to do everything her friends did. The diabetes was usually under control, except for a few heart-stopping moments when she lost consciousness from a sudden surge of insulin because of too much activity or too little food.

I learned to cope with these reactions, as did Kyle's older sister and the school nurse. After a reaction was over (they used to call it insulin shock, and that describes it much better), we all pretended she was just fine. I had no idea that when she grew up, all those side effects we had ignored would catch up with her.

When diabetic retinopathy caused Kyle to begin losing her sight at the age of twenty-one, I did what most mothers do when their child is threatened. I shifted into high gear and found what I thought was the best medical care possible. I had grown up in the metropolitan area and believed that New York doctors were the only ones who could help her. We were living in Pennsylvania at the time, and Kyle was in college in Boston. She would fly to New York, and I would drive up from Pennsylvania to meet her at the office of one of the leading laser specialists in the country. Then I would drive her back to Boston.

All her life, I had assured Kyle I would make sure she wouldn't be blind, that there were treatments the doctors could do to prevent blindness. I had her eyes examined every six months and there was never any problem—until she was twenty-one and the brittle diabetes that caused wild swings in her blood sugar began to attack the blood vessels in the back of her eyes and she needed laser treatment to stop the damage.

"There is only a mild discomfort," they told us.

Every time Kyle went into the doctor's office, I could hear the click, click, click of the laser from my seat in the waiting room. She stumbled from the room each time in agony, her eye bandaged, her words audible to the other people waiting for treatment. I held her, took her to the cafeteria in the hospital for lunch, and then drove her back to college, concentrating on the road, pushing back thoughts that she could be blind if these treatments didn't work.

Everyone assured me they would.

The specialist at Harkness may have been a skilled laser technician, but he needed a little help with his people skills. Whenever I tried to ask him any questions about my daughter's prognosis, what to do after the treatment, whether she should leave college, how many treatments she would need, he barely answered me, cold and unfriendly, at a time when I needed a friend badly.

Why don't they give doctors training in empathy in medical school?

The doctor said she could attend classes and continue with her studies, so I left Kyle there in Boston and drove the long way back to our house in one of Philadelphia's suburbs. We lived in a beautiful house with a swimming pool and eight apple trees and a garden. I sat by the fire during those terrible days and wrote a book on death and dying for my publisher. Not the most cheerful subject in the world.

We had lived in Pennsylvania for four years and I had made friends with other writers and neighbors, wives of my husband's colleagues, but my real friends were back in New Jersey, where I had lived most of my life. If they had been nearby, they would have comforted and helped me through the year I was struggling to save Kyle's sight.

There in Pennsylvania, not one person offered me any solace, or even a cup of coffee, a shoulder to cry on. Not one of them said, "Mary, what can we do to help?"

When the year was up and the laser treatments had caused the kind of glaucoma that can't be cured, Kyle was totally blind—not even a glimmer of light left.

I asked those people I had met in Pennsylvania why they had never even called or helped me. "Oh, Mary," they said, "you seemed to be doing so well, we thought you were fine. We didn't want to intrude."

One woman said, "I just didn't know what to say."

"Next time," I told them, "when a friend is going through a tough time, ask if she is all right, take her out to lunch, invite her to sit by your fireplace and offer her a cup of tea. If you can't think of anything to say, just put your hand on her arm and say, 'I'm so sorry.' It's not that hard."

If I had it to do all over again, I wouldn't hide my anguish and pretend that nothing terrible was happening to my child. I would tell people I needed extra help, extra kindness, extra compassion.

I had learned to stifle my feelings of grief and sorrow when I was growing up by watching my mother take care of my brother, who had cerebral palsy and mental retardation. To the rest of the world, she pretended that everything was fine, and she never complained. She would fix whatever was wrong, and she would listen to her friends complain about their problems with a compassion and understanding that came out of her own deep sorrow.

I watched my mother and admired her stoicism, and that's the way I reacted, too. But it's really not the best way to get through something as hard as watching your child become blind. You should call a friend and say, "Could we go someplace wonderful and have lunch? I need to talk to somebody." I was convinced that nobody really wanted to hear about problems. I thought they only wanted to hear the good stuff.

When Kyle had the last laser treatment and it seemed she would be blind, we went to see doctors in Philadelphia who tried but couldn't save her sight either. They, at least, were kind and answered all my questions as best they could. While we sat in the waiting room, I taught Kyle Braille by tapping the symbols on the back of her hand and telling her about the other people in the waiting room. It made her laugh and helped us both learn Braille.

The last month before she became blind was December. Christmas. She lay in bed, waiting, waiting, waiting for the last light to leave her eyes. I rubbed her back, bought her a talking clock, watched Judge Wapner with her, read to her, called agencies to find out what to do.

Then one morning when I went to wake her, she opened her eyes and said, "I can't see you anymore," and I held her tight while we both cried.

I went downstairs and sat in my kitchen and howled like Lear at God. "How could You do this to my child? Isn't it enough that I have a brother with retardation and cerebral palsy? Do You mean for me to live my mother's life all over again? Why? Why? Why?"

The worst part, for me, was that I had broken my promise to Kyle. She was going to be blind and there was nothing I could do to stop it. I had tried everything, taken her to the best doctors, prayed, convinced her the laser treatments would work.

But they didn't.

You always think you can protect your child from the bad

things in life. But sometimes you just can't. It took me a long time to come to terms with that.

It was Kyle who helped me understand that when bad things happen to good people, there is help waiting to get you through it. "God didn't cause my blindness," she would say. "Diabetes did. But ask for help and you'll get it—often from the most surprising sources."

She was right. But the guilt still lies there waiting in dark corners, ready to pounce when I'm vulnerable. There must have been something else I could have done, I tell myself.

On that terrible morning, I screamed and yelled, thinking Kyle was upstairs in her room with the door closed. But she had crept down the stairs and heard me crying. She went back upstairs, picked up the phone, and found a place to learn to walk, talk, and function as a blind person. She found a therapist who would help her through it. She was determined to go back to Boston University, get her degree, and live on her own.

And so she did.

One of the hardest things I ever had to do was let her go. I knew I had to let her lead her own life, but my heart was in my mouth when I kissed her good-bye and left her alone in her Boston apartment.

She finished B.U. and got a job with a state senator doing liaison with constituents. After five years with the senator, she went to the Kennedy School at Harvard, earned her master's in public administration, and became a consultant on health care.

She has worked at a mental hospital outside London, with a member of Parliament in Northern Ireland, and at a homeless shelter in Frankfurt. She has written a report on health care in Ukraine for the World Organization on Disability. I am so proud of her I could burst.

If I could give just one piece of advice to others going through an experience like mine I would say: Ask for help. People can't read your mind. If you act as if you are fine, they will treat you as if you are. But if you tell them you need them, most people will come through with flying colors.

• • •

Mary McHugh is a writer and editor. She is the author of Special Siblings: Growing Up with Someone with a Disability *(Hyperion, 1999). She lives with her husband, Earl, a retired attorney, in New Jersey. Kyle died in 1999 at age forty from complications of her diabetes. At the time of her death, she was living in Boston and working as a consultant on health care.*

62

YOU ARE NOT ALONE

by Patricia McGill Smith

When parents learn about any difficulty or problem in their child's development, it comes as a tremendous blow. The day my child was diagnosed, I was so devastated and confused that I recall little else other than the heartbreak. I've heard another parent describe her child's diagnosis as a "black sack" being pulled down over her head, blocking her ability to hear, see, and think in normal ways. Another parent described it as "having a knife stuck in [her] heart." While these descriptions may seem extreme to some, I know from personal experience that they don't even come close to describing the emotions parents feel at this time.

It may help you to know that your feelings are normal and almost universal. The emotions you are feeling now have been experienced by many, many others. You are not alone.

A common first reaction is *denial*: This cannot be happening to me, to my child, to our family. Denial can go hand in hand with *anger*—anger triggered by feelings of grief and inexplicable loss. Anger so intense it may color our communication with almost everyone, from the professionals who provided the diagnosis to our closest friends and relatives.

This essay is adapted from the article "You Are Not Alone: For Parents When They Learn That Their Child Has a Disability." The article first appeared in the NICHCY (National Information Center for Children and Youth with Disabilities) *News Digest*, vol. 3, no. 1, 1993. With permission.

Fear is another common emotion, and fears of the unknown can be the most difficult. Parents often fear an unknown and unpredictable future: What will happen when he is five years old, twelve, twenty-one? Will she be able to learn, go to college? Will she be able to love, laugh, live, and do all we had hoped for? What is going to happen to this child when I am gone?

Parents may also fear that the worst prognosis for their child is the one that will occur. Many parents have told me that their first thoughts were totally bleak. Many parents are haunted by long-forgotten memories of persons with disabilities from years past. There are also fears of society's rejection, fears about how siblings will be affected, concerns about whether family members will love and accept this child. Fear can be immobilizing.

Parents may feel *guilt* as they wonder if they could have done something to have caused their child's problem. These feelings may be related to religious interpretations of blame and punishment. Parents may cry, "Why me?" or, "Why my child?" But they may also be asking, "Why has God done this to me?" or, "What did I do to deserve this?"

Confusion also marks this period and may manifest itself as sleeplessness, inability to make decisions, and mental overload. Information can seem garbled and distorted. You want to find out everything, yet you cannot understand the information you are receiving.

Powerlessness to change a child's disability is difficult for parents who want to feel competent and capable. It is extremely hard to have to rely on the judgments, opinions, and recommendations of strangers.

Disappointment that a child is not perfect is a jolt to previous expectations and can create reluctance to accept one's child as a valuable, developing person.

When so many different feelings flood the mind and heart, there is no way to predict how intensely a parent may experience this constellation of emotions. Not all parents experience the same feelings. But it is important to acknowledge potentially troublesome feelings that arise and appreciate that you are traveling a road others have traveled before you.

One constructive response is to find another parent of a child with a disability, preferably one who has chosen to be a parent helper, and seek his or her assistance. Twenty-two hours after my child's diagnosis, another parent made a statement that I have never forgotten: "You may not realize it today, but there may come a time in your life when you will find that having a daughter with a disability is a blessing."

I remember being puzzled by these words. Nonetheless, they were a valuable gift that lit the first flame of hope. This parent gave me hope for the future. He told me that there would be programs, there would be progress, and there would be help of many kinds and from many sources. And he was right.

Here's some other advice:

• *Communicate.* Many parents have a difficult time communicating their feelings to each other. Many parents, especially dads, may believe it is a sign of weakness to talk about their feelings. But the strongest fathers understand that revealing feelings does not diminish one's strength. In fact, the more couples can communicate at difficult times like these, the greater their collective strength.

Try to understand that you each approach your roles as parents differently. This means that you may not respond to this new challenge the same way. Try to explain your individual feelings, and try to understand when you don't see things the same way.

If there are other children in the family, talk with them as well. If you do not feel emotionally capable of talking with your children or meeting their emotional needs at this time, identify others who can. Talk with significant others in your life—your best friend, your parents. It can be so beneficial to have reliable others who can help carry the emotional burden.

• *Reach out.* Turn to positive sources of strength and wisdom in your life—a spiritual leader, a good friend, or a counselor. Go to those who have been a source of strength before, or find new sources. A counselor gave me this recipe for living through a crisis: Each morning, when you arise, recognize your powerlessness over the situation at hand. Turn this problem over to God, as you understand Him, and begin your day.

Whenever feelings are painful, reach out. Call, write, or visit a real person who will talk with you and share that pain. Pain shared is not nearly so difficult as pain in isolation. Sometimes professional counseling is worthwhile. Do not be reluctant to seek this avenue of assistance.

• *Become informed.* For some parents, the search for as much information as possible becomes an obsession. The key is to request accurate information. Do not be intimidated by the credentials or manner of professionals. Do not be concerned that you are being a bother or are asking too many questions. Whenever someone uses a word that you don't understand, stop the conversation for an explanation. You do not have to apologize for wanting to know about your child.

When going to a meeting about your child, jot down your questions beforehand or as you think of them during the meeting. Use a notebook to save all information that is given to you. Always ask for copies of evaluations and reports. In the future, there will be many uses for the information; keep it in a safe place.

• *Acknowledge negative feelings.* Recognize your anger and learn to let go of it. You may need outside help to do this. By acknowledging and working through your negative feelings, you will be better equipped to meet new challenges. Bitterness and anger will no longer drain your energies and initiative.

• *Take one day at a time.* Fears of the future can immobilize anyone. Living with the reality of the day at hand is made more manageable if we throw out the "what if's" and "what then's." Worrying about the future will deplete emotional resources you need to get through each day, one step at a time.

Time is on your side. It may not feel like it, but life will get better, and the day will come when you will feel positive again.

This little person is your child, first and foremost. The child comes first; the disability comes second. Your child is not less valuable, less human, less important, or less in need of love and parenting than other children. If you can relax and take the positive steps just outlined above, one at a time, your child will benefit, and you can look forward to the future with hope.

* * *

Patricia McGill Smith is the executive director of the National Parent Network on Disabilities (www.npnd.org), an organization dedicated to serving families and individuals with disabilities. She has served as the acting assistant and deputy assistant secretary in the Office of Special Education and Rehabilitative Services in the

U.S. Department of Education and is the former deputy director of the National Information Center for Children and Youth with Disabilities (NICHCY), where she first wrote a longer article entitled "You Are Not Alone: For Parents When They Learn That Their Child Has a Disability."

Prior to relocating to Washington, D.C., Patty was the first paid parent coordinator for the Pilot Parent Program in Nebraska. She also spent five years as the parent activity consultant for the Meyer Children's Rehabilitation Center at the University of Nebraska Medical Center in Omaha.

Patty has traveled throughout the world to share her hope and experience with families who have a member with a disability. Patty is the parent of seven children. Jane (1970), her youngest, has multiple disabilities. She is also the grandparent of Sean, who has Down syndrome. Patty and Jane live in Fairfax, Virginia. Jane works as a clerk in a thrift store and enjoys her own apartment and her computer.

63

LESSONS LEARNED

by Donna L. Roberts

I was barely nineteen years old when my first child, my Kimi, was born. Because she was my first, I relied on support from my best friend, whose child was a few weeks older than my own.

For eleven months I watched as my friend's baby picked up her head, rolled over, and responded to her mother's care. And I watched as my baby—beautiful though she was—didn't do anything. Except for those horrible moments when she would stare off into space and appear totally unreachable. Except for those times when she choked on her formula or pureed food, often for no apparent reason at all. Except for the fact that she didn't seem to be developing any control over her arms or legs.

And for eleven months I tried to explain my concerns to Kimi's pediatrician—only to be patronized with, "Now don't be such a nervous new mother; all babies develop at their own rate. There's nothing wrong with Kimi."

But then came the morning when I could no longer use the pediatrician's assurances to ease my concerns. Shortly after breakfast, Kimi had her first grand mal seizure. During the next seven hours, she had fifty more.

Frantic, I called my pediatrician, who instructed me to take my child to a large nearby hospital. Six days later, after a myriad of confusing and frightening tests and procedures, an icy neurologist informed me that my child had Cornelia deLange syndrome and that the symptoms included profound mental retardation, cerebral palsy, epilepsy, and heart and respiratory problems. What he didn't tell me—but I learned later—was that at that time, in 1966, very few children with this condition survived to their tenth birthday.

The next few years are a blur. My family worried that I had done something to cause my child's disability; my husband withdrew from both of us; my friends alternated between pity and avoidance. A second child was born, then a third, and then there was a divorce—and I was all alone with an overwhelming sense of responsibility and fears that I was not up to the task.

Even grocery shopping became a major juggling act; babysitters were out of the question. When I think back now, I'm not sure *how* I managed; I knew only that there was no choice but to put one foot in front of the other and move forward.

I met other parents of children with disabilities, and together we started a school for our children, lobbied for federal and state legislation, held fund-raising events, and hung on to each other when the energy just wouldn't come. Those other parents were my salvation; they knew me and my life because they lived their own variations of the same story. I learned how to ask for help and how to give it. I learned how to fight—for my child, for myself, and for others. I learned how to lobby a legislator and how to solicit for donations. I learned how to run a bingo game and how to write a successful grant.

I wasn't a supermom, nor was I always graceful about accepting my responsibility. One of the toughest feelings I had to admit was the resentment I felt toward Kimi. There were days when I actually hated her for making my life so difficult—for taking so long to eat, for being so heavy, for having another seizure when I thought we'd finally gotten the medication level right. I hated her, and I hated myself. I hated the doctors and the teachers. I felt guilty for failing to produce a perfect child, for not fighting the doctors in the beginning, for failing to keep my marriage together, and for sometimes having to ignore the "hold-me-Mommy" looks of my other children because there was so much to do.

After more than a year of nearly constant hospitalization for respiratory infections, my sweet Kimi died just before her seventh birthday. My friends were there for me; so was the school that was eventually named after her. It took almost another year before I felt safe enough to grieve for the loss of my child—and the grieving came with a vengeance that threatened my mental health. Today, more than twenty-five years later, I still miss her and still have moments when the guilt and sadness creep over me.

But Kimi gave me lasting gifts. She taught me about unconditional love and about perseverance. She never gave up—despite the fact that her every attempt to walk resulted in a fall. She never held back her love. When I finally looked in her direction after hours of racing around the house without even giving her a glance, she greeted me with a smile and open arms—ready to love me no matter what. Through her, my other children, who are now adults, have learned to judge others by who they are rather than who we expect them to be. Finally, Kimi taught me to appreciate little things—like a day without a seizure, or her silly giggle, or the total beauty of all three of my children asleep in their beds. She guided me into a thirty-four-year career which has given me back far more than I could ever have given.

I've never been a religious person, especially during those times when I was furious with God for visiting this burden on me. But I do believe that everything—every *person*—has a purpose and that most pain is followed by relief, even pleasure. I learned that my first job was to love my children and myself. I learned that *every* day—no matter how difficult—has its moments of wonder and joy.

I'm grateful to Kimi for showing me how to find and appreciate that joy and for helping me discover the strength inside myself that carried us all through the rough spots.

And I'm finally learning that last lesson that all parents of children with disabilities must learn—the ability to forgive myself and others. I'm starting to believe that I did everything I could for my child. I'm starting to let go of my anger at the neurologist who was the messenger of a diagnosis no one wanted. I've forgiven others within "the system" who, for the most part, did the best they could. And I've come to realize how grateful I am for the strength, joy, and satisfaction I've gained from all those lessons learned.

● ● ●

Donna Roberts first became involved in the disability community in Massachusetts when her first child, Kimberly Ann (1966–1972), was born with Cornelia deLange syndrome. This rare syn-

drome causes profound mental retardation, epilepsy, cerebral palsy, and heart and respiratory complications.

After moving to New Hampshire and giving birth to two other children, Keith (1968) and Kristin (1971), Donna founded a school for children with severe disabilities and was an expert witness in a successful class action deinstitutionalization lawsuit that resulted in the closing of Laconia (New Hampshire) State School and Training Center. In 1984, she finally went to college and graduated with a degree in Human Services from New Hampshire College.

Moving to Indiana in 1987, Donna resumed her involvement in the field of disabilities. She has served as the executive director of the United Cerebral Palsy Association of Greater Indiana for ten years. She spends most of her spare time with volunteer work and with her new grandson, Tyler.

RESOURCES FOR PARENTS AND FAMILY MEMBERS

Parent Training and Information Centers

Parent centers in each state provide training and information to parents of infants, toddlers, school-aged children, and young adults with disabilities and the professionals who work with their families. This assistance helps parents participate more effectively with professionals in meeting the educational needs of children and youth with disabilities. Contact the nearest PTI for information about early intervention, parent support groups, and other local services.

U.S. military families, *see* STOMP in Washington
Native American families, *see* Idaho
Resource information source:

National Parent Network on Disabilities
1130 17th Street N.W., Suite 400
Washington, DC 20036
(202) 463-2299 (voice & TTY)
npnd@cs.com
http://www.npnd.org

Alabama

Special Education Action
  Committee, Inc.
P.O. Box 161274
Mobile, AL 36616-2274
(334) 478-1208 (voice & TDD)
(334) 473-7877 (fax)
(800) 222-7322 in AL
seacofmobile@zebra.net
http://home.hiwaay.net/~seachsv/

Alaska

PARENTS, Inc.
4743 E. Northern Lights
  Boulevard
Anchorage, AK 99508
(907) 337-7678 (voice)
(907) 337-7629 (TDD)
(907) 337-7671 (fax)
(800) 478-7678 in AK
parents@parentsinc.org
http://www.parentsinc.org

American Samoa

American Samoa PAVE
P.O. Box 3432
Pago Pago, AS 96799
(011-684)-699-6946
(011-684)-699-6952 (fax)
SAMPAVE@samoatelco.com
http://www.taalliance.org/ptis/
  amsamoa/

Arizona

Pilot Parents of Southern
  Arizona
2600 N. Wyatt Drive
Tucson, AZ 85712

(520) 324-3150
(520) 324-3152
ppsa@pilotparents.org
www.pilotparents.org

RAISING Special Kids
4750 N. Black Canyon
  Highway, Suite 101
Phoenix, AZ 85017-3621
(602) 242-4366 (voice & TDD)
(602) 242-4306 (fax)
(800) 237-3007 in AZ

Arkansas

Arkansas Disability Coalition
1123 University Avenue, Suite
  225
Little Rock, AR 72204-1605
(501) 614-7020 (voice & TDD)
(501) 614-9082 (fax)
(800) 223-1330 in AR
adc@alltel.net
http://www.adcpti.org

FOCUS, Inc.
305 West Jefferson Avenue
Jonesboro, AR 72401
(870) 935-2750 (voice)
(870) 931-3755 (fax)
(888) 247-3755
focusinc@ipa.net
http://www.grnco.net/~norre/

California

DREDF
2212 Sixth Street
Berkeley, CA 94710
(510) 644-2555 (voice & TDD)

(510) 841-8645 (fax)
(800) 466-4232
dredf@dredf.org
http://www.dredf.org

Exceptional Family Support,
  Education and Advocacy
  Center
6402 Skyway
Paradise, CA 95969
(530) 876-8321
(530) 876-0346 (fax)
(888) 263-1311
sea@sunset.net
http://www.sea-center.org

Exceptional Parents Unlimited
4120 N. First Street
Fresno, CA 93726
(559) 229-2000
(559) 229-2956 (fax)
epu1@cybergate.com
http://www.exceptionalparents.org

Loving Your Disabled Child
4528 Crenshaw Boulevard
Los Angeles, CA 90043
(323) 299-2925
(323) 299-4373 (fax)
lydc@pacbell.net
http://www.lydc.org

Matrix
94 Galli Drive, Suite C
Novato, CA 94949
(415) 884-3535
(415) 884-3555 (fax)

(800) 578-2592
matrix@matrixparents.org
http://www.matrixparents.org

Parents Helping Parents of San
  Francisco
594 Monterey Boulevard
San Francisco, CA 94127-2416
(415) 841-8820
(415) 841-8824 (fax)
sfphp@earthlink.com

Parents Helping Parents of
  Santa Clara
3041 Olcott Street
Santa Clara, CA 95054-3222
(408) 727-5775 (voice)
(408) 727-7655 (TDD)
(408) 727-0182 (fax)
info@php.com
http://www.php.com

Parents of Watts
10828 Lou Dillon Avenue
Los Angeles, CA 90059
(323) 566-7556
(323) 569-3982 (fax)
egertonf@hotmail.com

Support for Families of
  Children with Disabilities
2601 Mission, #710
San Francisco, CA 94110-3111
(415) 282-7494
(415) 282-1226 (fax)
sfcdmiss@aol.com

TASK (Team of Advocates for
Special Kids)
100 W. Cerritos Avenue
Anaheim, CA 92805
(714) 533-8275
(714) 533-2533 (fax)
taskca@aol.com

TASK, San Diego
3750 Convoy Street, Suite 303
San Diego, CA 92111-3741
(619) 874-2386
(619) 874-2375 (fax)
tasksd1@aol.com

Vietnamese Parents of Disabled
Children Association, Inc.
7526 Syracuse Avenue
Stanton, CA 90680
(310) 370-6704
(310) 542-0522 (fax)
luyenchu@aol.com

Colorado

PEAK Parent Center, Inc.
6055 Lehman Drive, Suite 101
Colorado Springs, CO 80918
(719) 531-9400 (voice)
(719) 531-9403 (TDD)
(719) 531-9452 (fax)
(800) 284-0251
info@peakparent.org
http://www.peakparent.org

Connecticut

Connecticut Parent Advocacy
Center
338 Main Street
Niantic, CT 06357
(860) 739-3089 (voice & TDD)

(860) 739-7460 (fax; call first
to dedicate line)
(800) 445-2722 in CT
cpacinc@aol.com
http://members.aol.com/cpacinc/
cpac.htm

Delaware

Parent Information Center of
Delaware (PIC/DE)
700 Barksdale Road, Suite 16
Newark, DE 19711
(302) 366-0152 (voice)
(302) 366-0178 (TDD)
(302) 366-0276 (fax)
(888) 547-4412
picofdel@picofdel.org
http://www.picofdel.org

District of Columbia

Advocates for Justice and
Education
2041 Martin Luther King
Avenue, S.E., Suite 301
Washington, DC 20020
(202) 678-8060
(202) 678-8062 (fax)
(888) 327-8060
justice1@bellatlantic.net
http://www.aje.qpg.com/

Florida

Family Network on Disabilities
2735 Whitney Road
Clearwater, FL 33760-1610
(727) 523-1130
(727) 523-8687 (fax)
(800) 825-5736 in FL
fnd@fndfl.org
http://www.fndfl.org

Parent to Parent of Miami, Inc.
c/o Sunrise Community
9040 Sunset Drive, Suite G
Miami, FL 33173
(305) 271-9797
(305) 271-6628 (fax)
PtoP1086@aol.com

Georgia

Parents Educating Parents and
  Professionals for All Children
  (PEPPAC)
6613 E. Church Street, Suite
  100
Douglasville, GA 30134
(770) 577-7771
(770) 577-7774 (fax)
peppac@bellsouth.net
http://www.peppac.org

Hawaii

AWARE
200 N. Vineyard Boulevard,
  Suite 310
Honolulu, HI 96817
(808)536-9684 (voice)
(808) 536-2280 (voice & TTY)
(808) 537-6780 (fax)
(800) 533-9684
ldah@gte.net

Palau Parent Network
Center on Disability Studies,
  University of Hawaii
1833 Kala Kaua Avenue, #609
Honolulu, HI 96815
(808) 945-1432
(808) 945-1440 (fax)
dotty@hawaii.edu; patric@palaunet.
  com

Idaho

Idaho Parents Unlimited, Inc.
4696 Overland Road, Suite 568
Boise, ID 83705
(208) 342-5884 (voice & TDD)
(208) 342-1408 (fax)
(800) 242-4785
ipul@rmci.net
http://home.rmci.net/ipul

Native American Parent
  Training and Information
  Center
129 E. Third
Moscow, ID 83843
(208) 885-3500
famtog@moscow.com

Illinois

Designs for Change
6 N. Michigan Avenue, Suite
  1600
Chicago, IL 60602
(312) 857-9292 (voice)
(312) 857-1013 (TDD)
(312) 857-9299 (fax)
dfc1@aol.com
http://www.dfc1.org

Family Resource Center on
  Disabilities
20 E. Jackson Boulevard,
  Room 300
Chicago, IL 60604
(312) 939-3513 (voice)
(312) 939-3519 (TTY & TDY)
(312) 939-7297 (fax)
(800) 952-4199 in IL
frcdptiil@ameritech.net
http://www.ameritech.net/users/
  frcdptiil/index.html

Family T.I.E.S. Network
830 S. Spring
Springfield, IL 62704
(217) 544-5809
(217) 544-6018 (fax)
(800) 865-7842
ftiesn@aol.com
http://www.taalliance.org/ptis/fties/

National Center for Latinos
  with Disabilities
1915-17 S. Blue Island Avenue
Chicago, IL 60608
(312) 666-3393 (voice)
(312) 666-1788 (TTY)
(312) 666-1787 (fax)
(800) 532-3393
ncld@ncld.com
http://homepage.interaccess.com/
  ~ncld/

Indiana

IN*SOURCE
809 N. Michigan Street
South Bend, IN 46601-1036
(219) 234-7101
(219) 239-7275 (TDD)
(219) 234-7279 (fax)
(800) 332-4433 in IN
insourc1@aol.com
http://www.insource.org

Iowa

Access for Special Kids (ASK)
321 E. 6th Street
Des Moines, IA 50309
(515) 243-1713
(515) 243-1902 (fax)
(800) 450-8667
ptiiowa@aol.com
http://www.taalliance.org/ptis/ia/

Kansas

Families ACT
555 N. Woodlawn
Wichita, KS 67203
(316) 685-1821
(316) 685-0768 (fax)
nina@mhasck.org
http://www.mhasck.org

Families Together, Inc.
3340 W. Douglas, Suite 102
Wichita, KS 67203
(316) 945-7747
(316) 945-7795 (fax)
(888) 815-6364
fmin@feist.com
http://www.kansas.net/~family/

Kentucky

Kentucky Special Parent
  Involvement Network (KY-
  SPIN)
2210 Goldsmith Lane, Suite
  118
Louisville, KY 40218
(502) 456-0923
(502) 456-0893 (fax)
(800) 525-7746
spininc@aol.com

Louisiana

Pyramid Parent Training
  Program
4101 Fontainbleau Drive
New Orleans, LA 70125
(504) 827-0610
(504) 827-2999 (fax)
dmarkey404@aol.com

Project PROMPT
4323 Division Street, Suite 110
Metairie, LA 70002-3179
(504) 888-9111
(504) 888-0246 (fax)
(800) 766-7736
fhfgno@ix.netcom.com
http://www.projectprompt.com

Maine

Special Needs Parent Info
  Network
P.O. Box 2067
Augusta, ME 04338-2067
(207) 582-2504
(207) 582-3638 (fax)
(800) 870-SPIN in ME
jlachance@mpf.org
http://www.mpf.org

Maryland

Parents Place of Maryland, Inc.
7484 Candlewood Road, Suite S
Hanover, MD 21076-1306
(410) 859-5300 (voice & TDD)
(410) 859-5301 (fax)
info@ppmd.org
http://www.ppmd.org

Massachusetts

Federation for Children with
  Special Needs
1135 Tremont Street, Suite 420
Boston, MA 02120-2140
(617) 236-7210 (voice & TTY)
(617) 572-2094 (fax)
(800) 331-0688 in MA
fcsninfo@fcsn.org
http://www.fcsn.org/

Michigan

CAUSE
3303 W. Saginaw, Suite F-1
Lansing, MI 48917-2303
(517) 886-9167 (voice & TDD
  & TDY)
(517) 886-9775 (fax)
(800) 221-9105 in MI
info-cause@voyager.net
http://www.pathwaynet.com/cause/

Parents Are Experts
23077 Greenfield Road, Suite 205
Southfield, MI 48075-3745
(248) 557-5070 (voice & TDD)
(248) 557-4456 (fax)
(800) 827-4843
ucp@ameritech.net
http://www.taalliance.org/ptis/
  mi-parents/

Minnesota

PACER Center, Inc.
4826 Chicago Avenue South
Minneapolis, MN 55417-1098
(612) 827-2966 (voice)
(612) 827-7770 (TTY)
(612) 827-3065 (fax)
(800) 537-2237 in MN
pacer@pacer.org
http://www.pacer.org

Mississippi

Parent Partners
1900 N. West Street, Suite C-100
Jackson, MS 39202
(601) 714-5707
(601) 714-4025 (fax)
(800) 366-5707 in MS
ptiofms@misnet.com
http://www.taalliance.org/ptis/ms/

Project Empower
136 S. Poplar Avenue
Greenville, MS 38701
(601) 332-4852
(601) 332-1622 (fax)
(800) 337-4852
empower@tecinfo.com

Missouri

Missouri Parents Act
2100 S. Brentwood, Suite G
Springfield, MO 65804
(417) 882-7434
(417) 882-8413 (fax)
(800) 743-7634 in MO
ptijcj@aol.com
http://www.crn.org/mpact/

Montana

Parents Let's Unite for Kids
516 N. 32nd Street
Billings, MT 59101
(406) 255-0540
(406) 255-0523 (fax)
(800) 222-7585 in MT
plukinfo@pluk.org
http://www.pluk.org

Nebraska

Nebraska Parents Center
1941 S. 42nd Street, #122
Omaha, NE 68105-2942
(402) 346-0525 (voice & TDD)
(402) 346-5253 (fax)
(800) 284-8520
gdavis@neparentcenter.org
http://www.neparentcenter.org

Nevada

Nevada Parents Encouraging
  Parents (PEP)
2810 W. Charleston Boulevard,
  Suite G-68
Quall Park IV
Las Vegas, NV 89102
(702) 388-8899
(702) 388-2966 (fax)
(800) 216-5188
nvpep@vegas.infi.net
http://www.nvpep.org

New Hampshire

Parent Information Center
P.O. Box 2405
Concord, NH 03302-2405
(603) 224-7005 (voice &
  TDD)
(603) 224-4379 (fax)
(800) 232-0986 in NH
picnh@aol.com
http://www.taalliance.org/ptis/nhpic/

New Jersey

Statewide Parent Advocacy
  Network (SPAN)
35 Halsey Street, 4th Floor
Newark, NJ 07102
(973) 642-8100
(973) 642-8080 (fax)
(800) 654-SPAN
span@spannj.org
http://www.spannj.org

New Mexico

Parents Reaching Out, Project
  ADOBE
1000-A Main Street NW
Los Lunas, NM 87031
(505) 865-3700 (voice & TDD)
(505) 865-3737 (fax)
(800) 524-5176 in NM
nmproth@aol.com
http://www.parentsreachingout.org

New York

The Advocacy Center
277 Alexander Street, Suite 500
Rochester, NY 14607
(716) 546-1700
(716) 546-7069 (fax)
(800) 650-4967 in NY
advocacy@frontiernet.net
http://www.advocacycenter.com

Advocates for Children of NY
151 W. 50th Street, 5th Floor
New York, NY 10001
(212) 947-9779
(212) 947-9790 (fax)
info@advocatesforchildren.org
http://www.advocatesforchildren.org

Resources for Children with
  Special Needs, Inc.
200 Park Avenue South, Suite
  816
New York, NY 10003
(212) 677-4650
(212) 254-4070 (fax)
resourcesnyc@prodigy.net
http://www.resourcesnyc.org

Sinergia/Metropolitan Parent
  Center
15 West 65th Street, 6th Floor
New York, NY 10023
(212) 496-1300
(212) 496-5608 (fax)
Sinergia@panix.com
http://www.panix.com/~sinergia/

United We Stand
c/o Casa del Barrio
728 Driggs Avenue
Brooklyn, NY 11211
(718) 302-4313, ext. 562
(718) 302-4315 (fax)
uwsofny@aol.com
http://www.taalliance.org/ptis/uws/

North Carolina

ECAC, Inc.
P.O. Box 16
Davidson, NC 28036
(704) 892-1321
(704) 892-5028 (fax)
(800) 962-6817 in NC
ECAC1@aol.com
http://www.ecac-parentcenter.org/

North Dakota

ND Pathfinder Parent Training
  and Information Center
Arrowhead Shopping Center
1600 2nd Avenue S.W,, Suite 19
Minot, ND 58701-3459
(701) 837-7500 (voice)
(701) 837-7501 (TDD)
701-837-7548 (fax)
(800) 245-5840 in ND
ndpath01@minot.ndak.net
http://www.pathfinder.minot.com

Ohio

Child Advocacy Center
1821 Summit Road, Suite 303
Cincinnati, OH 45237
(513) 821-2400
(513) 821-2442 (fax)
CADCenter@aol.com

OCECD
Bank One Building
165 W. Center Street, Suite 302
Marion, OH 43302-3741
(740) 382-5452 (voice & TDD)
(740) 383-6421 (fax)
(800) 374-2806
ocecd@gte.net
http://www.taalliance.org/PTIs/regohio/

Oklahoma

Parents Reaching Out in OK
1917 S. Harvard Avenue
Oklahoma City, OK 73128
(405) 681-9710
(405) 685-4006 (fax)
(800) 759-4142
prook1@aol.com
http://www.taalliance.org/ptis/ok/

Oregon

Oregon COPE Project
999 Locust Street N.E.
Salem, OR 97303
(503) 581-8156 (voice & TDD)
(503) 391-0429 (fax)
(888) 505-COPE
orcope@open.org
http://www.open.org/~orcope

Pennsylvania

Hispanos Unidas para Niños
con Impedimentos
(Hispanics United for Special
Needs Children)
Buena Vista Plaza
166 W. Lehigh Avenue, Suite
101
Philadelphia, PA 19133-3838
(215) 425-6203
(215) 425-6204 (fax)
hupni@aol.com

Parent Education Network
2107 Industrial Highway
York, PA 17402-2223
(717) 600-0100 (voice & TTY)
(717) 600-8101 (fax)
(800) 522-5827 in PA
(800) 441-5028 (Spanish in PA)
pen@parentednet.org
http://www.parentednet.org

Parents Union for Public Schools
1315 Walnut Street, Suite 1124
Philadelphia, PA 19107
(215) 546-1166
(215) 731-1688 (fax)
ParentsU@aol.com

Puerto Rico

APNI
P.O. Box 21301
Ponce de Leon 724
San Juan, PR 00928-1301
(787) 250-4552
(787) 765-0345 (fax)
(800) 981-8492
(800) 949-4232
apnipr@prtc.net

Rhode Island

RI Parent Information
  Network
175 Main Street
Pawtucket, RI 02860
(401) 727-4144 (voice)
(401) 727-4151 (TDD)
(401) 727-4040 (fax)
(800) 464-3399 in RI
collins@ripin.org
http://www.ripin.org/

South Carolina

Parent Training & Resource
  Center
c/o Family Resource Center
135 Rutledge Avenue
P.O. Box 250567
Charleston, SC 29425
(843) 876-1519
(843) 876-1518 (fax)
mccarthyb@musc.edu

PRO-PARENTS
2712 Middleburg Drive, Suite
  203
Columbia, SC 29204
(803) 779-3859 (voice)
(803) 252-4513 (fax)
(800) 759-4776 in SC
pro-parents@aol.com
http://community.columbiatoday.
  com/realcities/proparents

South Dakota

South Dakota Parent
  Connection
3701 W. 49th Street, Suite 200B
Sioux Falls, SD 57106

(605) 361-3171 (voice & TDD)
(605) 361-2928 (fax)
(800) 640-4553 in SD
bpete@dakota.net
http://www.sdparent.org

Tennessee

Support and Training for
  Exceptional Parents, Inc.
  (STEP)
424 E. Bernard Avenue, Suite 3
Greeneville, TN 37745
(423) 639-0125 (voice)
(636) 8217 (TDD)
(423) 636-8217 (fax)
(800) 280-STEP in TN
tnstep@aol.com
http://www.tnstep.org

Texas

El Valle Community Parent
  Resource Center
530 S. Texas Boulevard, Suite J
Weslaco, TX 78596
(956) 969-3611
(956) 969-8761 (fax)
(800) 680-0255 in TX
texasfiestaedu@acnet.net
http://www.tfepoder.org

Grassroots Consortium
P.O. Box 61628
Houston, TX 77207-6958
(713) 734-5355
(713) 643-6291 (fax)
speckids@pdq.net
http://www.gcod.org

The Arc of Texas in the Rio
Grande Valley
Parents Supporting Parents
Network
601 N. Texas Boulevard
Weslaco, TX 78596
(956) 447-8408
(956) 973-9503 (fax)
(888) 857-8688
dmeraz@gtemail.net
http://www.thearcoftexas.org

Partners Resource Network,
Inc.
1090 Longfellow Drive, Suite B
Beaumont, TX 77706-4819
(409) 898-4684 (voice & TDD)
(409) 898-4869 (fax)
(800) 866-4726 in TX
txprn@pnx.com
http://www.PartnersTX.org

Project PODER
1017 N. Main Avenue, Suite
207
San Antonio, TX 78212
(210) 222-2637
(210) 475-9283 (fax)
(800) 682-9747 in TX
poder@tfepoder.org
http://www.tfepoder.org

Utah

Utah Parent Center
2290 E. 4500 Street, Suite 110
Salt Lake City, UT 84117-4428
(801) 272-1051
(801) 272-8907 (fax)
(800) 468-1160 in UT
upc@inconnect.com
http://www.utahparentcenter.org

Vermont

Vermont Parent Information
Center
1 Mill Street, Suite A7
Burlington, VT 05401
(802) 658-5315 (voice & TDD)
(802) 658-5395 (fax)
(800) 639-7170 in VT
vpic@together.net
http://homepages.together.net/~vpic

Virgin Islands

VI Find
#2 Nye Gade
St. Thomas, US VI 00802
(340) 774-1662
(340) 774-1662 (fax)
vifind@islands.vi
http://www.taalliance.org/ptis/vifind/

Virginia

PADDA, Inc.
813 Forrest Drive, Suite 3
Newport News, VA 23606
(757) 591-9119
(757) 591-8990 (fax)
(888) 337-2332
webmaster@padda.org
http://www.padda.org

Parent Educational Advocacy
Training Center
6320 Augusta Drive
Springfield, VA 22150
(703) 923-0010
(703) 923-0030 (fax)
(800) 869-6782 in VA
partners@peatc.org
http://www.peatc.org

Washington

Parent to Parent Power
1118 S. 142nd Street
Tacoma, WA 98444
(253) 531-2022
(253) 538-1126 (fax)
ylink@aa.net

PAVE/STOMP
6316 S. 12th Street
Tacoma, WA 98465
(253) 565-2266 (voice &
  TTY)
(253) 566-8052 (fax)
(800) 572-7368 in WA
wapave9@washingtonpave.org
http://washingtonpave.org/stomp.
  html

West Virginia

West Virginia PTI
371 Broaddus Avenue
Clarksburg, WV 26301
(304) 624-1436 (voice & TTY)
(304) 624-1438
(800) 281-1436 in WV
wvpti@aol.com
http://www.iolinc.net/wvpti

Wisconsin

Native American Family
  Empowerment Center
Great Lakes Inter-Tribal
  Council, Inc.
2932 Highway 47 North
P.O. Box 9
Lac du Flambeau, WI 54538
(715) 588-3324

(715) 588-7900
(800) 472-7207 in WI
drosin@newnorth.net

Parent Education Project of
  Wisconsin
2192 S. 60th Street
West Allis, WI 53219-1568
(414) 328-5520 (voice)
(414) 328-5525 (TDD)
(414) 328-5530
(800) 231-8382 in WI
PMColletti@aol.com
http://members.aol.com/pepofwi/

Wisconsin Family Assistance
  Center for Education,
  Training and Support
2714 N. Dr. Martin Luther
  King Drive, Suite E
Milwaukee, WI 53212
(414) 374-4645
(414) 374-4635 (TTD)
(414) 374-4655 (fax)
wifacets@execpc.com

Wyoming

Parent Information Center
5 N. Lobban
Buffalo, WY 82834
(307) 684-2277 (voice & TDD)
(307) 684-5314
(800) 660-9742 in WY
tdawsonpic@vcn.com
http://www.wpic.org

Parent-Matching Resources

These organizations provide services that help "match" parents of children with rare disorders or parents who have specialized concerns about their children.

Alliance of Genetic Support
  Groups
4301 Connecticut Avenue,
  N.W., #404
Washington, DC 20008-2304
(202) 966-5557
(202) 966-8553 ((fax))
(800) 336-GENE
info@geneticalliance.org
http://www.geneticalliance.org

Association of Birth Defect
  Children (ABDC)–National
  Birth Defect Registry
930 Woodcock Road, Suite 225
Orlando FL 32803
(800) 313-ABDC
(407) 245-7035
abdc@birthdefects.org
http://birthdefects.org

MUMS: National Parent to
  Parent Network
150 Custer Court
Green Bay, WI 54301-1243
(920) 336-5333
(920) 339-0995 ((fax))
(877) 336-5333 (parents only
  please)
mums@netnet.net
http://www.netnet.net/mums/

National Parent to Parent
  Support and Information
  System (NPPSIS)
P.O. Box 907
Blue Ridge, GA 30513
(706) 374-3822
(706) 374-3826
(800) 651-1151 for parents
nppsis@ellijay.com
http://www.nppsis.org

Parent-to-Parent Web Board
The Family Village
Waisman Center
University of
  Wisconsin–Madison
1500 Highland Avenue
Madison, WI 53705-2280
familyvillage@waisman.wisc.edu
http://www.familyvillage.wisc.edu/

Early Intervention, ages 0–2

The Program for Infants and Toddlers with Disabilities, Part C of Individuals with Disabilities Act (IDEA), is a federal grant program that assists states in operating a comprehensive statewide program of early intervention services for infants and toddlers with disabilities, ages birth through 2 years, and their families. In order for a state to participate in the program it must assure that early intervention will be available to every eligible child and its family.

Note: States have some discretion in setting the criteria for child eligibility, including whether or not to serve at-risk children. As a result, definitions of eligibility differ significantly from state to state.

Resource information source:

National Early Childhood
  Technical Assistance System
Frank Porter Graham Child
  Development Center
University of North Carolina at
  Chapel Hill
137 E. Franklin Street, Suite 500
Chapel Hill, NC 27514-3628
(919) 962-2001
(919) 962-8300 (TDD)
(919) 966-7463 (fax)
nectas@unc.edu
http://www.nectas.unc.edu/

Alabama

Early Intervention Program
2129 E. South Boulevard
P.O. Box 11586
Montgomery, AL 36111-0586
(334) 613-2393
(334) 613-3541 (fax)
http://www.rehab.state.al.us/
  intervention.html

Alaska

Maternal and Child Health
State Department of Health
  and Social Services
1231 Gambell Street
Anchorage, AK 99501-4627
(907) 269-3419
(907) 269-3465 (fax)

American Samoa

Department of Health
Government of American
  Samoa
Pago Pago, AS 96799
(684) 633-4929
(684) 633-2167 (fax)

Arizona

Arizona Early Intervention Program
Department of Economic Security
3839 North 3rd Street, Suite 304
Site Code #801.A-6
Phoenix, AZ 85012
(602) 532-9960 x113
(602) 200-9820 (fax)

Arkansas

Developmental Delay Services,
  Department of Human
  Services
Donaghey Plaza North
7th and Main Streets
P.O. Box 1437, Slot 2520
Little Rock, AR 72203-1437
(501) 682-8699
(501) 682-8687 (fax)

Bureau of Indian Affairs

Branch of Exceptional
  Education
Bureau of Indian Affairs
MS 3512, MIB-Code 523

1849 C Street N.W.
Washington, DC 20240-4000
(202) 208-4975
(202) 273-0030 (fax)

California

Early Intervention Program
Department of Developmental
  Services
1600 9th Street, Room 310
P.O. Box 944202
Sacramento, CA 95814
(916) 654-2716
(916) 654-3255 (fax)
http://www.dds.ca.gov/prev004.htm

Colorado

Prevention Initiatives
Colorado Department of
  Education
201 E. Colfax Avenue, Room 301
Denver, CO 80203
(303) 866-6709
(303) 866-6662 (fax)

Connecticut

Birth to Three System
Department of Mental
  Retardation
460 Capitol Avenue
Hartford, CT 06106-1308
(860) 418-6147
(860) 418-6003 (fax)
http://www.birth23.org/

Delaware

Division of Management
  Services
Department of Health and
  Social Services
1901 N. Dupont Highway,
  Room 204
New Castle, DE 19720
(302) 577-4647
(302) 577-4083 (fax)

District of Columbia

DC-EIP Services
Office of Early Childhood
  Development
609 H Street N.E., 5th Floor
Washington, DC 20002
(202) 698-4660
(202) 727-5971 (fax)

Florida

Early Intervention Unit
Children's Medical Services
Department of Health
2020 Capital Circle S.E., BIN
  # A06
Tallahassee, FL 32399-1700
(850) 245-4444
(850) 414-7350 (fax)

Georgia

Children With Special Needs
  Unit
Babies Can't Wait Program
Division of Public Health,
  Family Health Branch
2 Peachtree Street N.E,, 11-204
Atlanta, GA 30303-3186

(404) 657-2727
(404) 657-2763 (fax)
http://www.ph.dhr.state.ga.us/bcw/
bcw.htm

Guam

Vince Leon Guerrero, Associate
Superintendent
Division of Special Education
Department of Education
P.O. Box DE
Agana, GU 96932
(671) 475-0549
(671) 475-0562 (fax)

Hawaii

Zero-to-3 Hawaii Project
Department of Health
Pan Am Building
1600 Kapiolani Boulevard,
Suite 1401
Honolulu, HI 96814
(808) 957-0066
(808) 946-5222 (fax)

Idaho

Infant/Toddler Program
Department of Health and
Welfare
450 W. State Street, 5th Floor
P.O. Box 83720
Boise, ID 83720-0036
(208) 334-5523
(208) 334-6664 (fax)
http://www2.state.id.us/dhw/
InfToddler/index.htm

Illinois

Department of Human Services
Bureau of Early Intervention
623 E. Adams, 2nd Floor
P.O. Box 19429
Springfield, IL 62794-9429
(217) 782-1981
(217) 524-6248 (fax)

Indiana

First Steps
Bureau of Child Development
Division of Family and
Children
402 W. Washington Street, #W-
386
Indianapolis, IN 46204
(317) 232-2429
(317) 232-7948 (fax)
Web site: http://www.state.in.us/
fssa/first_step/

Iowa

Iowa's System of Early
Intervention Services
Bureau of Children, Family,
and Community Services
Grimes State Office Building,
3rd Floor
Des Moines, IA 50319-0146
(515) 281-7145
(515) 242-6019 (fax)

Kansas

Infant Toddler Program
Department of Health and
  Environment
Landon State Office Building
900 S.W. Jackson Street, Suite
  1052-S
Topeka, KS 66612-1290
(785) 296-6135
(785) 296-8626 (fax)
http://www.kdhe.state.ks.us/bcyf/
  its/index.html

Kentucky

Infant-Toddler Program
Division of Mental Retardation
Department of MH and MR
  Services
100 Fair Oaks Lane, 4E-E
Frankfort, KY 40621-0001
(502) 564-7722
(502) 564-0438 (fax)

Louisiana

Office of Special Education
  Services
State Department of Education
P.O. Box 94064
Baton Rouge, LA 70804-9064
(225) 342-3730
(225) 342-5297 (fax)
http://www.doe.state.la.us/DOE/
  specialpop/ITPDisab/ITPDhome.asp

Maine

Child Development Services
Department of Education
State House Station #146
Augusta, ME 04333

(207) 287-3272
(207) 287-3884 (fax)

Maryland

MD Infant/Toddler/Preschool
  Services Division
Division of Special Education
State Department of Education
200 W. Baltimore Street
Baltimore, MD 21201
(410) 767-0261
(410) 333-2661 (fax)
http://www.msde.state.md.us/

Massachusetts

Early Intervention Services
Department of Public Health,
  4th Floor
250 Washington Street
Boston, MA 02108-4619
(617) 624-5969
(617) 624-5990 (fax)

Michigan

Early On Michigan
Office of Special Education and
  EI Services
Michigan Department of
  Education
P.O. Box 30008
Lansing, MI 48909
(517) 335-4865
(517) 373-7504 (fax)
http://www.earlyon-mi.org/

Minnesota

Interagency Early Intervention
Project
Department of Children,
Families and Learning
1500 Highway 36 West
Roseville, MN 55113-4266
(651) 582-8436
(651) 582-8494 (fax)
http://cfl.state.mn.us/ecfi/

Mississippi

Infant and Toddler Program
Mississippi State Department
of Health
2423 N. State Street, Room
105A
P.O. Box 1700
Jackson, MS 39215 1700
(601) 576-7427
(601) 576-7540 (fax)

Missouri

Early Childhood Special
Education
Department of Elementary and
Secondary Education
State Department of Education
P.O. Box 480
Jefferson City, MO 65102-0480
(573) 751-0185
(573) 526-4404 (fax)
http://www.dese.state.mo.us/
divspeced

Montana

Developmental Disabilities
Program
Division of Disability Services
Department of Public Health
and Human Services
P.O. Box 4210
Helena, MT 59604-4210
(406) 444-4181
(406) 444-0230 (fax)
http://www.dphhs.state.mt.us/dsd/
index.htm

Nebraska

Nebraska Department of
Health and Human Services
Special Services for Children
and Adults (Early Intervention)
301 Centennial Mall South
P.O. Box 95044
Lincoln, NE 68509
(402) 471-9329
(402) 471-6252 (fax)
http://www.nde.state.ne.us/ECH/
ECSE/ecse.html

Nevada

Janelle Mulvenon, Clinical
Program Manager
Community Connections
Division of Child and Family
Services
3987 S. McCarran Boulevard
Reno, NV 89502
(775) 688-2284
(775) 688-2558 (fax)

New Hampshire

Family Centered Early
  Supports and Services
Department of Health and
  Human Services
Division of Developmental
  Services
105 Pleasant Street
Concord, NH 03301
(603) 271-5122
(603) 271-5166 (fax)

New Jersey

Early Intervention Program
Department of Health and
  Senior Services
Division of Family Health
  Services
P.O. Box 364
Trenton, NJ 08625-0364
(609) 777-7734
(609) 292-3580 (fax)

New Mexico

Cathy Stevenson, Part C
  Coordinator
Long Term Services Division
Department of Health
1190 Street Francis Drive
P.O. Box 26110
Santa Fe, NM 87502-6110
(505) 827-0119
(505) 827-2455 (fax)
http://cdd.unm.edu/ec/doh.html

New York

Early Intervention Program
State Department of Health
Corning Tower, Room 208
Empire State Plaza
Albany, NY 12237-0618
(518) 473-7016
(518) 473-8673 (fax)
http://www.health.state.ny.us/
  nysdoh/eip/index.htm

North Carolina

Early Intervention Section
Division of Educational
  Services
Dobbin Building
2302 Mail Service Center
Raleigh, NC 27699-2302
(919) 715-7500 ext.233
(919) 733-9455 (fax)

North Dakota

Developmental Disabilities Unit
Department of Human Services
600 S. 2nd Street, Suite 1A
Bismarck, ND 58504-5729
(701) 328-8936
(701) 328-8969 (fax)

Northern Mariana Islands

CNMI Public Schools
P.O. Box 1370 CK
Saipan, MP 96950
(670) 664-3754
(670) 664-3796 (fax)

Ohio

Bureau of EI Services
State Department of Health
P.O. Box 118
Columbus, OH 43266-0118
(614) 644-8389
(614) 728-9163 (fax)

Oklahoma

Special Education Office,
  Department of Education
Oliver Hodge Memorial
  Education Building, 4th Floor
2500 N. Lincoln Boulevard
Oklahoma City, OK 73105-
  4599
(405) 521-4880
(405) 522-3503 (fax)
http://sde.state.ok.us/pro/ei.html

Oregon

Early Intervention /Early
  Childhood Special Education
Oregon State Department of
  Education
Public Services Building
255 Capitol Street NE
Salem, OR 97310-0203
(503) 378-3598 X651
(503) 373-7968 (fax)

Palau

Bureau of Education
Republic of Palau
P.O. Box 189
Koror, Palau, PW 96940
(011-680) 488-2537
(011-680) 488-2830 (fax)

Pennsylvania

Division of Early Intervention
  Services
Office of Mental Retardation
Department of Public Welfare
P.O. Box 2675
Harrisburg, PA 17105-2675
(717) 783-4873
(717) 787-6583 (fax)

Puerto Rico

Part C Program
Department of Health
Office of the Secretary
Call Box 70184
San Juan, PR 00936
(787) 274-5659
(787) 274-3301 (fax)

Rhode Island

Rhode Island Department of
  Health
Division of Family Health
Cannon Building, Room 302
3 Capitol Hill
Providence, RI 02908-5097
(401) 222-5926
(401) 222-1442 (fax)
http://www.health.state.ri.us/

South Carolina

BabyNet
Division of Community Health
  Services
Department of Health and
  Environmental Control
Robert Mills Complex, Box
  101106

Columbia, SC 29201
(803) 898-0591
(803) 898-0389 (fax)
http://www.scbabynet.org/

South Dakota

Office of Special Education
700 Governors Drive
Pierre, SD 57501
(605) 773-4478
(605) 773-6846 (fax)

Tennessee

Office of Special Education
State Department of Education
Andrew Johnson Tower, 5th
  Floor
710 James Robertson Parkway
Nashville, TN 37243-0375
(615) 741-3537
(615) 532-9412 (fax)
http://child.etsu.edu/center/
  projects/teis/index.htm

Texas

Texas ECI Program
Brown-Heatly State Office
  Building
4900 N. Lamar
Austin, TX 78751-2399
(512) 424-6754
(512) 424-6749 (fax)
http://www.eci.state.tx.us/

Utah

Baby Watch Early Intervention
State Department of Health
P.O. Box 144720
Salt Lake City, UT 84114-4720
(801) 584-8441
(801) 584-8496 (fax)

Vermont

Family, Infant and Toddler
  Project
P.O. Box 70
Burlington, VT 05402
(802) 651-1786
(802) 863-7635 (fax)
http://www.state.vt.us/health/hi/
  cshn/fitp/fitp.htm

Virgin Islands

Birth to Three Project
Charles Harwood Complex
Christiansted
3500 Richmond
St. Croix, VI 00820-4370
(340) 773-1311 X3006
(340) 773-9376 (fax)

Virginia

Infant and Toddler Program
Department of MH/MR/SA
  Services
P.O. Box 1797
Richmond, VA 23218
(804) 371-6592
(804) 371-7959 (fax)
http://www.dmhmrsas.state.va.us/
  vababiescantwait/

Washington

Infant Toddler Early
Intervention Program
Department of Social and
Health Services
12th and Franklin Streets
P.O. Box 45201
Olympia, WA 98504-5201
(360) 902-8492
(360) 902-8497 (fax)
http://www.wa.gov/dshs/iteip/iteip.
html

West Virginia

Early Intervention Program
Office of Maternal and Child
Health
Department of Health and
Human Resources
1116 Quarrier Street
Charleston, WV 25301
(304) 558-6311
(304) 558-4984 (fax)

Wisconsin

Birth to 3 Program
Division of Supportive Living
Department of Health and
Family Services
P.O. Box 7851
Madison, WI 53370-7851
(608) 267-3270
(608) 261-6752 (fax)
http://www.dhfs.state.wi.us/
disabilities/

Wyoming

Division of Developmental
Disabilities
1413 First Floor West
Herschler Building
122 W. 25th Street
Cheyenne, WY 82002-0050
(307) 777-6972
(307) 777-6047 (fax)
http://ddd.state.wy.us/

Early Intervention, ages 3–5

The Preschool Grants Program, authorized under Section 619 of Part B of IDEA, was established in 1981 to provide grants to states to serve young children with disabilities, ages 3 through 5 years.

Resource information source:

National Early Childhood
Technical Assistance System
Frank Porter Graham Child
Development Center
University of North Carolina
at Chapel Hill
137 E. Franklin Street, Suite
500
Chapel Hill, NC 27514-3628
(919) 962-2001
(919) 962-8300 (TDD)
(919) 966-7463 (fax)
http://www.nectas.unc.edu/

Alabama

Program for Exceptional
  Children
State Department of Education
Gordon Persons Building,
  Room 3346
P.O. Box 302101
Montgomery, AL 36130-2101
(334) 242-8114
(334) 242-9192 (fax)

Alaska

State Department of Education
801 W. Tenth Street, Suite 200
Juneau, AK 99801-1894
(907) 465-2970
(907) 465-2806 (fax)

American Samoa

Special Education Division
Department of Education
P.O. Box 434
Pago Pago, AS 96799
(684) 258-2416
(684) 633-1641 (fax)

Arizona

Division of Special Education
Arizona Department of
  Education
1535 W. Jefferson Street
Phoenix, AZ 85007
(602) 542-4013
(602) 542-5404 (fax)
http://www.state.az.us/

Arkansas

Special Education Section
State Department of Education
4 Capitol Mall, Room 105-C
Little Rock, AR 72201
(501) 682-4225
(501) 682-5168 (fax)

Bureau of Indian Affairs

Branch of Exceptional
  Education
Bureau of Indian Affairs
MS 3512, MIB-Code 523
1849 C Street N.W.
Washington, DC 20240-4000
(202) (208) 4975
(202) 273-0030 (fax)

California

Special Education Division
State Department of Education
515 L Street, Suite 270
Sacramento, CA 95814
(916) 327-4216
(916) 327-3706 (fax)

Colorado

Prevention Initiatives
Early Childhood Initiatives
Colorado Department of
  Education
201 E. Colfax Avenue, Room
  306
Denver, CO 80203-1799
(303) 866-6712
(303) 866-6662 (fax)

Connecticut

State Department of Education
25 Industrial Park Road
Middletown, CT 06457
(860) 807-2054
(860) 807-2062 (fax)
http://www.state.ct.us/sde/early/
index.htm

Delaware

Dept of Public Instruction
Townsend Building
P.O. Box 1402
Dover, DE 19903-1402
(302) 739-4667
(302) 739-2388 (fax)
http://www.doe.state.de.us/
exceptional_child/Early%20
Childhood%20Site/
earlychildhoodhome.htm

District of Columbia

DC Public Schools, 6th Floor
Webb School
1375 Mt. Olive Road N.E.
Washington, DC 20002
(202) 724-6676

Federated States of Micronesia

Division of Education
Department of Health,
Education and Social Affairs
P.O. Box PS87, Pohnpei State
Palikir, Pohnpei, FM 96941
(691) 320-2302
(691) 320-5500 (fax)

Florida

Division of Public Schools
Department of Education and
Community Services
325 W. Gaines Street, Room 614
Tallahassee, FL 32399-0400
(850) 488-1106
(850) 922-7088 (fax)

Georgia

Department for Exceptional
Students
State Department of Education
1870 Twin Towers East
Atlanta, GA 30334-5010
(404) 657-9955
(404) 651-6457 (fax)

Guam

Division of Special Education
Department of Education
P.O. Box DE
Agana, GU 96932
(671) 475-0549
(671) 475-0562 (fax)

Hawaii

Special Needs Branch
Hawaii Department of
Education
Building C, Room 102
637 18th Avenue
Honolulu, HI 96816
(808) 733-4840
(808) 733-4404 (fax)

Idaho

Bureau of Special Education
Idaho Department of
  Education
650 W. State Street
P.O. Box 83720
Boise, ID 83720-0027
(208) 332-6915
(208) 334-4664 (fax)
http://www.sde.state.id.us/SpecialEd/

Illinois

Division of Early Childhood
  Education
State Board of Education
100 N. First Street, E-230
Springfield, IL 62777-0001
(217) 524-4835
(217) 785-7849 (fax)
http://www.isbe.state.il.us/

Indiana

Division of Special Education
Indiana Department of
  Education
State House, Room 229
Indianapolis, IN 46204-2798
(317) 232-0567
(317) 232-0589 (fax)

Iowa

Bureau of Children, Family,
  and Community Services
State Department of Education
Grimes State Office Building
Des Moines, IA 50319-0146
(515) 281-5502
(515) 242-6019 (fax)

Kansas

Special Education
  Administration
Department of Education
120 E. 10th Avenue
Topeka, KS 66612-1182
(785) 296-1944
(785) 296-1413 (fax)
http://www.ksbe.state.ks.us/
  specialeducation

Kentucky

Division of Preschool Services
Department of Education
1711 Capitol Plaza Tower
Frankfort, KY 40601
(502) 564-7056
(502) 564-6952 (fax)
http://www.kde.state.ky.us/

Louisiana

Office of Special Education
  Services
State Department of Education
P.O. Box 94064
Baton Rouge, LA 70804-9064
(225) 342-3730
(225) 342-5297 (fax)
http://www.doe.state.la.us/DOE/
  specialpop/ITPDisab/ITPDhome.asp

Maine

Child Development Services
Department of Education
State House Station, #146
Augusta, ME 04333
(207) 287-3272
(207) 287-3884 (fax)

Marshall Islands

Ministry of Education
Republic of the Marshall Islands
P.O. Box 3179
Majuro, MH 96960
(692) 625-5261
(692) 625-3861 (fax)

Maryland

Division of Special Education
State Department of Education
200 W. Baltimore Street
Baltimore, MD 21201
(410) 767-0234
(410) 333-2661 (fax)

Massachusetts

Bureau of Early Childhood
  Programs
Massachusetts Department of
  Education
350 Main Street
Malden, MA 02148-5023
(781) 338-6357
(781) 338-3394 (fax)
http://www.doe.mass.edu/

Michigan

Office of Special Education and
  Early Intervention Services
Michigan Department of
  Education
P.O. Box 30008
Lansing, MI 48909
(517) 241-2591
(517) 241-3690 (fax)

Minnesota

Department of Children,
  Families and Learning
1500 Highway 36 West
Roseville, MN 55113-4266
(651) 582-8343
(651) 582-8494 (fax)
http://cfl.state.mn.us/ecfi/

Mississippi

Office of Special Education
Mississippi Department of
  Education
359 N. West Street
P.O. Box 771
Jackson, MS 39205-0771
(601) 359-3498
(601) 359-2198 (fax)

Missouri

Early Childhood Special
  Education
Department of Elementary and
  Secondary Education
State Department of Education
P.O. Box 480
Jefferson City, MO 65102-0480
(573) 751-0185
(573) 526-4404 (fax)
http://www.dese.state.mo.us/
  divspeced

Montana

Office of Public Instruction
State Capitol
P.O. Box 202501
Helena, MT 59620-2501

(406) 444-4425
(406) 444-3924 (fax)
http://www.metnet.state.mt.us/main.
 html

Nebraska

Special Education Office
Nebraska Department of
 Education
301 Centennial Mall South
P.O. Box 94987
Lincoln, NE 68509-4987
(402) 471-4319
(402) 471-5022 (fax)

Nevada

Educational Equity/Special
 Education—South
Nevada Department of
 Education
1820 E. Sahara, Suite 208
Las Vegas, NV 89104
(702) 486-6454
(702) 486-6474 (fax)

New Hampshire

Bureau of Early Learning
New Hampshire Department of
 Education
State Office Park, South
101 Pleasant Street
Concord, NH 03301
(603) 271-2178
(603) 271-1953 (fax)

New Jersey

Office of Special Education
 Programs
CN 500
Riverview Executive Plaza
 Building 100
Trenton, NJ 08625
(609) 984-4950
(609) 292-5558 (fax)
http://www.state.nj.us/education/

New Mexico

Special Education Unit
State Department of Education
300 Don Gaspar Avenue
Santa Fe, NM 87501-2786
(505) 827-6788
(505) 827-6791 (fax)

New York

Office of Special Education
 Services
Special Education Policy and
 Quality Assurance
1 Commerce Plaza, Room 1607
Albany, NY 12234
(518) 473-4823
(518) 486-4154 (fax)

North Carolina

Exceptional Children Division
Department of Public Instruction
301 N. Wilmington Street
Raleigh, NC 27601-2825
(919) 715-1598
(919) 715-1569 (fax)
http://www.dpi.state.nc.us/

North Dakota

Special Education Division
Department of Public
Instruction
600 E. Boulevard Avenue
Bismarck, ND 58505-0440
(701) 328-2277
(701) 328-4149 (fax)

Northern Mariana Islands

CNMI Public Schools
P.O. Box 1370 CK
Saipan, MP 96950
(670) 664-3754
(670) 664-3796 (fax)

Ohio

Division of Early Childhood
Education
Department of Education
65 S. Front Street, Room 309
Columbus, OH 43215 4183
(614) 466-0224
(614) 728-3223 (fax)
http://www.ode.state.oh.us/SE/

Oklahoma

Special Education Services
State Department of Education
2500 N. Lincoln Boulevard,
Room 411
Oklahoma City, OK 73105-
4599
(405) 521-3351 X4867
(405) 522-3503 (fax)
http://sde.state.ok.us/default.html

Oregon

Special Education Programs
State Department of Education
Public Service Building
255 Capitol Street N.E.
Salem, OR 97310-0203
(503) 378-3598 X625
(503) 373-7968 (fax)
http://www.ode.state.or.us/

Palau

Special Education
Bureau of Education
Republic of Palau
P.O. Box 278
Koror, Palau, PW 96940
(680) 488-2568
(680) 488-2830 (fax)

Pennsylvania

Bureau of Special Education
Department of Education
333 Market Street, 7th Floor
Harrisburg, PA 17126-0333
(717) 783-6882
(717) 783-6139 (fax)

Puerto Rico

Special Education Programs
G.P.O. Box 759
Hato Rey, PR 00919
(787) 759-7228
(787) 753-7691 (fax)

Rhode Island

Office Integrated Social
  Services RI Department of
  Education
Shepherd Building
255 Westminister Road
Providence, RI 02903-3400
(401) 222-4600 X2408
(401) 222-4979 (fax)

South Carolina

Programs for Exceptional
  Children
State Department of Education
Rutledge Building
1429 Senate Street
Columbia, SC 29201
(803) 734-8811
(803) 734-4824 (fax)

South Dakota

Office of Special Education
Department of Education and
  Cultural Affairs
700 Governors Drive
Pierre, SD 57501-2291
(605) 773-3678
(605) 773-3782 (fax)

Tennessee

Office of Special Education
State Department of Education
Andrew Johnson Tower, 5th
  Floor
710 James Robertson Parkway
Nashville, TN 37243-0375
(615) 741-2851
(615) 532-9412 (fax)

Texas

Special Education Programs
Texas Education Agency
1701 N. Congress Avenue,
  Room 5-120
Austin, TX 78701
(512) 463-9414
(512) 463-9560 (fax)

Utah

Special Education Services Unit
State Office of Education
250 East 500 South
Salt Lake City, UT 84111
(801) 538-7708
(801) 538-7991 (fax)
http://www.usoe.k12.ut.us/

Vermont

Special Education Unit
State Department of Education
120 State Street
Montpelier, VT 05620
(802) 828-5115
(802) 828-3140 (fax)

Virgin Islands

Division of Special Education
Department of Education
44-46 Kongens Gaden
Charlotte Amalie
St. Thomas, VI 00802
(340) 774-4399
(340) 774-0817 (fax)

Virginia

Office of Special Education
State Department of Education
P.O. Box 2120
Richmond, VA 23218-2120
(804) 225-2675
(804) 371-8796 (fax)
http://www.pen.k12.va.us/

Washington

Office of Superintendent of
  Public Instruction
Old Capitol Building, FG-11
600 S. Washington Street
P.O. Box 47200
Olympia, WA 98504
(360) 753-0317
(360) 586-0247 (fax)
http://www.k12.wa.us/

West Virginia

Office of Special Education Administration
State Department of Education
Capitol Complex, Building 6,
  Room 304
1900 Kanawha Boulevard East
Charleston, WV 25305-0330
(304) 558-2696
(304) 558-3741 (fax)

Wisconsin

Bureau for Exceptional Children
Department of Public Instruction
P.O. Box 7841
Madison, WI 53707
(608) 267-9172

(608) 267-3746 (fax)
http://www.dpi.state.wi.us/dpi/dltcl/
bbfcsp/ecspedhm.html

Wyoming

Department of Education
Special Education Unit
2300 Cheyenne Avenue, 2nd Floor
Cheyenne, WY 82002-0050
(307) 777-6236
(307) 777-6234 (fax)

National Resources

This list was adapted from the list compiled by the National Information Center for Children and Youth with Disabilities (NICHCY).

NICHCY
National Information Center
  for Children and Youth with
  Disabilities
P.O. Box 1492
Washington, DC 20013
(800) 695-0285 (voice & TTY)
(202) 884-8200 (voice & TTY)
nichcy@aed.org
http://www.nichcy.org

Internet Resource Sites

Disability Resources, Inc.
4 Glatter Lane
Centereach, NY 11720-1032

(631) 585-0290 weekdays from
9 A.M. to 5 P.M. EST
(631) 585-0290 (fax; call first)
info@disabilityresources.org
http://www.disabilityresources.org

The Family Village
Waisman Center
University of Wisconsin–
Madison
1500 Highland Avenue
Madison, WI 53705-2280
(608) 263-5973
(608) 263-0529 (fax)
familyvillage@waisman.wisc.edu
http://www.familyvillage.wisc.edu/

Clearinghouses

Clearinghouse on Disability
Information
Office of Special Education and
Rehabilitative Services
Room 3132, Switzer Building
330 C Street S.W.
Washington, DC 20202-2524
(202) 205-8241 (voice & TTY)

DB-LINK
National Information
Clearinghouse on Children
Who Are Deaf-Blind
345 N. Monmouth Avenue
Monmouth, OR 97361
(800) 438-9376 (voice)
(800) 854-7013 (TTY)
dblink@tr.wou.edu
http://www.tr.wou.edu/dblink/

ERIC Clearinghouse on
Disabilities and Gifted
Education
Council for Exceptional
Children (CEC)
1920 Association Drive
Reston, VA 20191-1589
(703) 264-9449 (TTY)
(800) 328-0272 (voice & TTY)
ericec@cec.sped.org
http://www.ericec.org

Laurent Clerc National Deaf
Education Center and
Clearinghouse
KDES PAS-6
800 Florida Avenue N.E.
Washington, DC 20002-3695
(202) 651-5340 (voice & TTY)
Ella.Gilbert@gallaudet.edu
http://www.gallaudet.edu/~
precpweb/

National Arthritis and
Musculoskeletal and Skin
Diseases Information
Clearinghouse
1 AMS Circle
Bethesda, MD 20892-3675
(301) 495-4484 (voice)
(301) 565-2966 (TTY)
http://www.nih.gov/niams\

National Diabetes Information
Clearinghouse
1 Information Way
Bethesda, MD 20892
(301) 654-3327
ndic@info.niddk.nih.gov
http://www.niddk.nih.gov/health/
diabetes/ndic.htm

National Digestive Diseases
  Information Clearinghouse
2 Information Way
Bethesda, MD 20892
(301) 654-3327
nddic@info.niddk.nih.gov
http://www.niddk.nih.gov/health/
  digest/nddic.htm

National Health Information
  Center
P.O. Box 1133
Washington, DC 20013-1133
(301) 565-4167
(800) 336-4797
nhicinfo@health.org
http://nhic-nt.health.org/

National Heart, Lung, and
  Blood Institute Information
  Center
P.O. Box 30105
Bethesda, MD 20824-0105
(301) 251-1222
(800) 575-9355
nhlbiic@dgsys.com
http://www.nhlbi.nih.gov

National Institute on Deafness
  and Other Communication
  Disorders Clearinghouse
1 Communication Avenue
Bethesda, MD 20892-3456
(800) 241-1044 (voice)
(800) 241-1055 (TTY)
nidcdinfo@nidcd.nih.gov
http://www.nih.gov/nidcd/

National Kidney and Urologic
  Diseases Information
  Clearinghouse
3 Information Way
Bethesda, MD 20892
(301) 654-3327
nkudic@info.niddk.nih.gov
http://www.niddk.nih.gov/health/
  kidney/nkudic.htm

National Lead Information
  Center and Clearinghouse
8601 Georgia Avenue, Suite 503
Silver Spring, MD 20910
(800) 424-5323
hotline.lead@epa.gov
http://www.epa.gov/lead

National Maternal and Child
  Health Clearinghouse
2070 Chain Bridge Road, Suite
  450
Vienna, VA 22182-2536
(888) 434-4624
nmchc@circsol.com
http://www.nmchc.org

National Organization for
  Rare Disorders (NORD)
P.O. Box 8923
New Fairfield, CT 06812-8923
(203) 746-6518 (Voice)
(203) 746-6927 (TTY)
(800) 999-6673
orphan@rarediseases.org
http://www.rarediseases.org

National Rehabilitation
  Information Center (NARIC)
8455 Colesville Road, Suite
  935
Silver Spring, MD 20910-3319
(301) 588-9284 (Voice)
(301) 495-5626 (TTY) Spanish
  speaker on staff
(800) 346-2742
http://www.naric.com

Research and Training Center
  on Family Support and Children's Mental Health
Portland State University
P.O. Box 751
Portland, OR 97207-0751
(503) 725-4040 (voice)
(503) 725-4165 (TTY)
(800) 628-1696
caplane@rri.pdx.edu
http://www.rtc.pdx.edu/

National Disability Organizations

Alexander Graham Bell
  Association for the **Deaf**
3417 Volta Place N.W.
Washington, DC 20007
(202) 337-5220 (voice & TTY)
agbell2@aol.com
http://www.agbell.org

American **Brain Tumor**
  Association
2720 River Road
Des Moines IA 60018

(847) 827-9910
(800) 886-2282 (Client
  Services)
info@abta.org
http://www.abta.org/

American Council of the **Blind**
1155 15th Street N.W., Suite
  720
Washington, DC 20005
(202) 467-5081
(800) 424-8666
ncrabb@erols.com
http://www.acb.org

American **Diabetes** Association
1701 N. Beauregard Street
Alexandria, VA 22311
(703) 549-1500
(800) 342-2383
customerservice@diabetes.org
http://www.diabetes.org

American Foundation for the
  Blind (AFB)
11 Penn Plaza, Suite 300
New York, NY 10001
(212) 502-7662 (TTY)
(800) 232-5463
afbinfo@afb.org
http://www.afb.org/afb

American Heart Association
  National Center
7272 Greenville Avenue
Dallas, TX 75231
(214) 373-6300
(800) 242-8721
inquire@amhrt.org
http://www.americanheart.org

American **Lung** Association
1740 Broadway
New York, NY 10019
(212) 315-8700
(800) 586-4872
info@lungusa.org
http://www.lungusa.org/

American Society for **Deaf**
 Children
1820 Tribute Road, Suite A
Sacramento, CA 95815
(916) 641-6084
(800) 942-2732
ASDC1@aol.com
http://www.deafchildren.org

Angelman Syndrome Foundation
P.O. Box 12437
Gainesville, FL 32604
(800) 432-6435
asf@adminsys.com
http://www.angelman.org

Aplastic Anemia & MDS
 International Foundation, Inc.
P. O. Box 613
Annapolis, MD 21404-0613
(410) 867-0242
(800) 747-2820
aamdsoffice@aol.com
http://www.aamds.org

The ARC (formerly the Association for **Retarded Citizens**
 of the U.S.)
500 E. Border Street, Suite 300
Arlington, TX 76010
(817) 261-6003 (voice)

(817) 277-0553 (TTY)
(800) 433-5255
Info@thearc.org
http://www.thearc.org

Asthma and Allergy Foundation of America
1125 15th Street N.W., Suite 502
Washington, DC 20005
(202) 466-7643
(800) 727-8462
info@aafa.org
http://www.aafa.org/

Autism Society of America
7910 Woodmont Avenue, Suite 300
Bethesda, MD 0814-3015
(301) 657-0881
(800) 328-8476
http://www.autism-society.org

Brain Injury Association
(formerly the National Head Injury Foundation)
105 North Alfred Street
Alexandria, VA 22314
(703) 236-6000
(800) 444-6443
FamilyHelpline@biausa.org
http://www.biausa.org

Children and Adults with
 **Attention Deficit/
 Hyperactivity Disorder**
 (CH.A.D.D.)
8181 Professional Place, Suite 201
Landover, MD 20785
(301) 306-7070

(800) 233-4050 (to request information packet)
national@chadd.org
http://www.chadd.org

Children's Craniofacial
  Association
P.O. Box 280297
Dallas, TX 75243-4522
(972) 994-9902
(800) 535-3643
http://www.childrenscraniofacial.com

Cornelia de Lange Syndrome
  Foundation
302 West Main Street, Suite
  100
Avon, Connecticut 06001
(860) 676-8166
(800) 223-8166
info@cdlsusa.org
http://www.cdlsoutreach.org

Craniofacial Foundation of
  America
975 E. Third Street
Chattanooga, TN 37403
(423) 778-9192
(800) 418-3223
farmertm@erlanger.org
http://www.erlanger.org/cranio

Easter Seals, National Office
230 W. Monroe Street, Suite
  1800
Chicago, IL 60606
(312) 726-6200 (voice)
(312) 726-4258 (TTY)
(800) 221-6827
info@easter-seals.org
http://www.easter-seals.org

Epilepsy Foundation
4351 Garden City Drive, 5th
  Floor
Landover, MD 20785-4941
(301) 459-3700
(800) 332-1000
postmaster@efa.org
http://www.efa.org

FACES: The National
  Craniofacial Association
P.O. Box 11082
Chattanooga, TN 37401
(423) 266-1632
(800) 332-2372
faces@faces-cranio.org
http://www.faces-cranio.org

Families of S.M.A. (Spinal
  Muscular Atrophy)
P.O. Box 196
Libertyville, IL 60048-0196
800-886-1762
info@fsma.org
http://www.fsma.org

Family Voices (children with
  special health care needs)
P.O. Box 769
Algodones, NM 87001
(505) 867-2368
(888) 835-5669
kidshealth@familyvoices.org
http://www.familyvoices.org

Federation of Families for
  Children's Mental Health
1021 Prince Street
Alexandria, VA 22314-2971
(703) 684-7710
(703) 836-1040 (fax)
ffcmh@ffcmh.com
http://www.ffcmh.org

Foundation for **Ichthyosis** &
Related Skin Types
P.O. Box 669
Ardmore, PA 19003
(610) 789-3995
(800) 545-3286
ICHTHYOSIS@aol.com
http://www.libertynet.org/~
ichthyos/

Hydrocephalus Association
870 Market Street, #955
San Francisco, CA 94102
(415) 732-7040
hydroassoc@aol.com
http://www.hydroassoc.org

International **Dyslexia**
Association
(formerly the Orton Dyslexia
Society)
Chester Building, #382
8600 LaSalle Road
Baltimore, MD 21286-2044
(410) 296-0232
(800) 222-3123
info@interdys.org
http://www.interdys.org

International **Rett Syndrome**
Association
9121 Piscataway Road, Suite
2B
Clinton, MD 20735-2561
(301) 856-3334
(800) 818-7388
irsa@rettsyndrome.org
http://www.rettsyndrome.org

Klinefelter Syndrome and
Associates
P.O. Box 119
Roseville, CA 95678-0119
(916) 773-2999
888-XXY-WHAT (888-999-
9428)
ksinfo@genetic.org
http://www.genetic.org/ks/

Learning Disabilities Association of America (LDA) (formerly ACLD)
4156 Library Road
Pittsburgh, PA 15234
(412) 341-1515
(412) 341-8077
(888) 300-6710
vldanatl@usaor.ne
http://www.ldanatl.org

Leukemia & Lymphoma
Society
600 Third Avenue
New York, NY 10016
(212) 573-8484
(800) 955-4LSA
infocenter@leukemia-lymphoma.org
http://www.leukemia-lymphoma.org

Lissencephaly Network, Inc.
716 Autumn Ridge Lane
Fort Wayne, IN 46804
(219) 432-4310
http://www.lissencephaly.org

Little People of America
P.O. Box 745
Lubbock, TX 79408
(888) LPA-2001
LPADataBase@juno.com
http://www.lpaonline.org/~lpa

March of Dimes **Birth Defects**
Foundation
1275 Mamaroneck Avenue
White Plains, NY 10605
(914) 428-7100
resourcecenter@modimes.org
http://www.modimes.org

Muscular Dystrophy
Association (MDA)
3300 E. Sunrise Drive
Tucson, AZ 85718
(520) 529-2000
(800) 572-1717
mda@mdausa.org
http://www.mdausa.org

Muscular Dystrophy Family
Foundation
615 North Alabama Street,
Suite 330
Indianapolis, IN 46204
(317) 632-8255
(800) 544-1213
mdff@prodigy.net
http://mdff.org

National Alliance for the
Mentally Ill (NAMI)
200 N. Glebe Road, Suite 1015
Arlington, VA 22203-3754
(703) 524-7600
(703) 516-7991 (TTY)
(800) 950-NAMI
namiofc@aol.com
http://www.nami.org

National Association of the
Deaf
814 Thayer Avenue, Suite 250
Silver Spring, MD 20910
(301) 587-1788
(301) 587-1789 (TTY)
nadinfo@nad.org
http://www.nad.org

National **Ataxia** Foundation
2600 Fernbrook Lane, Suite
119
Minneapolis, MN 55447
(612) 553-0020
naf@mr.net
http://www.ataxia.org

National **Brain Tumor** Foundation
785 Market Street, Suite 1600
San Francisco, CA 94103
(415) 284-0208
(800) 934-2873
nbtf@braintumor.org
http://www.braintumor.org

National Center for **Learning
Disabilities** (NCLD)
381 Park Avenue South, Suite
1401
New York, NY 10016
(212) 545-7510
(888) 575-7373
http://www.ncld.org

National **Chronic Fatigue**
Syndrome and **Fibromyalgia**
Association (NCFSFA)
P.O. Box 18426
Kansas City, MO 64133
(816) 313-2000
NCFSFA@aol.com

National **Down Syndrome**
Congress
1605 Chantilly Drive, Suite 250
Atlanta, GA 30324
(404) 633-1555
(800) 232-6372
NDSCcenter@aol.com
http://www.ndsccenter.org/

National **Down Syndrome**
Society
666 Broadway, 8th Floor
New York, NY 10012-2317
(212) 460-9330
(800) 221-4602
info@ndss.org
http://www.ndss.org

National **Fathers** Network
Kindering Center
16120 N.E. 8th Street
Bellevue, WA 98008
(425) 747-4004, ext. 218
http://www.fathersnetwork.org

National Federation for the
Blind
1800 Johnson Street
Baltimore, MD 21230
(410) 659-9314
nfb@access.digex.net
http://www.nfb.org

National **Fragile X** Foundation
1441 York Street, Suite 303
Denver, CO 80206
(303) 333-6155
(800) 688-8765
natlfx@sprintmail.com
http://nfxf.org

National **Limb Loss** Information Center
Amputee Coalition of America
900 E. Hill Avenue, Suite 285
Knoxville, TN 37915
(423) 524-8772
(888) 267-5669
ACAOne@aol.com
http://www.amputee-coalition.org

National **Marfan** Foundation
382 Main Street
Port Washington, NY 11050
516-883-8712
1-800-8-MARFAN
staff@marfan.org
http://www.marfan.org

National **Mental Health** Association
1021 Prince Street
Alexandria, VA 22314-2971
(703) 684-7722
(800) 969-6642
(800) 433-5959 (TTY)
nmhainfo@aol.com
http://www.nmha.org

National **Multiple Sclerosis**
Society
733 Third Avenue
New York, NY 10017
(212) 986-3240
(800) 344-4867
info@nmss.org
http://www.nmss.org

National **Neurofibromatosis**
Foundation
95 Pine Street, 16th Floor
New York, NY 10005

(212) 344-6633
(800) 323-7938
NNFF@aol.com
http://www.nf.org

National Organization on **Fetal Alcohol Syndrome** (NOFAS)
418 C Street N.E.
Washington, DC 20002
(202) 785-4585
(800) 666-6327
nofas@erols.com
http://www.nofas.org

National Organization for **Rare Disorders** (NORD)
100 Route 37
P.O. Box 8923
New Fairfield, CT 06812
(203) 746-6518
(203) 746-6927 (TTY)
(800) 999-6673
orphan@rarediseases.org
http://www.rarediseases.org

National **Parent Network on Disabilities**
1130 17th Street N.W., Suite 400
Washington, DC 20036
(202) 463-2299 (voice & TTY)
npnd@cs.com
http://www.npnd.org

National **Parent to Parent Support** and Information System, Inc.
P.O. Box 907
Blue Ridge, GA 30513
(706) 374-3822
(800) 651-1151
nppsis@ellijay.com
http://www.nppsis.org

National **Reye's Syndrome** Foundation
P.O. Box 829
Bryan, OH 43506
(419) 636-2679
(800) 233-7393
reyessyn@mail.bright.net
http://www.bright.net/~reyessyn

National **Scoliosis** Foundation
5 Cabot Place
Stoughton, MA 02072
(781) 341-6333
(800) 673-6922
scoliosis@aol.com

National **Spinal Cord Injury** Association
8300 Colesville Road, Suite 551
Silver Spring, MD 20910
(301) 588-6959
(800) 962-9629
nscia2@aol.com
http://www.spinalcord.org

National **Stuttering** Association
5100 E. La Palma Avenue, Suite 208
Anaheim Hills, CA 92807
(714) 693-7480
(800) 364-1677
nsastutter@aol.com
http://www.nspstutter.org

National **Tuberous Sclerosis** Association
8181 Professional Place, Suite 110
Landover, MD 20785-2226
(301) 459-9888

(800) 225-6872
ntsa@ntsa.org
http://www.ntsa.org

Neurofibromatosis, Inc.
8855 Annapolis Road, Suite 110
Lanham, MD 20706-2924
(301) 577-8984
(800) 942-6825
NFInc1@aol.com
http://www.nfinc.org

Obsessive Compulsive Foundation, Inc.
337 Notch Hill Road
North Branford, CT 06471
(203) 315-2190
info@ocfoundation.org
http://www.ocfoundation.org

Osteogenesis Imperfecta Foundation
804 Diamond Avenue, Suite 210
Gaithersburg, MD 20878
(301) 947-0083
(800) 981-BONE
bonelink@aol.com
http://www.oif.org

Prader-Willi Syndrome Association
5700 Midnight Pass Road, Suite 6
Sarasota, FL 34242
(941) 312-0400
(800) 926-4797
pwsausa@aol.com
http://www.pwsausa.org

Sibling Information Network
A.J. Pappanikou Center
University of Connecticut
249 Glenbrook Road, U64
Storrs, CT 06269-2064
(860) 486-4985

Sibling Support Project
Children's Hospital and Medical Center
P.O. Box 5371, CL-09
Seattle, WA 98105
(206) 527-5712
http://www.chmc.org/departmt/sibsupp

Special Olympics International
1325 G Street N.W., Suite 500
Washington, DC 20005
(202) 628-3630
specialolympics@msn.com
http://www.specialolympics.org/

Spina Bifida Association of America
4590 MacArthur Boulevard N.W., Suite 250
Washington, DC 20007-4226
(202) 944-3285
(800) 621-3141
sbaa@sbaa.org
http://www.sbaa.org

Stuttering Foundation of America
3100 Walnut Grove Road #603
P.O. Box 11749
Memphis, TN 38111

(800) 992-9392
stuttersfa@aol.com
http://www.stuttersfa.org

TASH (formerly the
Association for Persons with
Severe Handicaps)
29 W. Susquehanna Avenue,
Suite 210
Baltimore, MD 21204
(410) 828-8274 (voice)
(410) 828-1306 (TTY)
info@tash.org
http://www.tash.org

TEF/Vater International
Support Network (VACTERL
association)
15301 Grey Fox Road
Upper Marlboro, MD 20772.
(301) 952-6837
info@tefvater.org
http://www.tefvater.org

Tourette Syndrome Association
42-40 Bell Boulevard
Bayside, NY 11361
(718) 224-2999
(800) 237-0717
tourette@ix.netcom.com
http://tsa.mgh.harvard.edu/

United Cerebral Palsy
Associations, Inc.
1660 L Street N.W., Suite 700
Washington, DC 20036
(202) 776-0406
(202) 973-7197 (TTY)
(800) 872-5827
ucpnatl@ucpa.org
http://www.ucpa.org

United Leukodystrophy
Foundation
2304 Highland Drive
Sycamore, IL 60178
(800) 728-5483
ulf@tbcnet.com
http://www.ulf.org

Vestibular Disorders
Association
P.O. Box 4467
Portland, OR 97208 4467
(503) 229-7705
(800) 837-8428
veda@vestibular.org
http://www.vestibular.org

4p- Support Group (Wolf-
Hirschhorn Syndrome)
PO Box 1676
Gresham, OR 97030
(503) 661-1855
lbentley@orednet.org
http://members.aol.com/lbent503/
whs/

5p- Society (Cri du Chat
Syndrome)
7108 Katella Ave., #502
Stanton, CA 90680
(888) 970-0777
http://www.fivepminus.org

Editors' Note

We are planning another volume of essays in the future, and we would love to hear from readers with their essays for new parents. Please send your essay (up to 1,500 words) to:

Stanley D. Klein, Ph.D.
CanDo.com
P. O. Box 470715
Brookline, MA 02447-0715